Great
Battles
of
WORLD WAR II

Great *Battles* of WORLD WAR II

John Macdonald

Foreword by General Sir John Hackett

Michael Joseph
London

Great Battles of World War II
was conceived, edited and designed by
Marshall Editions Limited
170 Piccadilly
London W1V 9DD

© Marshall Editions Limited 1986

First published in Great Britain by
Michael Joseph Limited
27 Wrights Lane
London W8 5D2

Originated by Reprocolor Llovet SA, Barcelona, Spain
Typeset by Servis Filmsetting Limited, Manchester, UK
Printed and bound in Belgium by Usines Brepols SA

British Library Cataloguing in
Publication Data

Macdonald, John, 1945–
Great Battles of World War II.
1. World War, 1939–1945—
Campaigns
I. Title
940.54′2   D743

ISBN 0-7181-2727-7

Editor	**Gwen Rigby**	Art Director	**Paul Wilkinson**
Additional text	**Anthony Livesey**	Picture Research	**John and Diane Moore** (Military Archive and Research Services)
Assistant Editors	**Louise Tucker** **Carole Devaney**		
		Production	**Janice Storr**
		Chief Illustrator	**Harry Clow**

Contents

Picture captions, pages 1–6

Page 1: German Afrika Korps desert cap and sand goggles (**1**) and cuff band (**2**); German Army P38 automatic pistol (**3**).

Page 2: US ammunition pouch with magazine and .30 ammunition (**1**); US leather shoulder holster with M1911 A1 Colt .45 automatic pistol (**2**); US Army insignia of a Major-General or Vice-Admiral (**3**); Shoulder flash of US Army 3rd Infantry Division, which fought in North Africa,

Italy and Germany (**4**); Shoulder flash of US Army 85th Infantry Division—'Custer's Division' (**5**); Airplane Spotter playing cards, issued by the Coca Cola Company (**6**); Shoulder flash of US Seventh Army, which invaded Sicily under General George Patton (**7**); Pack of Lucky Strike cigarettes, smoked by many US troops (**8**).

Page 4: Polish banknote 1941, brought back to

England by a prisoner of war (**1**); Packet of 10 'V'—Victory—cigarettes, an unpopular brand produced in India for the troops in the Middle East (**2**); German World War II Iron Cross, 1st Class (**3**); An Egyptian banknote, issued in 1940 (**4**); Shoulder flash of the US 5th Army, which fought in North Africa and Italy under General Mark Clark and entered Rome on 6 June 1943 (**5**); Cap badge (**6**) and parachutist's wings (**7**) of

the Special Air Service Regiment, which came into being in the Western Desert in 1941.

Page 6: Luftwaffe officer's belt and buckle (**1**); 'Pegasus' shoulder flash of all British Airborne Divisions (**2**); German Red Cross armband, worn by all medical personnel. This armband was issued by the Germans to a corporal in the RAMC, who was captured at Arnhem, when he and

other prisoners of war were sent west in 1945, out of the path of the advancing Russians (**3**); The Victoria Cross, the highest award for bravery given to members of the British and Commonwealth forces (**4**); Action pictures, showing British paratroopers at Arnhem (**5**); The red beret, with its winged badge, worn by these men (**6**).

Jacket: Medal ribbon of the Atlantic Star 1939–45.

Foreword by General Sir John Hackett

As we approach the half-century mark in the passage of time since World War II, public interest in its course and conduct does not decline, and circumstances combine to encourage its further study. Though there has been much warfare in this time, there has been no world-wide conflict, and what happened in the last World War can now be seen in a clearer light and truer perspective.

Source material has become more readily available and much valuable work has been done upon it, offering considerable improvement upon a good deal of what was written and published sooner after the event. Though many of the principal actors are no longer around, there are still plenty of players of important minor parts to be consulted. The availability of first-hand personal evidence will not persist indefinitely, however, and this lends added emphasis and urgency to its exploitation.

A further cause of heightened interest in the last World War is the widespread and deep concern that there should never, with the weapons now available, be another. With the advent of nuclear weapons, we have passed over a watershed into a region where waging total war is no longer a rational act of policy. Moreover, apart from nuclear weapons, new and emerging technologies have radically modified military method, and battles on land or sea or in the air will never by the same again. Of those studied in this book more than one is already a historical curiosity. The Battle of Arnhem, in which I had myself a considerable part, inevitably comes to mind, and there are many others.

Some of the technology newly applied to warfare since World War II is already commonplace. Helicopters, lasers, remotely piloted vehicles, rocket propulsion, guided weapons, electronic techniques, proliferating automation, computers, fibre optics, new materials in metals, plastics and ceramics—the list from which a few items are here culled is a very long one. Brooding over the whole scene, moreover, is the question of what will happen in space. In studying the battles of World War II, we are already looking into a past whose material aspects will not be generally repeated, but in which we find continuing fascination and from which there is still much to learn.

An outstanding feature of the growing interest in the battles of World War II is the development of advanced techniques for their study, of which this book offers a notable example. The application of computer graphics to topography throws a new light on the dominant element in any land battle: what is generally called the terrain or the ground. The principal tool here is the map; but the better, more detailed and more accurate the map, the harder it often is to use, and sometimes it tells you nothing of what is vitally important.

One map sheet I had to use as a tank officer in the Western Desert in North Africa, during the fighting before Alamein, had 60 contiguous map squares containing nothing at all. Yet the movement of the desert terrain, with its small folds and undulations (let alone the going, as it varied from stones to soft sand) could easily be, in tank fighting, a matter of life and death. More dramatic features, bold enough to break a contour line, are easily noted on conventional maps, but even then portrayal in only two dimensions does not convey all the military operator wants to know.

The publication by Marshall Editions in 1984 of their splendid book *Great Battlefields of the World*, making free use of computer graphics, opened a new and exciting chapter. The present book, *Great Battles of World War II*, will be a revelation to many who have still to experience what this new and ingenious approach to battlefield reporting has to offer.

General Sir John Hackett, soldier and scholar, with Oxford degrees in Classics and in Medieval History, ended a military career (three times wounded and with three decorations for gallantry in World War II) as Commander of NATO's Northern Army Group before returning to university life. A devoted supporter of the Atlantic Alliance, he has particularly close affinities with US forces. His two books on a Third World War have sold more than two million copies worldwide.

Dunkirk/*May-June 1940*

In the closing days of May 1940 Britain teetered on the edge of a military disaster of unprecedented magnitude. To universal astonishment, German armies had blitzkrieged their way through the Low Countries and across northern France in just over two weeks. Allied resistance was disintegrating and almost the entire British Expeditionary Force was penned into a tiny pocket around the French Channel port of Dunkirk.

But how did such a reverse befall the pick of Britain's army? The long, hard road that ended on the shore at Dunkirk began on 10 May, when Nazi Germany invaded Holland, Belgium, Luxembourg and France, putting a violent stop to the inactivity of the so-called 'phoney war' which had prevailed since hostilities began in September 1939.

Although the French placed almost mystical faith in the deterrent power of the Maginot Line, a chain of sophisticated fortifications protecting their north-eastern frontier with Germany as far as the Belgian border, they were not unmindful of the possibility of an attack through the neutral Low Countries. Plan D, an unrehearsed advance into Belgium, was devised to meet such a threat.

That fateful 10 May (the same day that Winston Churchill became Prime Minister of Britain), the Supreme Allied Commander, the French General Maurice Gamelin, initiated Plan D. As poorly equipped Belgian forces recoiled before the Germans, three mechanized armies, the French First and Seventh and the British Expeditionary Force, moved up to the River Dyle.

The Allies, of course, knew nothing of the Germans' 'Plan Yellow' and by rushing their best troops north into Belgium they played into the enemy's hands.

What General Erich von Manstein had cleverly plotted and Adolf Hitler so exultantly approved was a two-fisted attack: General Fedor von Bock's Army Group B, comprising 29 divisions, was to swing down through Holland and Belgium while the 45 divisions of General Gerd von Rundstedt's Army Group A were to slip into France through the hilly Ardennes region, turning the flank of the vaunted Maginot Line.

Because they believed the terrain was impassable to enemy armour, the French had placed their weakest army, the Ninth, on the Ardennes front. They realized their error when the panzers, backed by the Luftwaffe, subjected the soft French opposition to the shock of blitzkrieg tactics.

As well as breaking the French line, the Germans were also poised to grip the

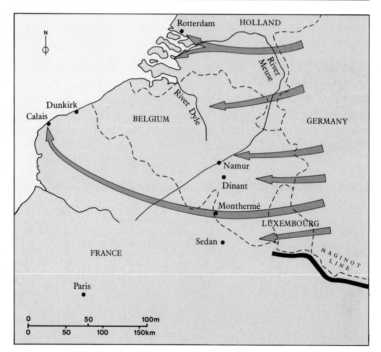

The Allied Plan D relied heavily on the Maginot Line. The best formations—the French Seventh and First Armies and the BEF—were stationed between the end of these defences and the North Sea. The weaker French Ninth, Second and Third Armies were placed where it was thought the Maginot Line and the hilly, forested Ardennes required minimum support.

If the Germans threatened Holland and Belgium, the three northern groups would swing forward to the natural defensive line of the River Dyle.

Had the Germans employed the 1914 Schlieffen Plan, which aimed at encircling Paris, Plan D might have been effective. Instead, they adopted General von Manstein's Plan Yellow.

By threatening the north, which enticed the BEF and the French Seventh and First Armies northeastward, a far superior force—Army Group A under von Rundstedt—was able to pour seven panzer divisions through the supposedly impassable Ardennes. These then headed for the north-coast ports.

Blitzkrieg tactics are simple in concept but potentially lethal. Objectives are selected, *right*, and the weakest points in the enemy's defensive line identified. The areas either side of the proposed armoured thrust are contained by conventional attacks (1), while a smokescreen camouflage is employed to conceal tanks assembling in the main sector.

The opening tank assault is preceded by heavy air attacks and artillery bombardment (2), designed to clear the area of attack and dislocate enemy communications and reserves. Paratroopers, dropped behind enemy lines, disrupt communications further and prevent the orderly advance of reinforcements.

The main armoured attack (3), closely supported by motorized divisions (4) and, behind them, infantry (5), strikes in maximum available strength at the weakly defended sector.

The breakthrough accomplished, the armoured spearhead fans out, bypassing and then enveloping defensive strongpoints. Supporting motorized troops, later replaced by infantry units, consolidate territorial gains. The weight, speed and ferocity of the attack causes panic among civilians.

Meanwhile, the armour is free to plunge deeper into enemy territory, encircling ever-widening areas. Speed is essential to ensure that defenders are captured before they have time to withdraw and regroup.

General Heinz Guderian (1888–1954), the creator of the German panzer force, was a decisive, bold commander. His methods were unusual for a man of his rank. At first light he would leave his headquarters in an armoured car, with a signals officer, his radio and an 'Enigma' cypher machine (*bottom left*). Accompanied by dispatch riders and a halftrack vehicle for difficult ground, he would direct operations from the front while keeping in continuous contact with his HQ.

In September 1939, Poland (1) was partitioned by Germany and Russia. The Russian invasion of Finland (2) in December was blocked, but in March 1940 the Finns accepted Russia's armistice terms. Germany occupied Denmark and Norway (3) in April 1940 and in May opened its lightning attack on the Low Countries and France (4). In North Africa (5), the Italians were preparing to attack Egypt, and in China the war with the Japanese, which had been in progress since 1937, continued.

Rommel's tanks and motorized infantry advanced so swiftly that their opponents had no time to destroy bridges and sections of road to delay them. Here an advancing

Blitzkrieg tactics

column is monitored by a Fiesler-Storch spotter aircraft, circling over the spot where a tank has toppled off the road. These craft were used to identify dangers and opportunities ahead and to radio information to headquarters. A German tank division, which could move at about 4.8kmh/3mph on roads, consumed around 4,546l/1,000gal of petrol an hour. German supplies were often augmented by tanks refuelling at French petrol stations.

Hitler, with highly trained paratroopers who had all won the Knight's Cross in the attack on Eben Emael, the supposedly impregnable Belgian fort. The Germans landed on the roof in gliders and attacked before the defenders knew that war had begun. They placed hollow-charge grenades on the gun cupolas, then threw high-explosives into ventilating shafts and stairwells. The fort quickly succumbed.

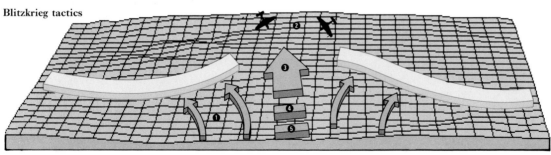

Dunkirk/2

million Belgian, French and British troops in the north in a classic double envelopment. There was little or no coordination between Allied fighting forces: confusion—and sometimes panic—prevailed on Luftwaffe-strafed roads, clogged with fleeing refugees and retreating soldiers.

Between 16 and 19 May the Allies withdrew to the River Scheldt in the face of Bock's steady advance. Meanwhile, in France, Rundstedt's panzers were now motoring along virtually unopposed. By 18 May lead elements were only 50km/31mls from the Channel coast. The German trap was closing.

Sunday 19 May was a momentous day in the Dunkirk campaign. In a desperate attempt to reverse the failing fortunes of its huge army, the French Government replaced the 68-year-old Gamelin with the brisk General Maxime Weygand, aged 73, who was then in Beirut and out of touch with events in Belgium and France.

At the same time as this change in command was being made, General the Viscount Gort VC, the Commander-in-Chief of the BEF, had reluctantly concluded that it was time to think in terms of a British withdrawal to rest on supply lines through the Channel ports. He also began to consider the possibility of evacuation.

Happily for the BEF, the Admiralty, at Churchill's instigation, had already started to make plans for such an eventuality. Operation Dynamo, as it was codenamed, was placed under the command of Vice-Admiral Sir Bertram Ramsay, Flag Officer Dover, who began assembling suitable vessels in harbours in the south of England.

Fight and fall back, fight and fall back became the daily norm of the tired men of the BEF and of those French and Belgian units still holding together. There was no cohesive front line, and the Allies were crumbling under sustained German pressure. When the action drifted down into the old World War I battlefields in the north of France, however, a small part of the BEF caused unexpected anxiety in German ranks. Seventy-four tanks from 'Frankforce', a mixed assault group commanded by Major-General H.E. Franklyn, counter-attacked enemy armour south of Arras, astonishing the commanding officer of the 7th Panzer Division, Major-General Erwin Rommel, by the ferocity of their offensive. Though the British were eventually beaten off, Rundstedt said later that this action had delayed his advance by two vital days.

The most serious threat to the German advance in northern France was the assault made on 21 May 1940 by 'Frankforce'. This scratch command, led by Major-General Franklyn, comprised tanks, infantry, field and anti-tank guns and motorcycle reconnaissance platoons.

Initially the 58 MkI and 16 MkII Matilda tanks made good progress. As Rommel wrote in his diary: 'The enemy tank fire had created chaos and confusion among our troops ... they were jamming up the roads ... with their vehicles instead of going into action.' But resistance stiffened immediately Rommel took charge, personally giving every gun its target.

In the nine-hour action, the British penetrated 16km/10mls before being beaten back; 46 tanks were lost.

The open fields near Beaurains (1) proved good tank country. By coincidence, the first-ever major tank action was fought only a few miles away at Cambrai in 1917.

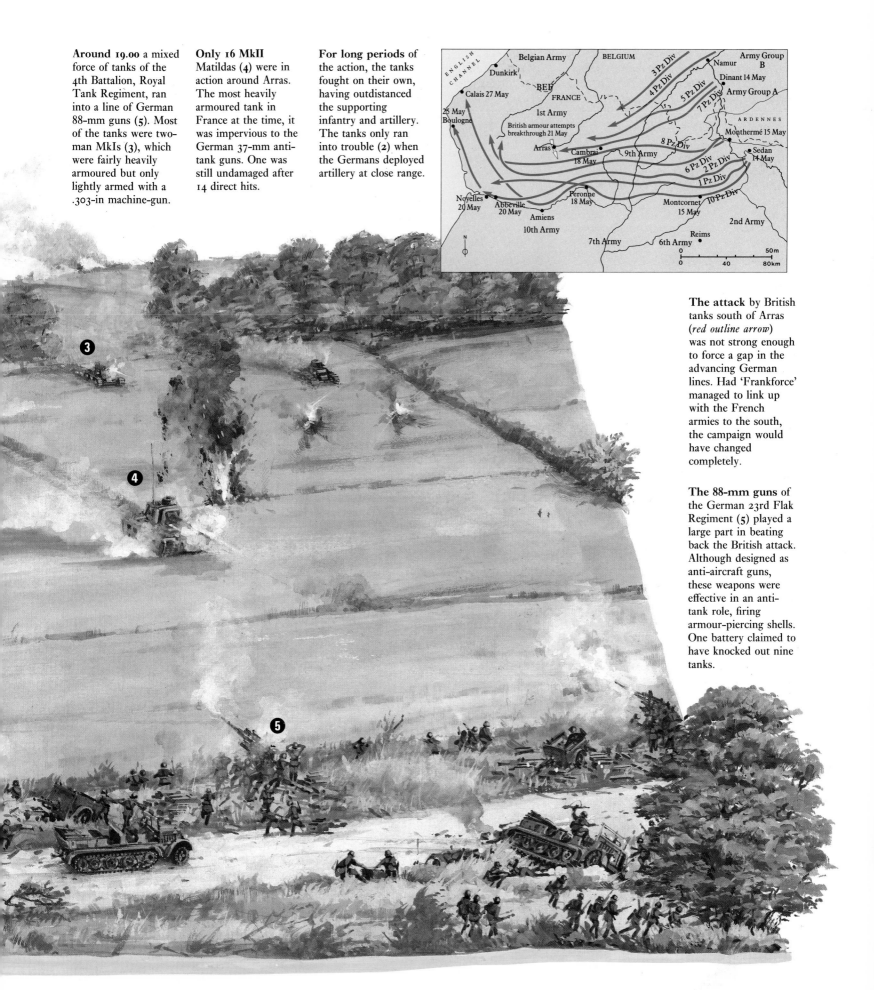

Around 19.00 a mixed force of tanks of the 4th Battalion, Royal Tank Regiment, ran into a line of German 88-mm guns (**5**). Most of the tanks were two-man MkIs (**3**), which were fairly heavily armoured but only lightly armed with a .303-in machine-gun.

Only 16 MkII Matildas (**4**) were in action around Arras. The most heavily armoured tank in France at the time, it was impervious to the German 37-mm anti-tank guns. One was still undamaged after 14 direct hits.

For long periods of the action, the tanks fought on their own, having outdistanced the supporting infantry and artillery. The tanks only ran into trouble (**2**) when the Germans deployed artillery at close range.

The attack by British tanks south of Arras (*red outline arrow*) was not strong enough to force a gap in the advancing German lines. Had 'Frankforce' managed to link up with the French armies to the south, the campaign would have changed completely.

The 88-mm guns of the German 23rd Flak Regiment (**5**) played a large part in beating back the British attack. Although designed as anti-aircraft guns, these weapons were effective in an anti-tank role, firing armour-piercing shells. One battery claimed to have knocked out nine tanks.

While General Weygand was laying impracticable plans for an Allied breakout to join up with those forces in the south cut off by Rundstedt's thrust, Gort put the BEF on half-rations. The situation grew worse, confounding Weygand's optimism. On Friday 24 May, Boulogne fell, Calais was just holding out, and panzers were within 25km/15½mls of Dunkirk, the last remaining port capable of handling a major evacuation.

The next day two events took place, one on either side of the lines, which ensured that the BEF would survive to fight another day. Hitler, inexplicably, ordered his tanks to halt and leave the Luftwaffe to mop up Allied resistance in the Dunkirk pocket—a job beyond his air arm's capability. And when the Führer later allowed the panzers to move forward again, heavy rain had made the terrain, laced with canals and ditches, unsuitable for rapid advance of armour.

On the other side, General Gort moved his two reserve divisions north to support his left flank, where the Belgian Army was on the verge of collapse and the danger to the BEF was real and imminent. On Sunday 26 May, while people at home in Britain attended church and went for walks in the sunshine, Calais fell and Operation Dynamo was put into effect.

That same day, the BEF, with the cooperation of the French and Belgians, who now accepted that evacuation was inevitable, began a phased pull-back to a prepared defensive perimeter. This was 25km/15½mls wide by about 12km/7mls deep, and stretched from a little below Dunkirk in the south to Nieuport in Belgium in the north. As the BEF began falling back, it disabled all its artillery and transport and destroyed massive quantities of stores to prevent the enemy making use of them.

Although embarkation had begun on the night of 26–27 May, with the arrival at Dunkirk of the troop transport *Mona's Isle*, the Royal Navy shore party under Captain W.G. Tennant did not arrive at the port until the Monday morning to begin coordinating the mammoth rescue mission. It was a bad day. German aircraft and artillery were pouring high explosive into the town, which was full of dazed, exhausted troops. The sickening débris of war was everywhere (including the bodies of 1,000 civilian casualties); and, to the sailors' dismay, the 8-km/5-ml network of docks had been put out of action.

Only the relatively fragile East and West Moles protecting the harbour entrance were intact, but they had not been designed for berthing big ships.

>

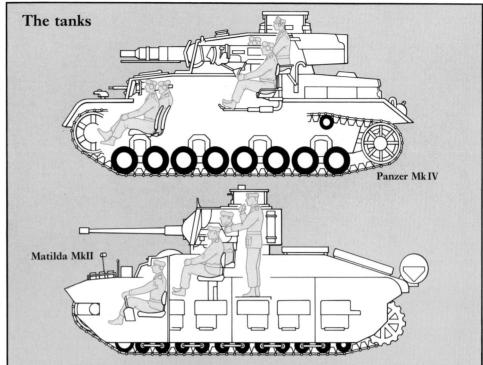

The tanks

Panzer Mk IV

Matilda MkII

The 20-ton Panzer MkIV tank had electro-welded body armour, up to 30mm/1¼in thick in places, particularly at the front. It was armed with a low-velocity, short-barrelled 75-mm gun and two 7.92-mm machine-guns. The crew of five—commander, gunner, loader, driver and wireless operator—were close enough to communicate by touch or lip-reading and to take over from each other. An exceptionally well-designed tank, the Panzer MkIV became the German Army's most widely used armoured fighting vehicle throughout the war.

The Matilda MkII was the most efficient British tank in the early years of the war, and almost 3,000 had been made by August 1943 when production ceased. Most of these 26.5 ton vehicles, with bolted and riveted armour up to 78mm/3in thick, mounted a high-velocity two-pounder gun. Caked mud from the tracks was ejected through apertures along the tank's sides. The hydraulically rotated turret was small and cramped for the three crewmen in it—commander, whose vision was restricted, gunner and loader/wireless operator.

The chilling whine of the Junkers Ju 87B dive-bomber—the Stuka—became synonymous with German blitzkrieg tactics in the early part of the war. The Allied retreat was harried by swarms of these rather clumsy-looking two-seater aircraft, which were used extensively by the Luftwaffe in support of infantry and armoured operations.

The Stuka had a top speed of 389kmh/242mph in level flight and a range of 600km/373mls and was an amazingly accurate bomber. Attacks were usually mounted by a wing of 30 aircraft, which swooped on the target in 10 sections of

three. It was common for a Stuka pilot to begin his dive at 15,000ft at an angle of 60°–90°, scream earthward at up to 740kmh/460mph, release his bombload at around 2,000ft, then overcome a force of four G to pull out of his headlong descent.

The Ju 87B, which had two forward-firing 7.92-mm machine-guns and one rearward-firing 7.92-mm machine-gun in the cockpit, usually carried four 50-kg/110-lb bombs under its wings and one 250-kg/551-lb bomb slung under the fuselage.

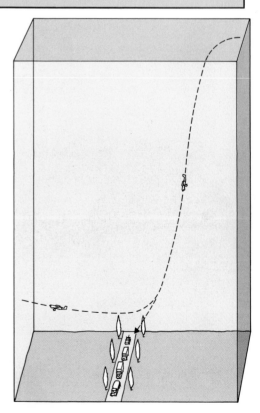

The Commanders

General Erich von Manstein (1887–1973) devised the German plan for the invasion of western Europe and himself commanded a corps. His greatest triumphs, however, came in the Russian campaign, when, in 1942, his Second Army defeated the Russians in the Crimea and, in 1943, he stabilized the German front after the disaster at Stalingrad.

Field Marshal Fedor von Bock (1880–1945), having served in the Polish campaign, commanded Army Group B in the western attack in 1940. A sharp-faced, rugged man, he was a thoroughly professional soldier who shunned political involvement. He commanded the central front during the invasion of the USSR in 1941, and the following year Army Group South; but in July he was relieved of his command by Hitler for being too cautious.

Like Bock, **Field Marshal Gerd von Rundstedt (1875–1953)** was a tough professional soldier of the Prussian school and he made little effort to disguise his patrician distaste for 'Corporal' Hitler. He commanded Army Group A during the invasion of France and later (1941–2) Army Group South in Russia.

The French Commander-in-Chief in 1939–40, **General Maurice Gamelin (1872–1958)** was confident of the strength of the French infantry, though less so of the artillery. He realized too late that German strategy aimed at the Channel, not Paris, and was replaced after the German breakthrough on 19 May. His successor, **General Maxime Weygand (1867–1965)** had had a long military career. On his appointment he remarked, 'I do not guarantee success.' Indeed, he was soon urging Marshal Pétain to conclude an armistice. Both Weygand and Gamelin were deported to Germany but were freed in 1945.

General the Viscount Gort VC (1896–1946) had served from 1937 as Chief of the Imperial General Staff until he was appointed to command the BEF in France in 1939. In 1942–4 he was responsible for the defence of Malta. A man of exceptional bravery, he was famous in the army for his coolness under pressure.

Retreating British trucks, including a tank transporter, brought to a standstill in the congested streets of Le Neubourg in northern France. Refugees, fleeing in confusion, greatly added to the chaos and to the army's difficulties. Many people in cars strapped a mattress on the roof as protection against Luftwaffe machine-gun fire; others, on bicycles or pushing carts, could only scatter when an aircraft dived on them. Since all main roads passed through town centres, these confused conditions were repeated along the entire line of the German advance.

Dunkirk/4

Between 26 May and 2 June 1940, most of the BEF and many French troops were evacuated from Dunkirk to England under the guns of the encircling Germans.

Braving mines, bombs and shells, a huge fleet of ships, both large and small, took part in a rescue mission codenamed Operation Dynamo.

Its success was due to several factors: the Royal Navy's superb organization; the fortitude and common sense of the waiting troops; and calm seas for nine days. In addition, long periods of poor visibility kept the Luftwaffe inactive, and it was constantly harassed by the RAF.

Columns of thick, black smoke from blazing oil tanks (**5**) marked the port of Dunkirk. They served to guide retreating Allied troops to the right part of the coast for embarkation.

On the first day of the evacuation, Captain Tennant RN realized that if most of the troops were to be saved they would have to be embarked from both the narrow and flimsy East Mole (**4**) and the broad beaches north of the town (**3**).

On the beaches, men in their thousands formed queues (**1**), waiting patiently for their turn to be taken off. German artillery, positioned some way inland, had the range of Dunkirk and the evacuation beaches and shelled them frequently, but to some extent the sand lessened the effect of the shells thudding into it. Many boats were hit and sunk (**9**).

To speed the embarkation from the beaches, army trucks were run into the sea at low water and lashed together to make improvised jetties (**2**) on which men could scramble out to shallow-draught boats waiting to pick them up.

About 600 large ships (**7**)—warships, ferry boats, merchantmen, Dutch barges—carried most of the troops back to England.

Troops were ferried out to larger ships, lying offshore by some 300 'little ships', such as cabin-cruisers (**8**). One of these was manned by Sea Scouts—boys of 16 or 17—but most of the civilians taking part were fishermen, lifeboatmen and the like.

The Luftwaffe appeared whenever the mist lifted. Time after time, Stuka dive-bombers (6) attacked both waiting soldiers and ships. Some aircraft were shot down by anti-aircraft guns on board.

Nieuport

Dunkirk East mole La Panne Furnes

Bergues–Furnes Canal

0 5m
0 4 8km

The Allies prepared a defensive perimeter around Dunkirk prior to their evacuation. The line shrank under German pressure but its strength gave many servicemen the chance to be taken off the beaches and East Mole.

Dunkirk/5

> Neither would they be sufficient for the Navy's purpose. The fierceness of the German bombardment, along with the great number of troops arriving in Dunkirk and the depressing fact that only 7,669 men had been taken off that day, led Captain Tennant to decide that the broad, flat beaches stretching northward from the flattened port would have to serve for embarkation, too.

He sent an urgent signal to the Admiralty requesting as many small boats as possible to come and ferry the waiting men from the sands to the bigger ships lying offshore. At the same time, Tennant made the crucial decision to try to use the long East Mole, which could accommodate several ships at a time. Tennant's decision proved the turning point at Dunkirk, and the salvation of the BEF.

'Bloody Monday', as it was called, ended with the news that King Leopold of the Belgians had concluded an armistice with the Germans to take effect at midnight. This spurred on the British withdrawal, to prevent the enemy pouring through the gap between their left flank and the coast, which until then had been defended by the courageous remnants of the Belgian Army.

While a spirited defence was sustained on the perimeter by British and French infantry, more and more hungry, weary units joined the long, snakelike and, for the most part, orderly queues forming on the sands. The first of the 'little ships' arrived off the French coast on the night of 29 May and began picking up troops. Before the end of the evacuation, nearly 300 of these frail vessels were engaged in this perilous task.

Through mining, bombing and shellfire, troop carriers of all shapes and sizes continued to run the gauntlet to and from Dunkirk. Some made it, several did not, and wrecks became an additional hazard for tired seamen. By 30 May, 125,000 men of the BEF had arrived back in England, and on that day Winston Churchill, fearful that the Germans might enjoy the propaganda coup of capturing the British Commander-in-Chief, ordered General Gort home. Two days later he complied, handing over command to Major-General Harold Alexander.

On 31 May, 68,014 men were taken off, the largest daily total of the whole evacuation; yet many, many more still remained. The next day, 1 June, dawned clear, one of only two and a half fine days in what was to be a nine-day operation, and the Luftwaffe arrived back over the beaches in force, strafing and bombing. Frustrated soldiers fired their rifles at the low-flying

Exhausted by their long, fighting retreat, men sleep on the deck of a troopship while waiting for her to set out for England. The decks were often so crowded that the sailors were prevented from operating the ship's guns. There were insufficient life-jackets to give one to every man.

Troops on a destroyer arriving safely at Dover. Many ships were damaged during their passage across the Channel, and scrambling nets were left hanging over the ships' sides so that men could be more easily rescued from the water if a sinking vessel were encountered.

The Red Cross and women's voluntary organizations quickly established an efficient service to provide the tired, hungry men of the BEF with food and hot tea. Most soldiers managed to save their personal weapons; everything else—including huge stockpiles of equipment made in anticipation of an increase in the BEF's strength—was lost.

Escaping the chaos

Large ships, requiring deep water, could not be used to evacuate troops because of shoals off the coast. Destroyers could get inshore, but although Britain had had more than 200 at the outbreak of war some had been sunk or damaged and many could not be spared from other duties. As a result, civilian vessels of all types—'the little ships'—were called upon.

The shortest route from Dunkirk to Dover, Route Z, was some 72km/45mls and took the boats within range of the newly established German gun batteries around Calais. Route X, farther to the northeast,

was out of range, but was dangerous because of shoals and unswept mines, so Route Y, a longer passage to the Kwinte Buoy, northeast of Ostend, then north of the Goodwin Sands had to be made. This route was almost 88km/55mls more than the shortest route, perilously prolonging exposure to German air attack.

There were other hazards, too. The sea in the embarkation area was soon littered with foundered ships, floating débris and hundreds of corpses. Ships loading soldiers were temporarily immobilized, presenting easy targets for the Luftwaffe. Every space

available was used to accommodate men and overloaded boats listed alarmingly when manoeuvring to avoid air attacks. In the dark, ships collided, adding to the general chaos.

Yet, despite the difficulties and the losses sustained, more than seven times the expected 45,000 men were rescued and, as Churchill was to write, 'There was a feeling of intense relief, melting almost into triumph', in Britain. Nevertheless, he was quick to remind Parliament of the danger of complacency. 'Wars', he declared, 'are not won by evacuations.'

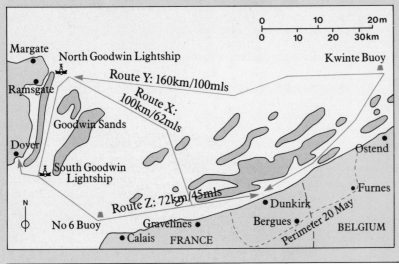

Captain William G. Tennant (1890–1963) offered his help to Ramsay and was sent to Dunkirk as Senior Naval Officer ashore. An imposing figure, he exuded authority and calm and gave confidence to the exhausted troops.

Vice-Admiral Sir Bertram Ramsay (1883–1945), Flag Officer Dover, knew the Channel well. He was an aloof but highly intelligent and decisive man, in whom Churchill had absolute confidence.

The destroyer HMS *Vivacious* alongside the mole. On her starboard is the hulk of a trawler, which has received a direct hit.

Destroyers could take off more soldiers, more quickly than other vessels but, when shipping losses mounted alarmingly, Admiral Sir Dudley Pound, the First Sea Lord, knowing that destroyers were an essential safeguard to Great Britain, ordered all but the 15 oldest out of action. The number of men rescued daily at once dropped.

Pound's duty was to preserve the British Fleet, Ramsay's to save the BEF. Early in the afternoon of 30 May Ramsay telephoned the First Sea Lord and forcefully made his point: unless destroyers were returned to Dunkirk much of the BEF would be captured. Whether the final decision was Churchill's is uncertain, but at 15.30 six modern destroyers were immediately ordered back to the beaches.

aircraft, muttering, 'Where's the bloody RAF?' The Royal Air Force came in for many unjustified jibes during and after the Dunkirk campaign, for it had, in fact, been in the thick of the fighting since the German blitzkrieg and had suffered heavy losses in both aircraft and crews.

When the retreat to the coast began in earnest, it was decided to provide air cover by flying sorties from England rather than risk sending more squadrons to France. That the RAF did its best with limited resources is beyond doubt, bombing enemy positions and installations at night and sending up regular fighter patrols by day. The British lost 177 aircraft, 31 of them on 1 June; the Germans lost 240. The figures speak for themselves.

Mist returned on 2 June, and the Channel continued uncannily calm while the remainder of the BEF, as well as large contingents of waiting French soldiers, boarded ships. One of the last British soldiers to leave that coast, littered with corpses and débris, was General Alexander; and just before midnight Captain Tennant, doubtless with relief, signalled to Admiral Ramsay, 'BEF evacuated'. A staggering 338,226 men had been snatched to safety, many of them still carrying their small arms.

Thousands upon thousands of French troops had been evacuated, too, but many kept up a gallant and desperate rearguard action as the Germans fought their way into the town. Operation Dynamo continued until 02.23 on 4 June, when it became clear that French resistance had collapsed and the 30–40,000 men still in Dunkirk were beyond rescue. Altogether, 139,911 French soldiers had been rescued and taken to safety in Great Britain.

The elation that followed relief at the deliverance of so many men led Winston Churchill to caution that evacuations did not win wars. Indeed, the figures underline the fact that the Allied cause had endured a punishing reverse. Of the 850-odd assorted vessels which had made Operation Dynamo's success possible, 235 had been sunk. The BEF had lost 68,111 men killed, wounded, missing and taken prisoner, all its guns and transport, and an enormous quantity of supplies. The French suffered terribly, with casualties estimated in the region of 2,000,000, of whom more than 90,000 died; Dutch and Belgian losses amounted to 9,779 and 23,350 respectively. Enemy casualties were reported to number 150,000.

On the credit side as far as Britain was concerned, most of the BEF's trained soldiers were safe and ready to renew the fight against Nazi Germany.

A German cameraman filming the scene on the front at Dunkirk shortly after the British evacuation. The Germans were masters of propaganda and used such films both for home consumption and to overawe the people of occupied Europe.

German soldiers on the beach at Dunkirk inspect a makeshift pier made from British army trucks.

Between 27 May and 4 June 1940, 338,226 Allied troops were brought safely back to England from the beaches and the East Mole at Dunkirk. Some, however, such as these at Calais, were taken prisoner, as were thousands who held the defensive perimeter around Dunkirk, so giving their comrades the chance of escape.

Operation Sealion

After Dunkirk and the Fall of France, Britain braced itself for invasion. But in early June 1940, Hitler thought his triumphs in Europe would persuade the British Government to sue for peace; he himself suggested an armistice.

By the time Hitler realized that Britain would not yield voluntarily, his best chance of a successful invasion had been lost. In the opinion of General Karl Student, commander of Germany's crack airborne forces, Hitler had left it six weeks too late. Early in the war Student had made plans for an airborne landing around the Kent Channel ports and for the capture of an airfield. He believed his scheme ought to have been implemented during the chaos of Dunkirk, but it was only in July that the German High Command began hurried planning for 'Operation Sealion'.

But Sealion suffered constant delay. The Luftwaffe lost control of airspace over the Channel; Hitler became convinced that Britain was on the brink of revolution, so making military intervention unnecessary; then, following the Battle of Britain, he turned his thoughts to attacking Russia.

Operation Sealion called for assaults on a front stretching from Portland to Dover, with a landing at a bridgehead already secured by airborne troops, as Student had planned.

The forces were available and efforts were made to gather a fleet of invasion barges, but the plan was never put into action.

Capitulation of France

On 13 June, Winston Churchill, already 65 and after a mere month in office as Prime Minister, donned a holster with loaded revolver and was flown, with fighter escort, to Tours, to which city the French Government had decamped. There he found all in chaos—the airport bombed, the streets crammed with refugees' cars and most of the ministers dispersed. The French Government was now divided between those who despaired and those who advocated fighting to the last. Four days earlier, however, the Germans had renewed their offensive, and on 10 June, Mussolini, 'the Italian miscalculator' in Churchill's contemptuous phrase, attacked in the south of France without warning.

On 16 June, Great Britain, in an act of remarkable generosity in her most perilous hour, released France from her solemn treaty obligation never to make a separate peace with Nazi Germany. Next day, a new French Government, led by the aged and defeatist Marshal Pétain, asked for an armistice and soon the puppet Vichy Government was established in unoccupied France. The Battle of France was over; the Battle of Britain would inexorably and swiftly follow.

Newspaper headlines on 15 July proclaimed Churchill's defiant broadcast of the previous evening. In the few weeks since Dunkirk, the British had achieved a high state of readiness against any attack. Posters enjoined civilians, in the event of an invasion, not to flee before the enemy as the French had, blocking the roads, but to stay at home.

ENEMY INVASION.

WHAT YOU MUST DO.

Remain at work: when unable to do so and you have no invasion duty

CONTACT YOUR LOCAL WARDEN.

He will arrange for you to help the City to carry on.

If you are in Civil Defence, that is your job.

If you have no invasion duty, stand firm.

Do not leave your district; do not block the roads.

Do not listen to rumours; only obey orders given by the military, police, Civil Defence personnel or Ministry of Information.

Be on your guard against Fifth Columnists.

Apply to your local Warden for more detailed instructions.

Keep by you a 48 hours' supply of food and water.

(P30780-9B-P) *Issued by the Birmingham Invasion Committee.*

The Battle of Britain/*July-October 1940*

Before Hitler could seriously consider launching 'Operation Sealion', the sea-borne assault on Britain, the Luftwaffe had to win control of the airspace over the English Channel. If it did not, the German fleet would present an easy target for the Royal Air Force. The Führer spelled it out plainly in Directive No 16, which outlined his requirements for the proposed invasion: 'The English Air Force must be so reduced morally and physically that it is unable to deliver any significant attack against the German crossing.'

Even though Germany's air arm had not fully recovered from its exertions in assisting Hitler's conquest of most of western Europe, it still outnumbered the RAF by three to one overall on the eve of what Winston Churchill called the 'Battle of Britain'. In fighters, the linchpins of aerial warfare, the Germans held a two to one advantage, having 1,290 single-engined Messerschmitt Bf 109 and twin-engined Messerschmitt Bf 110 aircraft compared with Britain's home defence force of 591 single-engined Hawker Hurricanes and Supermarine Spitfires.

That the combat-hardened Luftwaffe, confidently commanded by Reichsmarschall Hermann Goering, expected to annihilate RAF opposition was in little doubt as the battle opened on 10 July 1940, with heavy raids on convoys in the Channel and on military targets in the south of England. As the air war progressed, however, German fliers' optimism gave way to cynicism. 'Here come Britain's last 50 fighters', they would repeat as they arrived over England on yet another mission, to be confronted yet again by resolute interceptors.

Britain succeeded in standing off the Luftwaffe threat between July and October by a combination of shrewd leadership, unfailing courage, and determination from overworked aircrews and groundcrews. In addition, the RAF entered the Battle of Britain with both a technological and tactical advantage over the Luftwaffe, for it had a highly developed early warning system, backed by Observer Corps tracking stations once intruders had crossed the coast. There were also steady supplies of replacement Hurricanes and Spitfires—as well as a generous measure of luck.

At the head of RAF Fighter Command was 60-year-old Air Chief Marshal Sir Hugh Dowding, who directed its activities from his headquarters at Bentley Priory, a mansion near London. This officer had fought throughout World War I with the Royal Flying Corps and stayed on after 1918 in the newly formed Royal Air Force.

On 10 June 1940, Italy (1) declared war on Britain and France; on 14 June, German troops entered Paris (2) and on 22 June France signed an armistice with Germany. On 3 July, Britain, now standing alone in Europe save for Malta, crippled the French fleet at Oran (3).

Range of high-level radar

Range of low-level radar

Luftflotte 5
from Norway and Denmark

NORTH SEA

Fighter Command Group 13

Fighter Command Group 12

Amsterdam
NETHERLANDS

London

Fighter Command Group 10

Fighter Command Group 11

BELGIUM

Luftflotte 2

ENGLISH CHANNEL

Paris

Luftflotte 3

FRANCE

| 0 | 50 | 100 | 150m |
| 0 | 100 | 200 km |

In the opening days of the Battle of Britain, Germany had overwhelming air superiority, with more than 3,000 aircraft, roughly a third of which were fighters. Three Luftflotten were in striking range of Great Britain. British Fighter Command possessed 591 single-engined Spitfires and Hurricanes. This disparity in strength was offset by a number of factors. First, the British commander, Dowding, was experienced in all aspects of aerial warfare, whereas Goering knew little about commanding large air units in battle. Second, British pilots on baling out usually landed on native soil, to fight again. German pilots who escaped were often short of fuel, and many who had to bale out were swept back over the Channel by the prevailing winds.

Finally, thanks to radar, the British were forewarned of enemy attacks, so they could save fuel and make the most of rest periods by waiting until the last moment to 'scramble'.

Radar finds the attackers

Radar, first known as Radio Direction Finding, worked via a cathode ray tube, rather like a small television screen, on which an impulse or 'blip' appeared when the transmitter sent out a radio signal.

A radar station consisted of a pair of tall metal masts, one to transmit and one to receive signals. At the foot of these was a receiver hut housing the cathode ray tubes. If there were no aircraft in the area covered by the signal, the screen showed only one blip. But when an aircraft appeared, the signal bounced off it and was picked up by the station's receiving antennae, which translated it into another blip on the cathode ray tube.

Operators were then able to calculate the range and bearing of the approaching aircraft by the time that elapsed between the signal being transmitted and received. RAF aircraft were fitted with 'friendly' recognition signals, so radar operators could distinguish between them and the enemy. A system of base to fighter control had also been worked out that gave the RAF a tactical advantage over the Luftwaffe.

Two types of radar were operating during the Battle of Britain. Chain Home, or high-level radar, had a range of around 160km/100mls and could detect aircraft below 15,000ft. Chain Home Low sets were amazingly accurate at up to 48km/30mls in detecting low-flying aircraft.

When aircraft were picked up on a radar screen, a warning was flashed to Fighter Command Headquarters (FCH) at Bentley Priory, which in turn alerted the Fighter Group protecting the predicted target area. The Group Operations Room decided how many aircraft were needed to respond to the coming attack, ordered fighters to stand by to 'scramble', then handed over the direction of the interception to Sector Airfield Control. This was in radio contact with the pilots and guided them toward the enemy with coded messages. The early warning and other target information was also given to anti-aircraft batteries in the path of the Luftwaffe formation.

The position of the closing enemy aircraft was constantly updated by the radar stations and fed along the chain of command to the airborne fighters. Once intruders had crossed the coast, the radar stations, which operated only to seaward, could not track them. The task of following their progress then fell to Observer Corps watching posts, whose crews passed on their sightings to the Filter Room at FCH.

All this data, combined with radio reports to base from the aircraft once they were airborne, enabled the RAF to plot the development and course of every attack. This was done by moving symbols on large-scale table maps in operations rooms from FCH down to sector airfield level.

Radar masts, 110m/360ft high, carried fixed transmitting aerials which gave 'floodlight' cover at Chain Home long-range warning stations.

Plotters in Operations Rooms moved red and black counters (for enemy and friendly aircraft), marked with figures showing estimated height and strength, on map tables. The coloured direction arrow of each raid was changed to match differently coloured five-minute segments on a special clock as reports were updated. Information was then passed to Sector Controllers who scrambled the aircraft needed to deal with the enemy.

Hawker Hurricanes of 501 Squadron, County of Gloucester, take off to intercept attacking German aircraft on 16 August 1940.

The Battle of Britain/2

Dowding had done more than anyone else to ensure that Britain would be properly protected in the event of an air attack. Before taking over Fighter Command in 1936 he had been in charge of research and supply. In this capacity, he had been closely involved with the introduction of fast, well-armed monoplane fighters, as well as with the development of radar. This radio direction-finding system was capable of distinguishing approaching enemy aircraft and accurately plotting their course.

In the run-up to World War II, Dowding divided Fighter Command into four groups: 10 Group to cover southwest England; 11 Group, the southeast; 12 Group, the Midlands; and 13 Group, the north of England, Scotland and Northern Ireland. All of these were further subdivided into smaller defensive sectors. From a chain of coastal radar stations, stretching from the Orkney Islands in the north round as far as the Severn estuary in the southwest, information about hostile aircraft nearing British shores would be flashed to Dowding's operations room at Bentley Priory. Here was the nerve centre of the fighter control system that was to prove its worth throughout the Battle of Britain.

Aware of the strength, height, speed and direction of the incoming raiders, the controllers could alert not only the appropriate group but individual sectors within it. In this way the minimum number of interceptors required to meet the attack could be scrambled, thereby husbanding valuable aircraft and pilots.

In fact, in July 1940, pilots were more important than aircraft, which were by then coming off the assembly lines in ever-increasing numbers thanks to the dynamism of the newspaper tycoon Lord Beaverbrook, the new Minister of Aircraft Production. In the twenties and thirties, Britain had concentrated on building up a crack regular bomber force, so the RAF entered the war short of trained fighter pilots. Many of the young men destined to put up such an illustrious struggle against the Luftwaffe were weekend fliers from the Auxiliary Air Force and the Royal Air Force Volunteer Reserve, reinforced by

On Sunday 18 August 1940, the Luftwaffe launched the biggest raid of the Battle of Britain on RAF installations in the south of England. The attack on the fighter base at Kenley was carried out by two waves of Dorniers from Bomber Geschwader 76: a low-level raid followed by a high-level raid. The low-level attackers did most damage. The Kenley area was hit by 100 50-kg/110-lb bombs, but the base was out of operation for only two hours. Nine servicemen were killed and 10 seriously injured; there were 6 civilian dead and 21 badly hurt. Five fighters were destroyed on the ground and 3 damaged; of the 9 raiders, 5 were shot down and 4 damaged. The raid lasted only five and a half minutes.

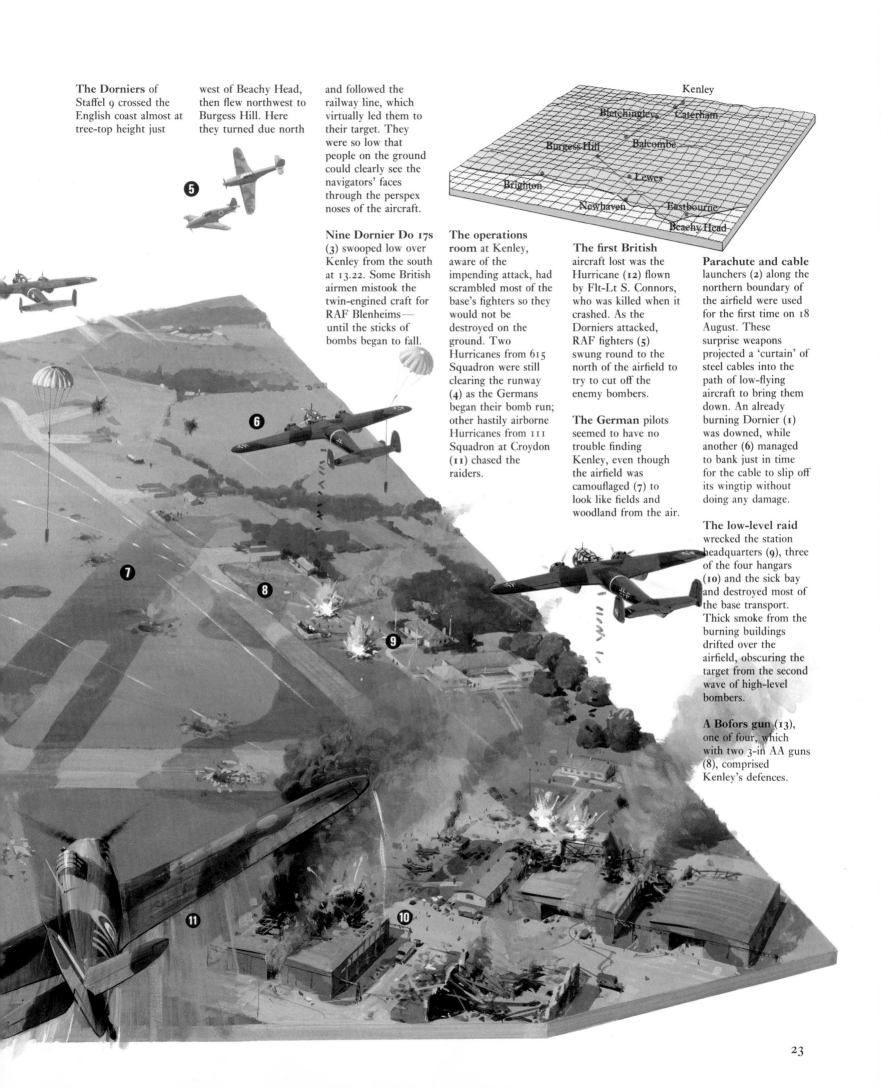

The Dorniers of Staffel 9 crossed the English coast almost at tree-top height just west of Beachy Head, then flew northwest to Burgess Hill. Here they turned due north and followed the railway line, which virtually led them to their target. They were so low that people on the ground could clearly see the navigators' faces through the perspex noses of the aircraft.

Nine Dornier Do 17s (3) swooped low over Kenley from the south at 13.22. Some British airmen mistook the twin-engined craft for RAF Blenheims— until the sticks of bombs began to fall.

The operations room at Kenley, aware of the impending attack, had scrambled most of the base's fighters so they would not be destroyed on the ground. Two Hurricanes from 615 Squadron were still clearing the runway (4) as the Germans began their bomb run; other hastily airborne Hurricanes from 111 Squadron at Croydon (11) chased the raiders.

The first British aircraft lost was the Hurricane (12) flown by Flt-Lt S. Connors, who was killed when it crashed. As the Dorniers attacked, RAF fighters (5) swung round to the north of the airfield to try to cut off the enemy bombers.

The German pilots seemed to have no trouble finding Kenley, even though the airfield was camouflaged (7) to look like fields and woodland from the air.

Parachute and cable launchers (2) along the northern boundary of the airfield were used for the first time on 18 August. These surprise weapons projected a 'curtain' of steel cables into the path of low-flying aircraft to bring them down. An already burning Dornier (1) was downed, while another (6) managed to bank just in time for the cable to slip off its wingtip without doing any damage.

The low-level raid wrecked the station headquarters (9), three of the four hangars (10) and the sick bay and destroyed most of the base transport. Thick smoke from the burning buildings drifted over the airfield, obscuring the target from the second wave of high-level bombers.

A Bofors gun (13), one of four, which with two 3-in AA guns (8), comprised Kenley's defences.

23

a few squadrons manned superbly by refugee Poles and Czechs. (Indeed, some of the highest scores for shot-down enemy planes were recorded by these expatriates.)

When casualties began to mount in the thick of the fighting, training wings were hard pressed to provide an adequate supply of fresh pilots. At the very height of the battle, some youngsters were joining operational squadrons after only 24 hours in a Spitfire's cockpit and an inadequate amount of gunnery practice.

One of the advantages that helped tip the balance in favour of the RAF was the fact that the dogfights with enemy aircraft took place over Britain or close to its coast. This ensured the swift recovery of baled-out or crash-landed pilots who, provided they were not injured, simply collected a reserve fighter and went straight back into the front line.

When Goering, a fighter ace of World War I and a staunch Nazi, planned the destruction of Britain's air defences, he had at his command three Luftflotten, or air fleets. Luftflotte 2 (Field Marshal Albert Kesselring) had bases in Holland, Belgium and northern France; Luftflotte 3 (Field Marshal Hugo Sperrle) operated from bases in Normandy, and Luftflotte 5 (General Hans-Jurgen Stumpff) from Denmark and Norway.

Because of the limited range of German fighters escorting bomber squadrons, the majority of enemy operations was directed at southeast England. The defence of this area was entrusted to Fighter Command's 11 Group, commanded by Air Vice-Marshal Keith Park, a 44-year-old New Zealander who was an expert on fighter interception. His Spitfire and Hurricane squadrons bore the main burden of the Battle of Britain.

A measure of the intense pressure on Park's command was clearly revealed to Prime Minister Churchill the day he visited 11 Group's operations room at Uxbridge during a particularly strong series of attacks. Watching the to and fro of aerial combat on the controllers' plotting table, he enquired about Park's reserve only to be told, 'There is none.'

Soon after the Luftwaffe began its attempt to win control of the Channel skies, its aircrews realized that the stream of coded radio telephone messages from the ground to RAF fighters were explicit interception instructions based on radio direction-finding techniques far more advanced than anything employed by the Third Reich. In an effort to black out Fighter Command's communications system, the Germans began a tactically

Maximum speed: 580kmh/362mph; armament: eight .303-in Browning machine-guns sited in the wings.

Maximum speed: 523kmh/328mph; armament: eight .303-in Browning machine-guns sited in the wings.

Maximum speed: 489kmh/304mph; armament: four .303-in Browning machine-guns sited in the turret.

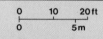

Maximum speed: 515kmh/321mph; armament: four 20-mm Hispano cannon and six .303-in Browning machine-guns sited in the wings.

British aircraft

Supermarine Spitfire IA Although more Hurricanes had actually been produced, the Spitfire was the outstanding single-seater fighter aircraft of the Battle of Britain.

Hawker Hurricane I An older single-seater than the Spitfire, the Hurricane was inferior in speed and climb but was capable of taking great punishment. Almost as manoeuvrable as the Spitfire, it accounted for 80% of enemy losses.

Boulton Paul P82 Defiant I Originally designed for defensive patrol, this two-seater was used as an interceptor and night fighter but few had been built by 1940. The Defiant, with its strong turret armament, was effective against bombers but vulnerable to Messerschmitts.

Bristol Beaufighter I A powerful two-seater fighter, painted black and equipped with AI (Airborne Interception) radar, this was the first of a series of aircraft designed to intercept and destroy German night raiders.

Maximum speed: 573kmh/357mph; armament: two 7.9-mm MG 17 machine-guns on the engine and two 20-mm MG FF cannon in the wings.

Maximum speed: 562kmh/349mph; armament: four 7.9-mm MG 17 machine-guns, two 20-mm MG FF cannon and a rear 7.9-mm machine-gun.

Maximum speed: 426kmh/265mph; armament: up to eight 7.9-mm MG 15 machine-guns and a bombload of 998kg/2,200lb.

Maximum speed: 398kmh/247mph; armament: three 7.9-mm MG 15 machine-guns, and a bombload of 1,800kg/3,968lb.

Maximum speed: 460kmh/286mph; armament: three 7.9-mm MG 15 machine-guns, and a bombload of 1,800kg/3,968lb.

Maximum speed: 373kmh/232mph; armament: three 7.9-mm machine-guns, and a bombload of 1,000kg/2,205lb.

0 10 20 ft
0 5m

German aircraft

Messerschmitt Bf 109E-4 Designed to combine the smallest practicable frame with the most powerful engine available, it was a stable craft and could dive faster than any British aircraft.

Messerschmitt Bf 110C-4 Designed both to prepare the way for German bombers and to protect home airspace, it proved ineffectual in the first role but highly successful in the second.

Dornier Do 17Z-2 A twin-engined bomber, which together with the Heinkel and the Junkers comprised the bulk of the German air arm, it was obsolescent by 1942 and virtually went out of production. The Dornier had a crew of either four or five, including a rear-facing gunner.

Heinkel He IIIP-2 Though inadequately equipped with firepower when confronted by Spitfires and Hurricanes, this twin-engined bomber had proved highly effective both in Spain and Poland, where opposition was less stiff. Subsequent versions failed to overcome this armament deficiency.

Junkers Ju 88A-1 This craft, the most versatile of all those developed during WWII, remained in service until 1945. It could be used either as a dive-bomber, a conventional bomber, a torpedo bomber or as a day or night fighter.

Junkers Ju 87B-2 This 'Stuka' or dive-bomber was generally used for precision bombing of small targets—bridges, road and rail junctions—ahead of blitzkrieg attacks, causing great disruption. In the face of stiff British resistance it proved extremely vulnerable.

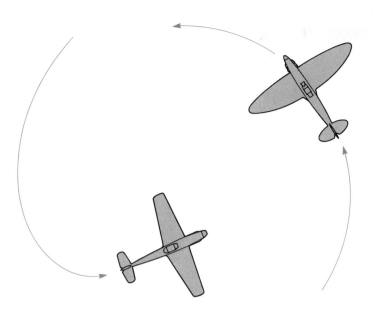

By **1940**, fighters on both sides could achieve high speeds and had the ability to make tight turns. In a dogfight, a pilot would make the tightest turn possible, in order either to get behind his opponent or to attack him with deflection fire. The Messerschmitt Bf 109E had a turning circle 40m/130ft tighter than the Spitfire IA.

This picture, viewed from 46cm/18in, shows what an enemy fighter, coming up behind and about to open fire, looked like at 549m/600yds. Constant vigilance was crucial, for the first pilot to sight an enemy had the advantage. A fighter coming in from behind, especially out of the sun, was lethal unless the pilot's marksmanship was inaccurate.

Cone of fire

Deflection angle

When firing on a turning target, a fighter pilot had to aim ahead of it by an amount called the deflection angle. To ensure that the cone of fire converged at the precise point aimed at, the pilot also had to judge the range accurately. These skills, essential during dogfights, were not mastered by all pilots.

229m/250yds

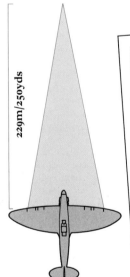

RAF regulations stipulated that a fighter's guns must be so aligned that their fire converged at 594m/650yds. This helped poor marksmen, but since the German bombers could sustain heavy punishment without being brought down, it was essential for pilots to get closer to their targets.
  Many British pilots, despite regulations, realigned their guns to converge at 183–274m/200–300yds. This often made the difference between damaging an aircraft and destroying it.

The Germans had armour-plated their aircraft and had perfected self-sealing fuel tanks by 1940. In consequence, many German bombers still reached home after sustaining 50 and more hits, *above left*.

A Dornier Do 17, engaged by a Spitfire, *above*. 'Sailor' Malan's philosophy was not necessarily to seek to destroy German aircraft but to inflict so much damage that repair would be lengthy and costly.

logical, but imperfectly coordinated, assault on the giant pylons of the coastal radar station chain, as well as on air-base installations. The 110 m/360 ft high masts were not, however, easy targets to hit. Their height made them impossible to dive-bomb, and their girder construction meant that they were not easily destroyed by the effects of blast.

This bid coincided with the all-out air attack called for by Hitler in early August as a prelude to invasion. Goering chose 13 August as 'Adlertag' (Eagle Day), when the massed might of his air fleets would, he predicted, pound the RAF into submission. But Eagle Day started badly when some German squadrons took off piecemeal, unaware that the Reichsmarschall had delayed the operation on hearing reports about deteriorating weather. Goering later changed his mind when conditions improved, and that afternoon waves of swastika-emblazoned fighters, dive-bombers and bombers were blasting RAF airfields and other military targets all over the south of England.

Altogether 1,485 sorties were flown that day by the Luftwaffe, which shot down 13 British fighters, knocked out 47 assorted aircraft during attacks on airfields, and did a fair amount of damage to buildings and stores. The RAF accounted for the loss of 34 German planes.

Bad weather on 14 August provided Fighter Command with a short breathing space. But German mass attacks were renewed on 15 August, when they lost 70 machines, compared with a loss of 29 by the defenders. This day saw also the intervention of some of the luck that was to help the RAF to endure the worst the Luftwaffe could throw at it, for Goering ordered his fliers to stop wasting their time attacking radar stations because it seemed to be having minimal effect. (Little did he know how well some of his bombers had been doing.)

That same day, 15 August, was crucial for another reason. The heavy, continuous fighting had mainly been over Kent and the Channel coast. Goering and his advisers, convinced that all British fighter squadrons had been drawn into the struggle, ordered a daylight raid on industrial cities north of the Wash. The distance was such that German bombers were escorted not by powerful Me 109s but by 110s, which had the range but not the dogfighting capability. One hundred bombers, with 40 escorts, were thrown against Tyneside. Unknown to the Germans, however, Dowding, despite the unremitting fighting in the south, had so disposed his forces that seven fighter

The most effective way to shoot down an enemy aircraft was for the pilot to dive out of the sun at maximum speed and to fire at the closest possible range below and behind his target as he pulled upward out of his dive.

Werner Mölders, *left*, the youngest Kommodore in the Luftwaffe, realized the vulnerability of tight formations to this type of attack and devised the 'pair' formation to overcome it. The leader (1) was accompanied by his wingman (2) who flew lower and on the sun side. The leader was the attacker, the wingman the defender, who watched the sun for an attack; (3) is the second pair's leader and (4) his wingman.

If they were attacked from behind, they employed a simple 'crossover' turn, *below*, which simply reversed the previous formation. Alternatively, one pair would wheel to the left, the other to the right. If the attacking pilot followed the pair turning right, the pair turning left completed a full circle and came in behind him, and vice versa.

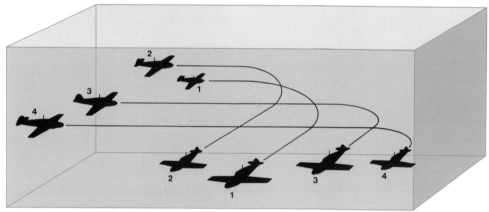

"SAILOR"

Sqn.Ldr. A.G. MALAN. D.S.O. D.F.C.   74 SQUADRON

At the outset of the battle, the British were still flying in V-formations, usually of three craft. They made a tight, vulnerable target, and the pilots of the two outside aircraft had to spend more time keeping formation than searching for the enemy.

Then Squadron Leader 'Sailor' Malan, an ace pilot, *left*, revealed his great tactical skill. Instead of dividing his squadron into four sections of three aircraft, he organized it into three sections of four fighters, *below*. This seemingly slight rearrangement was in fact of the greatest significance, for when battle was joined each of his three units divided easily and rapidly into two units of two fighters. In this way no pilot was left without support from a comrade.

The home front

The British people, despite warning voices and the dreadful impact of Hitler's blitzkrieg tactics against Poland, were slow to appreciate the peril of their position. Then, in the early summer of 1940, came the 'miracle of Dunkirk' and the fall of France. In the space of a few sunny weeks, the awesome danger became obvious. There was an immediate transformation in the public's attitude.

As Churchill later wrote in *The Second World War*: 'This was a time when all Britain worked and strove to the utmost limit and was united as never before. Men and women toiled at the lathes and machines in the factories till they fell exhausted to the floor and had to be dragged away and ordered home, while their places were occupied by newcomers ahead of time. The one desire of all the males and many women was to have a weapon . . . Nothing moves an Englishman so much as the threat of invasion, the reality unknown for a thousand years. Vast numbers of people were resolved to conquer or die.'

It was not only the fit and young who answered the call. The defence of the home was paramount, and the elderly, often including the infirm, enlisted in great numbers in the Local Defence Volunteers, shortly renamed by Churchill, in a felicitous phrase, 'The Home Guard'. At first armed with little more than broomsticks for drill purposes, they were later issued with rifles, albeit for the most part obsolescent, and limited ammunition. As the weeks passed, however, the force, soon numbering almost one and a half million men, received efficient weapons. With their dedication and willingness to perish in the cause, they would have presented the Germans with formidable opposition had they attempted invasion. They were also useful in taking over guard duties from the army, and provided an organized look-out force.

All hands were occupied. Women, living too far from industrial centres to work in factories, shopped and cooked for children and the elderly; others acted as messengers or provided homes for children evacuated from the big cities. Men above service age flocked in their thousands to join the ARP or as auxiliaries to the fire service, while young girls volunteered for the female arms of the services or worked on the land to raise essential food. Even schoolchildren played their part as firewatchers. There was a feeling of unity, an uplifting sense of each belonging with his neighbour. Hitler was, for the first but not the last time, faced with the courage of a people resolved to defend their homeland and their freedom, regardless of the cost.

LEAVE THIS TO US SONNY — YOU OUGHT TO BE OUT OF LONDON

MINISTRY OF HEALTH EVACUATION SCHEME

POLICE NOTICE

AIR RAID DANGER

Conceal your Lights

All windows, skylights, glass doors, etc., in private houses, shops, factories, and other premises must, as from to-day, be completely screened after dusk, so that no light is visible from the outside. Dark coverings must be used so that the presence of a light within the building cannot be detected from outside.

All illuminated advertisements, signs and external lights of all kinds must be extinguished, excepting any specially authorised traffic or railway signal lights or other specially exempted lights.

Lights on all vehicles on roads must be dimmed and screened. The Police will issue leaflets describing the restrictions to be observed.

THESE MEASURES ARE NECESSARY FOR YOUR PROTECTION IN CASE OF AIR ATTACK.

The Government used all possible means to convey instructions and advice to the civilian population. The Ministry of Health, for example, produced posters to promote their scheme for the evacuation of children from the bomb-blasted cities to rural homes. The 'black-out' was rigorously enforced, *left*, some over-zealous wardens even admonishing people for striking a match in the street.

Notices such as these appeared not only on buildings in public places, including railway stations and factory canteens, but in newspapers and magazines. Even cigarette cards, *right*, explained how to remove a gas mask, deal with an incendiary bomb or build a shelter.

WILLS'S CIGARETTES

REMOVAL OF INCENDIARY BOMB WITH SCOOP AND HOE

WILLS'S CIGARETTES

THE CIVILIAN RESPIRATOR — HOW TO REMOVE IT

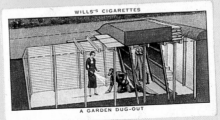

WILLS'S CIGARETTES

A GARDEN DUG-OUT

squadrons had been moved north, both to rest and to defend the area. They were on hand to greet the Germans. Thirty German aircraft, mostly bombers, were shot down; two British pilots were injured. The Germans never again attacked northern England by day.

Goering now urged his aircrews to concentrate on breaking the RAF, which he was sure was approaching its last gasp, by shooting down its machines, wrecking its airfields and destroying its aircraft factories and supporting industries. To help them, he cancelled Luftflotte 5's long-range operations against Britain from Scandinavia and transferred some of Stumpff's aircraft to Luftflotten 2 and 3, where they could play a more positive part in grinding down the opposition. Then, in contrast, he gradually withdrew all Junkers 87 'Stuka' dive-bombers from the offensive because they were proving vulnerable.

In the two weeks from 24 August to 6 September, the Luftwaffe committed around 1,000 planes a day against Britain, stretching Fighter Command's dwindling resources to the limit. Pilot casualties were crippling, and those who survived, exhausted and battle weary, were called upon to fly time and again, day in day out, in order to maintain an adequate defence. Meanwhile, on the ground, superhuman efforts had to be made to keep vital communications networks in operation despite heavy enemy damage.

Just when it seemed that the Luftwaffe's war of attrition might ultimately weigh against the valiant, but desperately hard-pressed, British defenders, Goering issued another edict. This time he supplied Dowding's men with just the reprieve they needed to get their second wind for what was to be the final stage of the Battle of Britain.

On the night of 26 August, the pilots of RAF Bomber Command shook the overconfident Third Reich by carrying out a raid on the German capital. It had been ordered by Churchill in response to enemy bombers offloading high explosives on civilians in London the night before. This retaliation for what had probably been poor bomb-aiming on the part of the Luftwaffe, which hitherto had pursued a strict policy of attacking military targets only, sparked a nine-week campaign of terror bombing against the British capital.

The turning point of the battle came on 7 September, when Goering diverted the Luftwaffe from its almost-successful effort to break Fighter Command in order to concentrate on mass bombing raids, principally on London. The Blitz had

Kommodore Helmut Wick joined the Luftwaffe in 1936 and, instructed by Mölders, rapidly proved himself a fighter pilot of the first order, indifferent to peril and always keen to fly and fight. He was respected by his fellow pilots, especially for his disregard of his superiors. Wick, then aged 25, achieved 56 'kills' before he was shot down and drowned in the Channel in November 1940.

Sergeant Pilot James ('Ginger') Lacey had joined the RAF Volunteer Reserve before the war and worked in civilian life as a flying instructor. Lacey served in France in the early summer of 1940 (he shot down three German aircraft on his first day in action) and during the Battle of Britain scored 15 'kills', possibly more. Lacey was fortunate and survived being shot down on several occasions.

Pilots of doomed aircraft, if over the Channel, always baled out since a fighter would sink instantly.

German pilots wore yellow skullcaps and were equipped with sea-dye, flare pistols and dinghies. Rescue rafts, *left*, sited in the Channel contained survival equipment for four men, as well as a mallet and wooden pegs for securing any holes made by machine-gun attacks. Heinkel HL 59 'floatplanes', supported by German naval rescue vessels, swept the Channel for survivors.

British pilots had to rely on a 'Mae West', which was almost impossible to inflate in rough water. No rescue organization for ditched RAF pilots had been formed, so they depended on chance encounters with coastal shipping or on one of the few high-speed rescue launches stationed along the coast.

The Commanders

Park

Goering

Dowding

Air Chief Marshal Sir Hugh Dowding (1882–1970), a solitary man with few friends, had a greater understanding of aerial warfare than any other British commander. A leader with the ability to delegate, he steadily enhanced the morale of Fighter Command and his choice of **Air Vice-Marshal Keith Park (1892–1975)** to command 11 Group, the front line of defence in the southeast, was inspired.

Park was an aggressive and brilliant tactician with many hours of flying experience gained in the fighting in France and at Dunkirk. He went on to take command in Malta in July 1942, when he at once introduced the plan of intercepting bomber raids on the island before they crossed the coast, saving time, lives and aircraft. In 1944 he became Air Commander-in-Chief in the Middle East, and in 1945 held the same position in Southeast Asia.

Air Vice-Marshal Trafford Leigh-Mallory (1892–1944), an intriguer of great ambition, resented not being given command of 11 Group and became one of Dowding's denigrators, doing much to undermine his authority. At the end of 1943, Leigh-Mallory was appointed to command the Allied Expeditionary Air Force during the Normandy landings.

Reichsmarschall Hermann Goering (1892–1946), Commander-in-Chief of the Luftwaffe, was a man of unbridled ambition and vanity. Though he had been an outstanding air ace in World War I, he had no experience of commanding large formations in war. Thus the bombing of Great Britain was without plan: he relied solely on numerical superiority and the effect of massed attacks. Targets were chosen haphazardly: Portsmouth one night, Coventry another, Liverpool a third. This gave each

city time to recover and did not cause the panic among the civilian population that he sought, as bombing one target for a number of nights in remorseless succession might have done.

Goering's commander of Luftflotte 2, **Field Marshal Albert Kesselring (1885–1960)**, had until seven years previously been an army officer, but by 1940 he had become an enthusiastic exponent of aerial warfare. A gifted improviser, he was later to show his great ability when, as commander in Italy, he was under Allied pressure.

Field Marshal Hugo Sperrle (1885–1953), a man of massive frame, was chief of Luftflotte 3. A pilot in World War I, he later commanded the Condor Legion during the Spanish Civil War and had more flying experience than any other German air commander. Like Goering, he was debased by an insatiable craving for luxury.

Luftwaffe pilots flew longer but less-frequent missions than the British and often enjoyed rest periods. Here they are playing cards on an airfield in northern France while awaiting the order to scramble.

Often flying up to six sorties a day for a week or more without respite, RAF pilots were driven to the point of exhaustion. They took whatever rest they could; as one pilot remarked, 'We were too tired even to get drunk.'

begun. With it came a breathing space for the RAF, especially battleworn 11 Group, during which to patch its wounds and recover some of its strength with an injection of fresh pilots and machines. Meanwhile, Hitler was still nursing plans for an imminent invasion of southern England (20 September was a likely date) and he pestered Goering to tell him when he could expect the Luftwaffe to overcome the British air force. It would be soon, the Reichsmarschall promised, and prepared a maximum-strength operation against London and other targets in the south for 15 September. However, the long series of raids that took place on that day, although they had 11 Group at full stretch, was dispersed with heavy loss to the intruders. Then, as the weather deteriorated and reports of undiminished Royal Air Force activity in the Channel area continued to

reach the Führer, 'Operation Sealion' was postponed and later cancelled.

By October, the vicious, swirling dogfights that characterized the Battle of Britain had dwindled, and the young Spitfire and Hurricane pilots had truly earned Churchill's immortal commendation: 'Never in the field of human conflict has so much been owed by so many to so few.' Since July, the Royal Air Force had destroyed some 1,500 German aircraft for the loss of about 900 of its own planes.

The architects of this great victory, Dowding and Park, did not receive the recognition that history has judged to be their due. Their jointly agreed tactic of sending up tightly controlled small forces of fighters to disrupt enemy formations before they could do much damage had many critics. Chief among them was Air Vice-Marshal Trafford Leigh-Mallory,

AOC 12 Group, who smarted at being required to play a supporting role while 11 Group led the action. He was an advocate of 'scrambling' (as the urgent take-off of fighter-interceptor aircraft was known in RAF jargon) large numbers of aircraft to meet the incoming enemy masses and shooting down as many of their planes as possible with minimum direction from operations rooms on the ground.

The Battle of Britain was hardly over before this controversy resulted in a showdown at the Air Ministry where, incredible as it may seem now, Dowding and Park were censured for proceeding too cautiously against the Luftwaffe. Dowding (due to retire on 15 July but required to stay on in the crisis) was relieved, and Park was switched to Training Command. Leigh-Mallory moved to head 11 Group and, later, Fighter Command.

On Saturday 7 September 1940, the Luftwaffe turned its attention to the mass bombing of London. This switch in tactics cost them the Battle of Britain, for they did not realize how close their sustained attacks against RAF Fighter Command had come to wearing out the Hurricane and Spitfire pilots. The first attack of the Blitz, as the raids on the capital became known, began in the late afternoon and, with only a two-hour break, continued until 04.30 next morning. Bombs rained down on the East End and the docks, causing huge fires, which burned for days. This scene shows what it was like looking east down the Thames from Tower Bridge shortly after 22.00. When the 'All clear' finally sounded, more than 300 people were dead, 1,300 badly injured and large areas were laid waste. It was, perhaps, as well that Londoners did not

know then that they were about to undergo another 56 consecutive nights of heavy bombing.

The Blitz on London started with almost 12 hours of bombing. Wave after wave of Heinkel He III bombers (8), Dorniers and Junkers, carrying incendiaries and high-explosive bombs attacked the city. Most of the bombs fell in and around the docks.

London was an inferno, but to Air Vice-Marshal Keith Park, watching the destruction from his personal Hurricane, it meant a desperately needed respite for the much-battered fighter airfields.

London Docks (1) were ablaze; the West India Docks (3) and Rotherhithe (6) were also burning fiercely. On the river, fireboats (7) made valiant attempts to fight the fires with their hoses.

Lines of barrage balloons (5) formed part of London's defence against low-flying aircraft. Tethered by steel cables, these giant balloons were flown at heights of 915m/3,000ft to 1,525m/5,000ft.

Every fire-fighting appliance for miles around was in action in London. More than 300 pumps were used in an effort to contain the enormous fire that started in the Surrey Docks (4) when vast

Elsewhere, warehouses full of paint, rum and rubber blazed, pepper stores exploded, and burning molten sugar set the surface of the Thames on fire.

stocks of timber caught alight. The searing heat forced fireboats to draw off to the other side of the river—even so, the paint was blistered on their hulls.

Searchlights traced geometric patterns across the night sky (2) as their operators tried to locate and hold enemy aircraft in the beams so that anti-aircraft gunners could shoot at them.

The civilian services

The Air Raid Precaution Service, set up in 1937, became one of the most effective Civil Defence services. Wardens were always local people who supervised shelters, enforced black-out regulations, warned of impending attack and provided invaluable, unstinting rescue work during and after bombing raids.

At the outbreak of war, the **Auxiliary Fire Service** was made up of full-timers backed by 60,000 volunteers, many of whom soon joined the armed forces. The rest laboured for long hours in dreadful conditions to contain the ferocious fires caused by the bombing. Equipment was often makeshift—early on, London taxis painted grey were used as fire tenders.

The **Ambulance Corps** was stretched to the limit. Mobile first-aid posts with a doctor and three nurses tended the wounded until they could be dug out of the rubble. Drivers of auxiliary ambulances, most of them women, then took the casualties to hospital along streets strewn with débris, with bombs falling about them, often only to find that it too had been destroyed.

The Sinking of the Bismarck/*May 1941*

Britannia ruled the waves on the outbreak of hostilities with Nazi Germany, but her powerful, wide-ranging fleet did not discourage Hitler's seriously understrength Kriegsmarine from reviving the German naval strategy of World War I. The Germans hoped that if it were pursued more vigorously this time, Great Britain might be starved into submission. This strategy was known as commerce raiding, and its success depended upon Germany sinking as many unarmed merchantmen as possible, while avoiding combat with Royal Navy warships. In this way it hoped to deprive its island enemy of vital raw materials, food and war supplies.

Between the wars the Germans, ignoring treaty limitations on the size and type of vessel allowed in their resurgent navy, secretly set about building more U-boats (submarines) than permitted and laying down destroyers, heavy cruisers (sometimes called pocket battleships) and, ultimately, full-blown battleships.

When war with Britain came sooner than expected, Grand Admiral Erich Raeder, Commander-in-Chief of the Kriegsmarine, was, however, a long way from possessing the fleet he needed to fight the Royal Navy on anything approaching equal terms. Nevertheless, he was able immediately to deploy U-boats and cruisers, such as the *Admiral Graf Spee* and *Deutschland*, against Allied cargo ships.

Despite the scuttling of the *Graf Spee* after the Battle of the River Plate in December 1939, and heavy naval losses incurred in Hitler's invasion of Norway, Raeder continued to encourage commerce raiding in the Atlantic.

Throughout the second half of 1940 and into early 1941, British convoys took an increasing battering in the Battle of the Atlantic and a heavy burden was falling on the Royal Navy, tasked as it was to shepherd vulnerable merchantmen on their dangerous voyages. In March 1941, the Germans achieved a monthly record of 350,000 tons of cargo shipping destroyed and, with the rate of sinkings continuing to rise, Raeder sensed that the time had come to exert even greater pressure on Britain's maritime lifeline.

In addition to his U-boat flotillas, he decided to release into the Atlantic trade routes a surface force which would cause consternation among convoys. His Fleet Commander, Admiral Günther Lütjens, was ordered to lead out the two battle-cruisers *Scharnhorst* and *Gneisenau*, both of which were already experienced in commerce raiding; the new heavy cruiser *Prinz Eugen*; and, fresh from

Germany's Z-Plan

Hitler made it clear to his service chiefs in November 1937 that he intended to seek war with Britain. Although superior both on land and in the air, Germany was weak at sea, and Hitler ordered a special committee to study how best to build up its naval strength. They reported, early in 1938, that there were only two options: to construct a fleet of pocket battleships, like *Graf Spee*, and U-boats, entailing a fairly short building schedule, or a fleet of battleships and cruisers to rival the Royal Navy's, a task that would take at least seven years. Hitler and Raeder opted for the latter.

This so-called 'Z-Plan Fleet' would be split into four groups: a force capable of containing the British Home Fleet and another to undertake raids against merchantmen, with two fast strike forces to

back it up. In total, 10 battleships, 3 pocket battleships, 16 cruisers, 2 aircraft-carriers, 190 U-boats and also a host of destroyers were required.

At the outbreak of war this programme had hardly begun. Great Britain, then the greatest naval power in the world, outnumbered Germany 7:1 in battleships, 6:1 in cruisers and 9:1 in destroyers. The German battleships *Bismarck* and *Tirpitz* and the carrier *Graf Zeppelin* had been launched but were incomplete; the first Z-Plan super battleship, 'H', had just been laid down and only a sixth of the U-boats deemed necessary to destroy the British merchant fleet had been built. Raeder decided, therefore, to employ his U-boats in swift and devastating attacks on Britain's shipping in the North Atlantic.

H44, one of the Z-Plan 60,000-ton battleships.

Graf Zeppelin, Germany's first aircraft-carrier.

The battleship *Bismarck* was launched by the granddaughter of Germany's famous Chancellor, whose name she bore, from the Blohm and Voss Shipyard in Hamburg in February 1939. A state occasion, the ceremony was attended by Hitler and many other Nazi leaders. *Bismarck* was commissioned in August 1940.

The most powerful vessel then afloat, her formidable armament consisted of eight 15-in guns mounted in pairs in four turrets, two forward, two aft. In addition, she bristled with secondary and close-range armament.

The British knew that to win the war against Germany they must safeguard the passage of convoys bearing supplies, food and military equipment from the United States and Canada. Once western Europe had been overrun, the Atlantic theatre became of even greater importance.

Fortunately for Britain, Hitler at first underrated this importance, even though his senior naval commanders argued for a total blockade. All hinged on Britain's ability to control the seaways of the western world, and she immediately established a convoy system based on that of WWI. Convoys were savaged, but they got through. Morale was given a further boost in December 1939 when, after harassment by three British ships, each of inferior gunpower, the German pocket battleship *Admiral Graf Spee* was ignominiously scuttled in the River Plate, Montevideo.

On 13–14 September 1940, at the height of the Battle of Britain, Italy invaded Egypt (1), and on 28 October, Greece (2). British naval vessels and aircraft mauled the Italian fleet at Taranto (3) on 11 November, and on 9 December launched their first offensive against the Italians in North Africa (4). On 6 April 1941, the Germans invaded Greece and Yugoslavia (5) and in May, Crete.

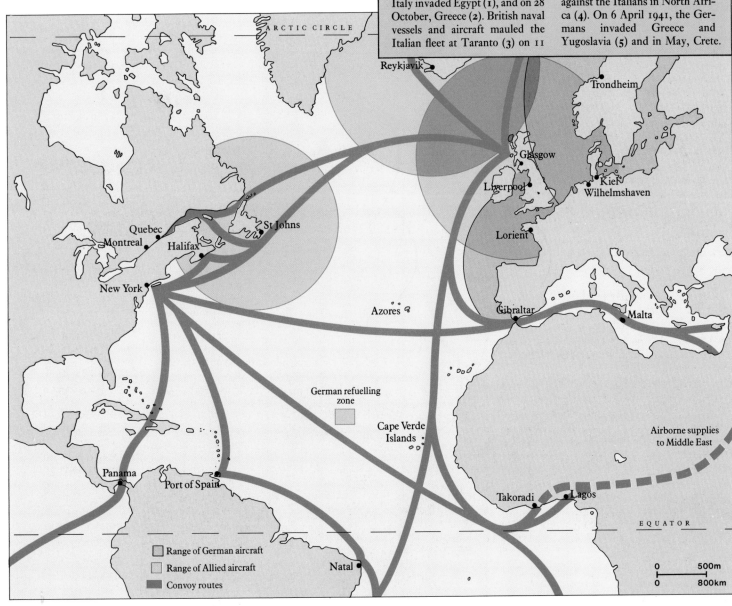

German refuelling zone

Airborne supplies to Middle East

☐ Range of German aircraft
☐ Range of Allied aircraft
▬ Convoy routes

| 0 | | 500m |
| 0 | | 800km |

Convoy routes were determined by many factors, not least the weather. For instance, in early 1943, at the height of the Battle of the Atlantic, conditions in the North Atlantic were the worst for 50 years, and many merchantmen were sunk by the mountainous seas.

Convoys could not take a calmer, more southerly route because this brought them beyond the range of the air patrols from Iceland, leaving them exposed to attack by U-boats. In the same way, convoys to ports in northern Russia had to brave the Arctic Circle in an attempt to avoid air attacks from German bases in Norway.

The safest route for convoys from North America was first to steam northeast, with air cover provided from Newfoundland, then to swing on an easterly course to ports in the north of England and Scotland, protected by the RAF.

A great expanse of the North Atlantic was still without air cover, as was the entire mid-Atlantic, where there was a German refuelling zone.

her working-up trials, the battleship *Bismarck*, commanded by Captain Ernst Lindemann. Eight months after her commissioning ceremony in August 1940, Lindemann reported his ship operational, having completed sea trials and the crew's battle training in record time.

Then the vicissitudes of war intervened to spoil Raeder's plan. First, *Scharnhorst* developed serious boiler trouble, then *Gneisenau* was torpedoed and badly damaged; finally the *Prinz Eugen* struck a mine. Of the three, only *Prinz Eugen* was capable of being repaired quickly. Raeder, in spite of the misgivings of Lütjens, decided to proceed with 'Exercise Rhine', as he called it, using only *Bismarck* and *Prinz Eugen*.

On 12 May, Lütjens and his staff joined Lindemann aboard the *Bismarck* at Gotenhafen, now Gdynia, in German-occupied Poland, and final preparations were made for a three-month-long foray into the North Atlantic. Six days later *Bismarck*, her fuel bunkers not quite filled with oil because of a malfunction while loading, and *Prinz Eugen* began their momentous voyage. They were accompanied in the initial stages of the voyage by an anti-submarine screen of destroyers as well as Luftwaffe air cover.

Though their departure was supposed to be secret, the ships were spotted by the neutral Swedes as they sailed through the Kattegat in daylight on 20 May. The British naval attaché in Stockholm was informed of the ships' movement by a member of the Swedish Secret Service sympathetic to the Allies' cause; he in turn duly alerted the Admiralty in London. A message from the Norwegian Resistance corroborated the signal.

Throughout 21 May, *Bismarck* sheltered in Grimstadfjord south of Bergen, while *Prinz Eugen* and the destroyers steamed on to rendezvous with an oil tanker. (*Bismarck*, although underfuelled, did not have orders to use this refuelling stop, a fact which would later have a bearing on her destiny.) During that time, a sharp-eyed Royal Air Force reconnaissance pilot located and photographed *Bismarck*, but when bombers arrived at the fjord in bad weather and darkness she had slipped away, though the aircrews, who were attacking blind, were not aware of the fact.

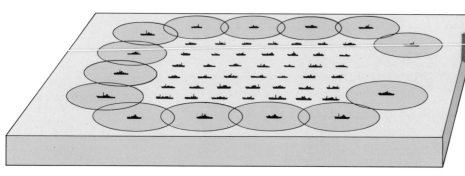

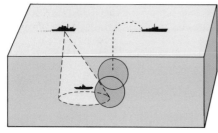

A submerged U-boat lost its great surface speed and became unaware of what was happening above. It was, therefore, vulnerable to attacks by depth charge.

The most effective attacks were those in which two escort vessels worked in tandem. One would maintain contact by means of Asdic, a device for detecting a submerged submarine by bouncing a sound wave off its hull. It would then radio the U-boat's position and depth to the second vessel, which would speed to the spot and drop depth charges.

The Asdic cone enlarged with distance, and at its extremity its accuracy became suspect; moreover, the cone, being narrow at source, was not effective at less than about 275m/300yds. The U-boat's best chance of escape was to change course, either directly toward or away from the destroyer.

Depth charges were detonated by firing a timer set to go off at the level of the submarine as shown by Asdic.

When encountering surface raiders, a convoy was ordered to scatter by the senior officer present only as a last resort if the attacking force was overwhelmingly strong. Thereafter, each merchantman had to keep radio silence and make for his destination without protection.

The signal 'Scatter fanwise and proceed at your utmost speed' entailed a simple and well-understood procedure. The centre column of ships or, when there was an even number of columns, the right-hand column of the central two, continued ahead. The columns either side turned away 10° to port or starboard. The next columns turned out 20° (10° more than their neighbours), and so on to the wings of the convoy.

In this way, a compact convoy dispersed in a slowly expanding fan. Marauders would then attack some vessels, but this manoeuvre usually ensured the safety of most.

When war broke out in 1939, the German navy quickly deployed U-boats and surface raiders to sink merchantmen bound for British ports, hoping to strangle Britain's supply lines across the Atlantic. The Admiralty at once reinstituted the convoy systems that had proved so successful in combating this threat in WWI.

Convoys often comprised 45–50 ships and occupied as much as 52sq km/20sq mls. There were usually several columns of ships about 1km/½ml apart.

In theory, as the diagram shows, escort vessels were stationed all around the edges of the convoy to protect the flanks. An advance force, with look-outs, radar and Asdic worked ahead of the convoy, which was also supported from the rear by a rescue ship.

When the convoy was attacked, ships of the escort force were to be detached to search out the attackers. This could be a perilous action, for it left a gap in the defence line through which other U-boats could penetrate.

In practice, there were often only two or three warships available to protect a convoy and early in the war U-boats were able to sink merchant ships almost at will.

Convoys were made up of large numbers of merchantmen (1), often 40 or more, escorted by a handful of Royal Navy corvettes and destroyers.

Four-engined Focke-Wulfe 200 Condors (2), operating from bases in France, often directed lone U-boats to convoy targets. With a then amazing range of 3,450km/ 2,150mls and a bombload of 1,633kg/ 3,600lb, they were able also to carry out their own raids on shipping.

were hard to see. U-boat commanders preferred to attack when surfaced, for they could then dominate most situations.

Whenever possible, attacks were made from windward: this was the most difficult side for a convoy's look-outs to scan, and the submarine's tell-tale bow waves were eliminated.

their great speed to get ahead of a convoy and, when it came into range, attacked at periscope depth. Surface attacks were made at night because then, U-boats, slender and low in the water,

'Wolf-packs'— groups of German submarines—usually attacked from the surface by night and submerged by day. Ideally, U-boats used

Ships carrying passengers or volatile cargoes, such as munitions or fuel, were usually placed in the centre of the convoy (3) in the belief that they would be less vulnerable to U-boat attack. This was not always so.

Anti-submarine escort work in the gruelling Battle of the Atlantic fell largely on corvettes (4), a class of small, eminently seaworthy warships built on the design of the well-tried Middlesbrough whaler. They carried Asdic and 113-kg/250-lb depth charges.

Each convoy was led by a Commodore, whose ship always headed the centre column (5). The Commodore was responsible for marshalling the convoy and seeing that the merchantmen, of all shapes, sizes and speeds, kept in formation. At night, in fog, and in high seas, his was a difficult and unenviable task.

In the early hours of 22 May, the two big German ships parted with their destroyer escort and set course for the narrow, foggy Denmark Strait separating Iceland and Greenland, in an attempt to slip undetected into the North Atlantic.

Meanwhile, the British had been preparing counter-measures. Admiral Sir John Tovey, the Commander-in-Chief, Home Fleet, warned his standing patrols in northern waters to keep a sharp look-out for the two enemy ships. Then, on 21 May, he sent Vice-Admiral Lancelot Holland and his squadron hurrying north from his Scapa Flow base toward Iceland to provide heavy firepower should it be needed. The squadron comprised the biggest warship in the world (as distinct from the most powerful), the 20-year-old, somewhat lightly armoured battle cruiser *Hood*, and the new battleship *Prince of Wales*, which was still having trouble with her 14-inch main armament, as well as half a dozen destroyers.

The next day, when aerial reconnaissance revealed that the German ships had vanished from Norwegian waters, Tovey realized they would be making a break for the Atlantic and took the bulk of the Home Fleet to join the hunt—the battleship *King George V*, together with the aircraft-carrier *Victorious*, four cruisers and seven destroyers. At sea he was to rendezvous with another battle cruiser, *Repulse*.

In the icy waters of the North Atlantic, British ships and aircraft scanned the heaving seas for the *Bismarck* and *Prinz Eugen*. At last, at 07.22 on 23 May, the cruiser *Suffolk* from Rear-Admiral Frederick Wake-Walker's command, which was patrolling the Denmark Strait, spotted the enemy. Holding the German ships on her new and powerful radar *Suffolk*, accompanied by *Norfolk*, Wake-Walker's flagship, began to shadow them while interception plans were laid. At 20.30 there was an unplanned brush with *Bismarck*, during which a few salvoes were fired. No damage was done to the British ships, but as a result of the jolt caused by firing her guns, *Bismarck*'s forward radar was put out of action, leaving her blind ahead, so the two ships proceeded with *Prinz Eugen* in the lead.

Shortly after 05.30 next morning, *Hood* and the *Prince of Wales* caught up with their quarry, which they considerably outgunned: they had eight 15-inch and ten 14-inch guns, compared with the German's eight 15-inch and eight 8-inch weapons. However, instead of bringing all his turrets to bear, Admiral Holland approached his targets obliquely, opening fire with just his forward batteries. In an

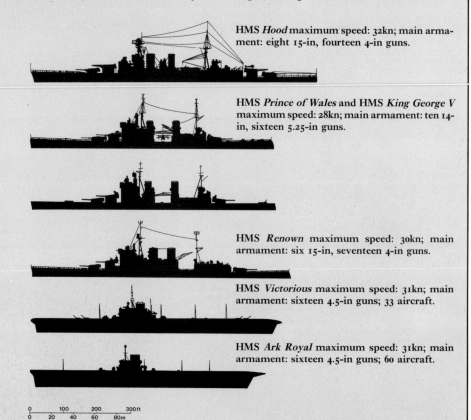

The opposing fleets

Bismarck maximum speed: 30kn; main armament: eight 15-in, twelve 5.9-in guns.

Prinz Eugen maximum speed: 32kn; main armament: eight 8-in, twelve 4.1-in guns.

Seen in silhouette, the heavy cruiser *Prinz Eugen* and the battleship *Bismarck* were identical, except that the *Prinz Eugen* was 52m/169ft shorter. British look-outs could only detect this difference if they sighted the two warships steaming in parallel formation. If they sighted either singly or any distance apart, it was almost impossible to judge whether the vessel they were

shadowing or about to attack was the cruiser or the *Bismarck*. This was one of the mightiest warships then afloat, with a displacement of 42,000 tons and thick, specially strengthened armour. HMS *Hood* made precisely this significant error in identification at the battle off the Greenland coast and opened fire on the *Prinz Eugen*, leaving *Bismarck* unmolested at first.

HMS *Hood* maximum speed: 32kn; main armament: eight 15-in, fourteen 4-in guns.

HMS *Prince of Wales* and HMS *King George V* maximum speed: 28kn; main armament: ten 14-in, sixteen 5.25-in guns.

HMS *Renown* maximum speed: 30kn; main armament: six 15-in, seventeen 4-in guns.

HMS *Victorious* maximum speed: 31kn; main armament: sixteen 4.5-in guns; 33 aircraft.

HMS *Ark Royal* maximum speed: 31kn; main armament: sixteen 4.5-in guns; 60 aircraft.

0 100 200 300ft
0 20 40 60 80m

At the outbreak of war, Great Britain was the world's greatest naval power despite Germany's intensive shipbuilding programme after Hitler renounced the Versailles Treaty in 1935. The battleships *Scharnhorst* and *Gneisenau*, among others, were laid down, as were U-boats, cruisers, destroyers and the mighty *Bismarck*.

The ten to one overall numerical superiority of warships in Great Britain's favour did not, however, confer the advantage that appeared on paper. Britain's resources were stretched, since her ships had to patrol the Atlantic, the Mediterranean and the waters of the Far East. Moreover, while almost all the German ships were of modern design and construction, many of Great Britain's capital ships were coming to the end of their serviceable lives. Of the major warships

involved in the pursuit of the *Bismarck*, HMS *Hood* had been commissioned 20 years earlier and, though fast and with impressive fire power, had inadequate armour. The battle cruiser *Repulse* was even older, had two fewer main guns than *Bismarck*, was weakly armoured and carried insufficient fuel for long voyages.

On the other hand, the battleship HMS *Prince of Wales* was too new. She had joined the Fleet only two months before and still carried workmen on board; her machinery had not been thoroughly run-in and her crew were not fully used to working together. The same applied to the aircraft carrier HMS *Victorious*, the pilots of whose squadron of Swordfishes had not even had time to master the drill of landing their aircraft on deck.

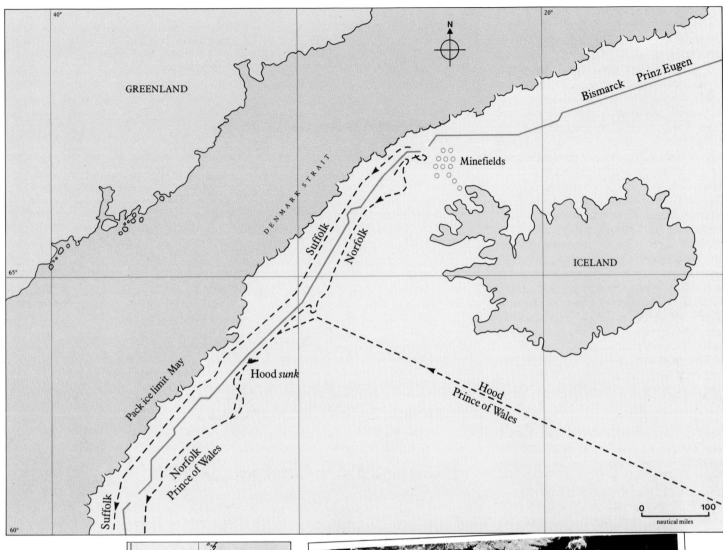

On 18 May 1941,
Bismarck and *Prinz Eugen*, under the command of Admiral Lütjens, sailed from Gotenhafen to a fjord near Bergen.

It was clear they were preparing to break into the Atlantic, but which route would they take? They could steam north of Scotland and south of the Shetland Isles or north of the Shetlands and south of the Faroe Islands. Alternatively, they could make passage north of the Faroes and south of Iceland, or between Iceland and Greenland, through the Denmark Strait.

In the event, Lütjens chose the last option but was sighted on 23 May by the cruiser HMS *Suffolk*. Equipped with the most up-to-date radar which could 'hold' the enemy even in the most adverse weather, *Suffolk* kept in touch with *Bismarck*, while using a fog bank to remain out of her sight. Meanwhile, HMS *Hood* and HMS *Prince of Wales*, with six destroyers, were moving to seal the southern end of the Denmark Strait.

The *Bismarck* was photographed in Grimstadfjord, near Bergen, on 21 May by Flying Officer Suckling in a Spitfire of Coastal Command. Air reconnaissance was vital in WWII because it was the quickest way to get information on the enemy.

Suckling's sighting of the *Bismarck* first alerted the British to her position; later in the pursuit, after contact had been lost, it was a Catalina flying boat of Coastal Command that again sighted her. Without this air reconnaissance, the *Bismarck* would probably have reached the mid-Atlantic undetected.

exchange of salvoes which lasted a mere six minutes, *Bismarck* blew up *Hood*, breaking her back and sending her and 1,417 men to the bottom.

Then *Bismarck* and *Prinz Eugen* corrected their aim and engaged *Prince of Wales*, which was having a recurrence of the main armament trouble that had dogged her since commissioning. Eight shells bored into her and her captain withdrew from the action. Lütjens let her go. The news of *Hood*'s sinking rocked the Royal Navy, shook Britain and sent tremors of disbelief around the world. *Prinz Eugen* escaped unscathed in the brief encounter, but *Bismarck* took three hits, two of which spelled the beginning of the end. She was now sailing bow down, with 2,000 tons of seawater slopping around in her forecastle, and she was trailing oil from a fractured tank. Already short of fuel, the

ship would have to sacrifice the speed needed to try to outrun her pursuers in order to preserve sufficient oil to reach a suitable port.

The best means to save the damaged ship was uppermost in the minds of her captain, Lindemann, and Lütjens, the Fleet Commander. The latter decided, against the former's advice, to steer a southerly course for St Nazaire and seek repairs in German-held western France, rather than to turn north and make a run for home. It was to be a fateful decision.

Recovering from the devastating news about *Hood*, the Admiralty set out to concentrate the might of the Royal Navy on the German raiders, which were still being shadowed by *Suffolk* and *Norfolk*, the damaged *Prince of Wales* and the destroyers from the late Admiral Holland's squadron. In addition to Tovey's

fleet, now steaming some 800km/500mls southeast of *Bismarck*, Force H—an aircraft-carrier, two cruisers and six destroyers under Vice-Admiral Sir James Somerville—was ordered up from Gibraltar. And just about every other British warship in the North Atlantic, whether it was on important convoy duty or not, was signalled to intercept the two ships.

Though fuelling difficulties would eventually mar its efforts to concentrate its forces, the Royal Navy had by the end of 23 May arranged to deploy 5 battleships, 2 aircraft-carriers, 14 cruisers and 21 destroyers against the enemy ships.

On board *Bismarck*, Lütjens was making plans of his own. Taking into account the damage to his flagship and the fact that the smaller *Prinz Eugen* would soon be running low on fuel, he decided they should part company. *Bismarck* would try

Commissioned in 1920, *Hood* was almost the last of a class of heavy British warships which had suffered at the Battle of Jutland in 1916 because their deck armour was not strong enough to withstand long-range plunging fire from

large-calibre guns. But this deficiency was never remedied, even when *Hood* was refitted in 1939.

The fatal salvo, fired at 19-km/12-mls range, screamed down almost perpendicularly and went straight

through *Hood*'s unstrengthened deck into the magazines deep below the waterline. *Hood* blew up

and sank within two minutes. Of her crew of 1,420, only three survived; their stations are shown below.

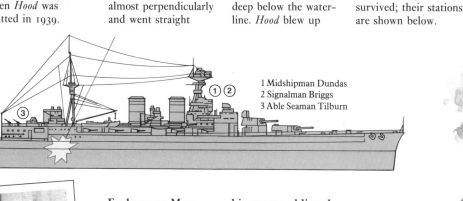

1 Midshipman Dundas
2 Signalman Briggs
3 Able Seaman Tilburn

Seaman Tilburn, one of the three survivors of HMS *Hood*. Details of his rescue were not released until much later.

Early on 24 May 1941, as *Bismarck* and *Prinz Eugen* raced south through the Denmark Strait, they were intercepted by HMS *Hood* and HMS *Prince of Wales* from Vice-Admiral Holland's battle-cruiser squadron. *Hood* was the biggest warship in the world and, between them, the two British ships outgunned the Germans.

But perhaps because *Hood*'s deck was somewhat lightly armoured, Holland approached

his quarry obliquely so that only half his main armament could be brought to bear on the enemy.

In an engagement which began at 05.52 and lasted about six minutes, *Hood* was blown out of the water by *Bismarck*.

Hood was hit in an early exchange of salvoes and a fire started. Then, as Admiral Holland ordered his ships 20° to port to bring the after guns into action, disaster overtook *Hood*. A 15-in shell from *Bismarck* penetrated to the magazines amidships and a tremendous explosion (4) blew the great ship in two.

An eye-witness on *Prinz Eugen* recalled seeing one of *Hood*'s huge 15-in after gun turrets (1) tossed into the air as if it were a feather. Inexplicably, nobody heard any sound of an explosion.

As the pillar of smoke and flame rose high in the sky, it was speckled with bright white flashes (2) as *Hood*'s shells exploded. One sailor later said it looked 'like a huge Chinese Christmas cracker'.

Watchers on *Bismarck* were amazed to see *Hood*'s two forward 15-in guns (3) fire a final salvo as the bows rose up and the stricken ship slipped beneath the waves, but it was probably an accidental detonation caused by electrical circuits connecting.

Seconds later, *Hood* went to the bottom, leaving only a dense, billowing cloud of smoke hanging over the empty sea.

to shake off her pursuers and set a straight course for St Nazaire; *Prinz Eugen* would break away to rendezvous with an oil tanker, then start commerce raiding.

Their first attempt to split up in bad weather on the afternoon of 24 May was foiled, but a second try a few hours later succeeded, even though *Bismarck* and Wake-Walker's shadowing force exchanged ineffectual fire in the process. Unlike her 'big brother', *Prinz Eugen* ultimately reached port in France.

While the Royal Navy continued to drive closer, Admiral Tovey made a last attempt that day to cripple *Bismarck*. He detached the aircraft-carrier *Victorious* to steam at full speed to within launching range—160km/100mls—and send in its torpedo bombers. Nine Swordfish biplanes braved the *Bismarck*'s spurting fire, but only one torpedo struck home and did no damage. No aircraft were shot down and, miraculously, considering the darkness of the night, all returned to *Victorious*. Before 24 May closed, *Bismarck* and *Prince of Wales* again fired on each other at extreme range, without either registering any hits.

On Sunday 25 May, *Bismarck* shook off the chasing ships for the first time in 31 hours. Then began a feverish effort by the Royal Navy and the Royal Air Force to make contact again. By coincidence, 31 hours would pass before a Catalina flying boat of RAF Coastal Command, from Northern Ireland, rediscovered *Bismarck* through a break in the clouds.

Tovey in *King George V* was running low on fuel and was too far behind to intercept. In fact, most of his Home Fleet ships had already turned back because of shortage of oil. However, aircraft from the carrier *Ark Royal* in Somerville's H Force coming up from the south would be able to attack before dark. Even if they could not stop *Bismarck*, they could at least slow her down enough to let British ships come up with her next morning.

That afternoon *Ark Royal*'s first Swordfish strike was flown, and it ended in embarrassment. The crews mistook HMS *Sheffield* for the *Bismarck* and, luckily for their comrades-in-arms, their torpedoes, fitted with new magnetic detonators, exploded harmlessly as soon as they hit the sea. Back on *Ark Royal* old, reliable contact detonators were fitted to the torpedoes on the craft being readied for the next sortie.

For just over half an hour that evening, 15 Swordfish of the Fleet Air Arm flew through the *Bismarck*'s blistering anti-aircraft fire to deliver their torpedoes. Only two hit: one did no damage, but the

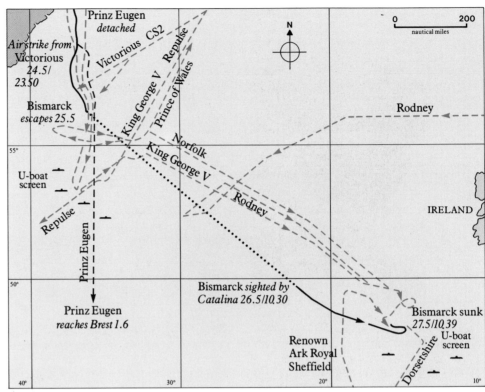

At Gibraltar, Force H (*Renown*, *Ark Royal* and *Sheffield*) under Admiral Somerville was ordered to the chase to bring maximum firepower to bear on the *Bismarck*. They were to be joined by the battleships *Ramillies* and *Revenge*, which were on escort duty in the western Atlantic.

The damage to *Bismarck*'s bow was causing steady loss of oil. At 08.00, Lütjens detached *Prinz Eugen* and himself set about trying to shake off his pursuers.

This he achieved on 25 May. Shadowing British ships, warned of possible U-boat attacks, adopted a zigzag anti-submarine course, which entailed briefly losing *Bismarck* from their radar screens on shifts to port. During one of these port turns, the *Bismarck* turned to starboard, made a loop behind *Suffolk* and *Norfolk* and set a southeasterly course for port in France.

At 10.36 on 26 May, a Catalina flying boat of RAF Coastal Command rediscovered her by chance 1,110km/690mls from the French coast.

Torpedo-carrying aircraft, such as the Swordfish, *above*, followed a set procedure when attacking ships. In groups of three, they dived steeply, one behind the other. At 46–76m/150–250ft, they pulled out of their dive, fanned out and approached the ship in line abreast, presenting anti-aircraft gunners, whose guns were optically ranged, with three targets, instead of one. About 823m/900yds before releasing their torpedoes they dropped to 15–30m/50–100ft above the surface of the sea.

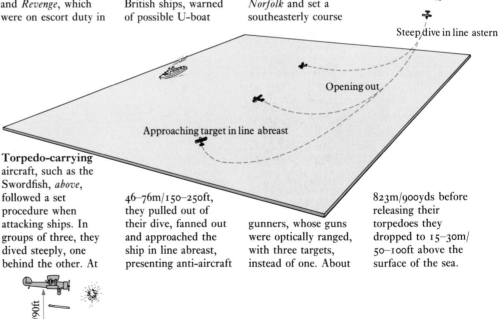

Steep dive in line astern

Opening out

Approaching target in line abreast

27m/90ft

The Commanders

Lütjens

Lindemann

Tovey

Admiral Günther Lütjens (1889–1941), the Fleet Commander, had joined the Imperial Navy in 1907 and, until World War II, had spent most of his professional life with Torpedo Boat flotillas. During the Norwegian campaign he had led the *Scharnhorst* and *Gneisenau* and in July 1940 was appointed commander of the *Bismarck* flotilla. A tall, quiet man, his high intelligence, physical courage and generous nature were recognized by all in the service. Lütjens had reservations as to the wisdom of 'Operation Rhine', yet when the *Bismarck* sustained three hits he insisted on continuing with the operation rather than turning for home. Why he made this disastrous decision is unknown, but it is possible that he was under pressure from a higher authority in Berlin.

Captain Ernst Lindemann (1894–1941), a gunnery expert, had been appointed captain of the *Bismarck* in early 1940. After the hits on his ship, he argued strongly with Lütjens that she should return to port. It was in every sense the correct course: not only was oil lost and speed reduced, but the element of surprise had gone. Moreover, at that moment the *Bismarck* had achieved the notable success of sinking HMS *Hood*. She had a good chance of safely reaching port and a hero's reception would await her. Lütjens, however, overruled him and the *Bismarck* was taken on to her doom.

Admiral Sir John Tovey (1885–1971), Commander-in-Chief of the British Home Fleet, was stationed at Scapa Flow in his flag ship *King George V*. A born leader, he gave confidence to all around him. He was deeply religious and, both in his private and professional life, always did what he thought was right, irrespective of what his superiors might want, or wish to hear. He also possessed an attribute of inestimable value—tenacity of purpose.

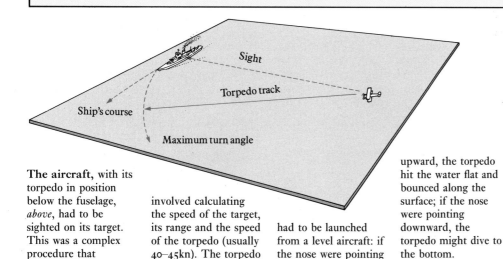

Sight

Torpedo track

Ship's course

Maximum turn angle

The aircraft, with its torpedo in position below the fuselage, *above*, had to be sighted on its target. This was a complex procedure that involved calculating the speed of the target, its range and the speed of the torpedo (usually 40–45kn). The torpedo had to be launched from a level aircraft: if the nose were pointing upward, the torpedo hit the water flat and bounced along the surface; if the nose were pointing downward, the torpedo might dive to the bottom.

Major warships were well equipped to withstand torpedo attacks. Many had a reinforced bulge below the water line, *see below*, which could sustain a hit without receiving irreparable damage. Once the attacking aircraft were sighted, ships could take rapid evasive action to move out of the torpedo's path. Meanwhile, ships fired not only at the aircraft but bombarded the sea around themselves to distract the pilot's concentration with massive spurts of water.

823m/900yds

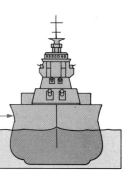

other—which the Germans described as a 100,000 to 1 chance—knocked out the big battleship's steering gear. As the aircraft broke off and returned safely to *Ark Royal*, *Bismarck* slowly executed a wide circle while fruitless efforts were made to regain some sort of control. Then she settled to a northwesterly course which would take her straight into the path of Admiral Tovey.

As she struggled along, *Bismarck* was intercepted by five destroyers, sent as an anti-submarine screen for Tovey's big ships, and a running fight developed in heavy seas and darkness, illuminated by frequent British starshells. Neither the destroyers' torpedoes nor *Bismarck*'s guns managed to find a mark, but the German sailors knew that, come daylight, their fate would be sealed.

The last act of this tragic maritime drama, which had lasted eight days and encompassed the whole North Atlantic, began a little after 08.45 on 27 May when the battleships *King George V* and *Rodney* engaged *Bismarck*. Her crew fought her as best they could until 09.31, when her last gun fell silent. For another hour the stricken German ship continued to be subjected to terrible punishment. Her topsides were shot to pieces and she was burning fiercely below decks, but she would not sink.

By then, most of the British ships in the area had to break off because they were in danger of running out of fuel. As he sailed away, Tovey ordered the cruiser *Dorsetshire*, which still had torpedoes left, to move in close and finish off *Bismarck*. However, the Germans claim that before this could happen scuttling charges were ignited in her hull and the sea-cocks opened. Whichever side was responsible for administering the *coup de grâce*, the result was the same. The great ship began to heel over and capsize, going down stern first at 10.39 with her colours still flying.

With the sinking of the *Bismarck*, the *Hood* was revenged. It was now Britain's turn to be cheered by victory, Germany's turn to mourn the sinking of its greatest battleship. Hitler, whose Kriegsmarine had never been strong, realized that a similar fate awaited the remaining handful of big surface ships once they were detected at sea. He therefore ordered that in future no battleships should be sent into the Atlantic, so the threat of *Scharnhorst*, *Gneisenau* and *Tirpitz* (*Bismark*'s sister ship) was greatly reduced, causing Grand Admiral Raeder to comment: 'The loss of the *Bismarck* had a decisive effect on the war at sea.'

In the short exchange of salvoes before *Hood* was sunk, *Bismarck* was holed forward and in a fuel tank. Limping bows down and trailing a tell-tale slick of oil, she parted from *Prinz Eugen* to try to reach port in German-occupied France. For 31 hours on 25 and 26 May, *Bismarck* managed to elude her pursuers, but then she was resighted 1,110km/690mls from the French coast.

British ships were running low on fuel and could not close with her unless she could be slowed even more. So, at 19.10 on 26 May, 15 Swordfish torpedo bombers from the carrier *Ark Royal* were launched against *Bismarck*, which they reached around 20.50. For half an hour they attacked through a fierce anti-aircraft barrage and succeeded in crippling her steering gear. Her fate was sealed: *Bismarck* was sunk by gunfire early next morning.

The Swordfish attack was made in dreadful weather. Low cloud and rain limited visibility for the three-man crews in the open cockpits of their obsolete aircraft, while *Bismarck* had to contend with a Force 8 gale and heavy seas.

Aircraft from sub-flights 3 and 4 attacked from the port quarter (1). One of their torpedoes struck home but did no significant damage.

Bismarck: the aftermath

The sinking of *Bismarck* was profoundly important. Churchill later wrote: 'Had she escaped, the moral effects of her continuing existence as much as the material damage she might have inflicted on our shipping would have been calamitous. Many misgivings would have arisen regarding our capacity to control the oceans, and these would have been trumpeted round the world to our great detriment and discomfort.'

There was another equally important outcome. Hitler began to lose faith in Grand Admiral Raeder (who was replaced by Dönitz) and in the concept of a large surface fleet. Indeed, he eventually came to believe that all the great German warships should be paid off, dismantled and their steel used to make tanks for deployment on the Eastern Front.

Henceforth, all naval building facilities were to be employed in the construction of U-boats. Had this been undertaken earlier, and the U-boat force increased to a strength of 300 as Dönitz had repeatedly requested, the outcome of the Battle of the Atlantic—which was, in any event, close run—might well have been different. Had Great Britain collapsed, this would have had appalling consequences, notably that there would have been no launching base for the Normandy landings in 1944.

Members of *Bismarck*'s crew struggled in the cold, oil-stained Atlantic, awaiting rescue by HMS *Dorsetshire* and the destroyer *Maori*. One hundred and ten had been taken on board when a U-boat alarm was sounded, and the ships had no choice but to steam quickly from the area, leaving about 700 survivors to drown. A German supply ship and a U-boat between them rescued a further five men, bringing the total saved to 115 out of a ship's company of 2,200.

The anti-aircraft armament on *Bismarck* (2) was formidable: 32 guns—sixteen 110-mm and sixteen 37-mm. Nevertheless, not one Swordfish was shot down and all returned to *Ark Royal*, although three crashed on landing.

The torpedo that smashed *Bismarck*'s steering gear came from one of two Swordfish of No 2 sub-flight approaching on the starboard quarter (3). The pilots, Lt 'Feather' Godfrey-Faussett and Sub-Lt Kenneth Pattisson, brought their biplanes down from 9,000ft almost to wave-top height to deliver their attack. At one time they were so low they were flying underneath *Bismarck*'s anti-aircraft fire: the gunners could not depress their weapons far enough to bring them to bear.

Bismarck was crippled by a 46-cm/18-in torpedo, which hit her below the waterline on the starboard side at the stern (4). With her steering gear smashed and rudders jammed, the ship made two circles out of control; then she settled on an unalterable course NNW, into the path of approaching British warships.

Adolf Hitler's euphoria over his swift subjugation of most of western Europe, and his hurried preparations for the invasion of Britain, did not eclipse his long-cherished ambition to take a greater prize—the Union of Soviet Socialist Republics.

That a German–Soviet non-aggression pact had been in force since August 1939 did not bother him. For almost a year, the two giants had been enlarging their frontiers at the expense of smaller countries without coming into confrontation. Now it was time for Hitler to revert to the goal of National Socialism expounded in *Mein Kampf*: the eastward expansion of the German nation to obtain *lebensraum* (living space), and with it the overthrow of Communism.

At the end of July 1940 the Führer announced to his staff his intention of attacking the USSR the following spring. A few days later, at a meeting with senior generals, he declared his aim: 'Wiping out the very power to exist of Russia.' There followed a build-up of the production of war material, an expansion of the German armed forces, and a massive transfer of troops and equipment to East Prussia and Nazi-occupied Poland. In December, Hitler dignified his huge military undertaking with the codename 'Operation Barbarossa', after the famous medieval German emperor.

Barbarossa was planned to commence in early May 1941 and, according to the Führer's optimistic estimate, would last two months, by which time Josef Stalin's Communist régime would have succumbed to German blitzkreig. However, an exceedingly wet spring which would have made the deployment of mechanized armies difficult, coupled with the unforeseen diversion of some German forces to occupy Yugoslavia and Greece, caused Hitler to hesitate. His Russian adventure was postponed until 22 June.

This critical six-week delay was resented by Field Marshal Walther von Brauchitsch, Commander-in-Chief of the Army, who correctly assumed that his troops in the east might not have accomplished all that the Führer required of them before the onset of winter. But Hitler would not relent, nor would he permit German factories to switch production to the manufacture of proper cold-weather equipment, maintaining that it would not be needed.

In Russia, meanwhile, life was proceeding normally. Despite repeated warnings that it was Germany's intention soon to turn on him, Stalin chose to ignore them. He believed them to be no more than

The Ribbentrop-Molotov pact

On 24 August 1939, the free world was astonished to learn that von Ribbentrop, the German Foreign Minister, and his Russian counterpart, Molotov, had signed a non-aggression pact.

The mutual loathing of the two despotisms was absolute and undisguised; the expedient, therefore, necessarily temporary. But for both Hitler and Stalin the benefits of this hypocritical agreement were clear: Germany would be a reduced danger to the USSR if she were engaged in warfare in the west, while Hitler could pursue his hitherto successful strategy of tackling one opponent at a time.

The crucial paragraph of the pact read: 'Both High Contracting Parties obligate themselves to desist from any act of violence, any aggressive action, and any attack on each other, either individually or jointly with other powers.'

Hitler had thus secured a free hand in western Europe, Stalin a breathing space. Yet even as the rival, jubilant diplomats toasted each other and their countries at a Kremlin banquet, suspicion poisoned their minds. Untrusting and devious, each side resorted to even more subterfuge and watched each other's every move with fearful apprehension. Spies proliferated, of whom perhaps the most effective was Dr Richard Sorge, a Communist working in Tokyo as correspondent for the German newspaper *Frankfurter Zeitung*. On 20 May 1941, he informed the Kremlin that the Germans planned to invade around 20 June. Subsequently he reported that Japan had no plans to attack the USSR, thus allowing Stalin to move his well-equipped Siberian troops to the Moscow area when the struggle for the capital developed.

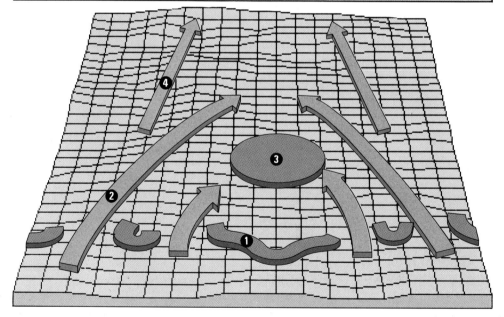

On 18 December 1940, some six months before the German attack on the USSR, Hitler signed Directive 21 in respect of Operation Barbarossa.

Instructions, though in the planning stage only, were precise. The objective was to destroy the first-line of the Red Army (1) stationed in the western parts of the USSR by thrusting deep into the interior (2) at maximum speed with spearheads of tanks (4) to encircle huge numbers of Russian troops (3). In this way, Hitler planned to prevent their retreat to, and re-formation within, central Russia.

At first the German plan proved hugely successful: within two weeks 323,898 Soviet troops had been encircled in two operations, one at Bialystok and the other near Minsk. The German Army, advancing at more than 80km/50mls a day, seemed likely to fulfil Hitler's demand for the conquest of the Caucasus before the end of 1941.

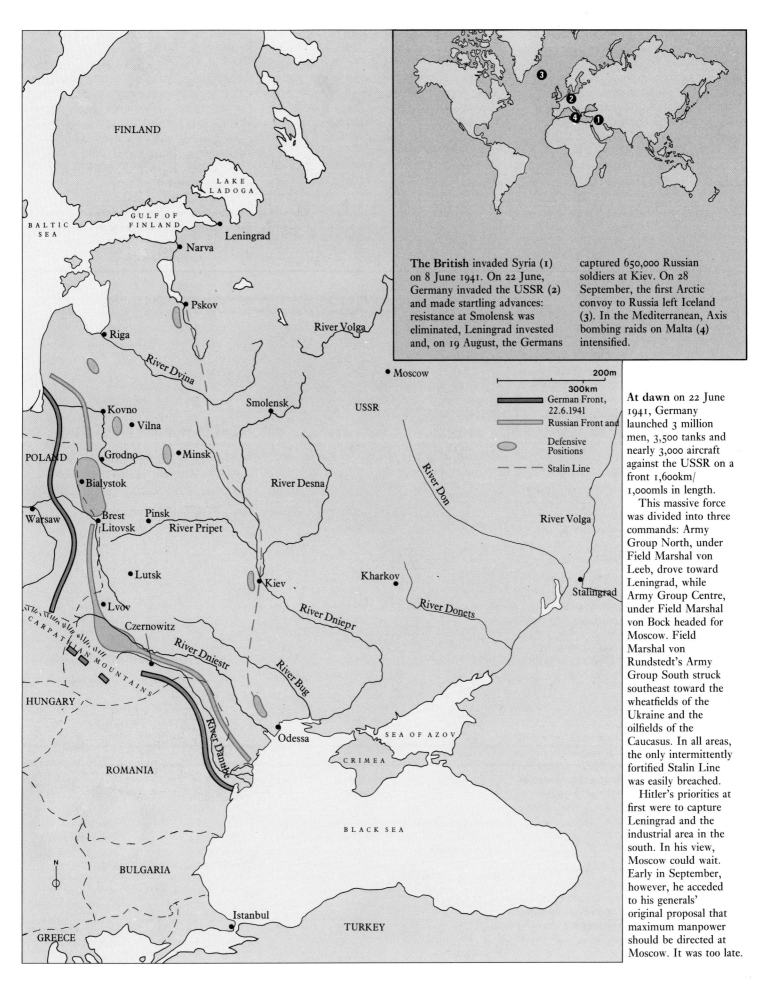

FINLAND

LAKE
LADOGA

GULF OF
FINLAND

BALTIC
SEA

Leningrad

● Narva

● Pskov

River Volga

● Riga

River Dvina

USSR

● Kovno

Smolensk ○

● Vilna

● Moscow

POLAND

Grodno ●

● Minsk

River Desna

River Don

● Bialystok

River Volga

Warsaw ●

Brest
Litovsk

Pinsk ●

River Pripet

● Lutsk

Kharkov ●

River Dniepr

Kiev ●

River Donets

Stalingrad ●

Lvov ●

Czernowitz

River Dniestr

River Bug

CARPATHIAN MOUNTAINS

HUNGARY

SEA OF AZOV

River Danube

Odessa ●

CRIMEA

ROMANIA

BLACK SEA

BULGARIA

N

Istanbul ●

TURKEY

GREECE

The British invaded Syria (1)
on 8 June 1941. On 22 June,
Germany invaded the USSR (2)
and made startling advances:
resistance at Smolensk was
eliminated, Leningrad invested
and, on 19 August, the Germans

captured 650,000 Russian
soldiers at Kiev. On 28
September, the first Arctic
convoy to Russia left Iceland
(3). In the Mediterranean, Axis
bombing raids on Malta (4)
intensified.

200m

300km

German Front,
22.6.1941

Russian Front and

Defensive
Positions

Stalin Line

At dawn on 22 June
1941, Germany
launched 3 million
men, 3,500 tanks and
nearly 3,000 aircraft
against the USSR on a
front 1,600km/
1,000mls in length.
    This massive force
was divided into three
commands: Army
Group North, under
Field Marshal von
Leeb, drove toward
Leningrad, while
Army Group Centre,
under Field Marshal
von Bock headed for
Moscow. Field
Marshal von
Rundstedt's Army
Group South struck
southeast toward the
wheatfields of the
Ukraine and the
oilfields of the
Caucasus. In all areas,
the only intermittently
fortified Stalin Line
was easily breached.
    Hitler's priorities at
first were to capture
Leningrad and the
industrial area in the
south. In his view,
Moscow could wait.
Early in September,
however, he acceded
to his generals'
original proposal that
maximum manpower
should be directed at
Moscow. It was too late.

crude attempts by third parties, Britain in particular, to undermine the Berlin–Moscow non-aggression treaty.

The Soviet Union was, therefore, unprepared for the gigantic Nazi onslaught that was unleashed against it at 03.15 on 22 June along an immense front, stretching from the Baltic to the Black Sea. The advancing Germans were, on the whole, better trained, better led and better equipped than the surprised Red Army, which was only just beginning to recover from Stalin's purges of its officer corps in the late thirties, and this superiority showed in the results of the early battles.

According to the German Chief of Staff of the Army, General Franz Halder, at the start of the campaign respective strengths were: Germany—102 infantry divisions, 19 armoured divisions, 14 motorized divisions, 5 special divisions, 1 cavalry division; USSR—154 infantry divisions, 25.5 cavalry divisions, 37 armoured brigades. In addition, the Germans were supported by Finnish, Hungarian, Slovak, Croat, Romanian and Italian troops, as well as a specially recruited Spanish contingent.

Brauchitsch had three huge army groups, each backed by a Luftwaffe air fleet, to pit against Russia in what was the biggest attack ever mounted in the history of land warfare. Army Group North was commanded by Field Marshal Wilhelm von Leeb, Army Group Centre by Field Marshal Fedor von Bock and Army Group South by Field Marshal Gerd von Rundstedt, all experienced leaders.

Facing them were Marshal Kliment Voroshilov in the north, Marshal Semën Timoshenko in the centre and Marshal Semën Budënny in the south, who had at their disposal masses of untried troops, still on a peacetime footing. They lacked transport and had to rely largely on the civilian communications network for the transmission of orders.

Hitler swept aside his generals' logical desire to strike boldly for Moscow as the primary objective because it was the seat of Stalin's government, the spiritual home of Communism, centre of the Russian rail network and a massive industrial base. He insisted on the capture first of Leningrad in the north and the Caucasus in the south, believing that the possession of these would guarantee the Soviet collapse.

In the early stages of the great offensive, German armoured forces moved far and fast, cutting off and capturing huge numbers of enemy troops and their equipment. Von Bock's Army Group Centre, which fought the first major battle of Operation

The German Army was virtually at the gates of Moscow by the end of November 1941. In the five months since Operation Barbarossa was launched, it had advanced some 966km/600mls and had inflicted crushing defeats on Soviet troops.

Near Istra, a town lying only 35km/22mls northwest of Moscow on a main road to the city, assault troops from Colonel-General Erich Hoepner's 4th Panzer Group were clearing out fortified villages. They had carried out such manoeuvres countless times before in the campaign, but the grip of winter, coupled with stiffening resistance by the Red Army, was slowing up the offensive, and although the Germans took Istra itself on 26 November they were unable to exploit their gain. The men were cold and hungry, they were short of fuel and essential supplies, and the Russians were bringing up more and more well-clad and well-fed reinforcements. The bid to capture Moscow had failed.

The Russian winter had set in when this typical attack on a village near Istra took place, but there was still only a light covering of snow and tanks and infantry could move freely across country.

German infantry (1) advanced with armour to take the village, which had been turned into a small fortress by Red Army troops. As the temperature plunged below zero, the German soldiers suffered greatly, for they were still clad in the uniforms issued in the summer at the start of the offensive.

Panzer MkIII tanks
(2) rumbled across the
frosty ground to lend
support to the infantry
as the final phase of
the attack opened.
The tanks were draped
with red swastika flags
(6) so that they would
be instantly
recognizable to the
Luftwaffe when they
were strafing and dive-
bombing.

The village (3) had
been set ablaze in a
bombardment before
the main attack went
in, ironically ensuring
that, when they finally
took it, the Germans
had no shelter.

The knocked-out
Russian T34 tank (5)
was probably a victim
of the same artillery
barrage.

Russian infantry (4)
lay in wait on the
outskirts of the village.
They were supported
by concealed anti-tank
guns, and more T34s
were close by.

Barbarossa, took a staggering 290,000 prisoners, 2,585 tanks and 1,449 guns. The Luftwaffe, too, had been busy, destroying most of the Soviet Air Force's obsolete planes before they could get off the ground. Before June was over, Leeb was well on his way to Leningrad, Bock was pushing toward Smolensk and Rundstedt was into the Ukraine.

There was understandable jubilation in the German camp at such astonishing successes across such a broad front, but in July came the first signs that any victory celebrations would be premature. From the first day of the invasion, German troops had been greeted almost everywhere by cheering crowds who looked on them as their liberators from the oppressions of Stalinism, but Hitler shunned this support. He regarded the Russians as subhuman and later, by way of special units of Himmler's SS, treated them with singular harshness. In doing so, he alienated the common people.

Stalin, on the other hand, cleverly forsook his daunting image to appeal directly to his 'brothers and sisters' (until then unheard-of terminology) to stand shoulder to shoulder in what he emotively painted as a great patriotic war to preserve the motherland. Sickened by German brutality, the Russians rallied to Stalin. Partisan groups started behind enemy lines, colossal numbers of reservists hurried to join their regiments, and by mid-July Red Army resistance was stiffening.

Nevertheless, the German leviathan continued to roll forward, often through vast tracts of country laced with forests and marshes, whose unmade roads were never meant to carry tanks and motor vehicles. That they got so far so fast is a tribute to the Germans' determination. Then, on 19 July, while Army Group Centre was fighting and winning a pitched battle at Smolensk, just 322km/200mls from Moscow on a direct route, Hitler decided to cut short Bock's inexorable drive for the Russian capital in favour of pursuing his objectives on the right and left flanks. In spite of prolonged opposition from his High Command, the Führer insisted on the 3rd Panzer Group (General Hermann Hoth) turning north to assist Leeb in the assault on Leningrad, and the 2nd Panzer Group (General Heinz Guderian) moving south to help Rundstedt around Kiev in the heart of the Ukraine.

On 21 August, Hitler made his wishes clear in Directive 34, which read in part: 'The principal objective that must be accomplished before the onset of winter is not the capture of Moscow but rather, in

Infantry of General Guderian's 29th Motorized Division entering a village in July 1941, with the close support of a 37-mm gun mounted on a halftrack.

Russian BT type tanks, forerunners of the T34, being loaded for dispatch to the front in July 1941. Most were overrun before they could be used against the Germans.

The race for supplies

Throughout 1941, German weaponry was not more plentiful or of better quality than that of the Russians, but it was more expertly handled. Although the Russians possessed huge stockpiles of tanks and other equipment, the German advance was so rapid that some forward depots were encircled before stores could be withdrawn.

This disparity would in time be redressed: in the short term by the advent of winter, which rendered many German— but no Russian—tanks, artillery and small arms inoperable. In the long term, it was offset by the construction of enormous factories in the Russian interior that produced an unending flow of arms and war machines. Still later in the campaign on the Eastern Front, *matériel* from Russia's allies, Britain and the USA, was to reach her northern ports, brought in at great cost in ships and men by the Arctic convoys.

The mainstay of the Russian tank armies was the T34, regarded by some as the best armoured fighting vehicle of WWII. They were mass produced throughout the war in different marks. Utilitarian yet formidable, this 26-ton tank, with its 45mm-/1¾in-thick sloped armour, hard-hitting 76.2-mm gun and two 7.62-mm machine-guns, took the Germans by surprise at Smolensk in July 1941.

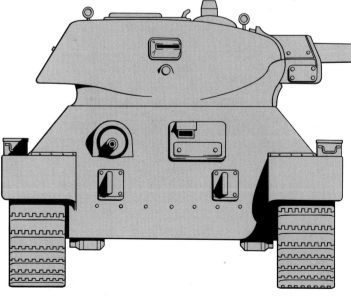

The T34s, powered by a 373kW/500hp diesel engine, giving a top speed of 51kmh/32mph and a range of 306km/190mls, were more than a match for Panzer IIIs and IVs. They were manned by a crew of four— commander/gunner, loader, driver and hull gunner/ wireless operator, though usually only squadron commanders' tanks had radios.

The Commanders

Hoepner

Zhukov

Vlasov

The Germans had almost all the advantages in the opening phases of Operation Barbarossa. Many of their soldiers, airmen and commanding officers had fought in Spain, Poland and France.

Few of the Russians had experience of warfare on so massive a scale. Stalin's purges of 1937–9 had left the officer corps depleted and demoralized. In total, some 35,000 officers were dismissed, imprisoned or murdered. Another factor of huge importance in Germany's favour was Stalin's refusal to believe warnings that an attack on the USSR was imminent. When the blow fell, it is said that he was so shocked that for two crucial weeks he was incapable of directing his staff or issuing any orders.

Not all senior commanders, however, were docile lackeys of the two dictators. **General Erich Hoepner (1886–1944)**, commander of the 4th Panzer Group, who had led the attack on Moscow, later disobeyed Hitler's order to stand firm. He withdrew his endangered right flank to prevent its annihilation. For this action he was cashiered; in 1944 he was hanged for his participation in the 20 July plot to kill Hitler.

Marshal Georgi Zhukov (1896–1974), who had escaped Stalin's purges, was a brilliant strategist and improviser. He was probably the most independently minded of all the senior Russian commanders, with courage enough to disagree with Stalin to

his face. Zhukov stabilized the front and held Leningrad. In 1942–3 he directed the defence of Stalingrad and led the forces that captured Berlin in 1945.

General Andrei Vlasov (1900–46), at the head of the Russian Twentieth Army, played a decisive role in the defence of Moscow. In May 1942 he was captured at Sevastopol after he had commanded a vigorous counter-attack to a German advance but had been cut off. He defected to the Germans in the hope of assisting in Stalin's overthrow. At the end of hostilities he was, however, returned to Russia and was hanged as a traitor.

The Panzer MkIII tank was the brainchild of Nazi Germany's leading tank expert, General Heinz Guderian, who regarded it as the Army's standard armoured fighting vehicle. Certainly it filled this role for much of the first half of the war.

Manufactured by Daimler-Benz, this tank was first produced with a 37-mm gun and one 7.92-mm machine-gun. Later the 37-mm gun was replaced by a 50-mm weapon and another machine-gun was added. The Panzer MkIII was powered by a 224kW/

300hp Maybach petrol engine, giving a top speed of 40kmh/25mph and a range of 160km/100mls. It had 30-mm/$1\frac{1}{4}$-in thick armour and weighed 21 tons.

Several marks of this tank saw service on the Russian Front. They carried a crew of five—commander, gunner, loader, driver, wireless operator—in comparative comfort. The smoothness of the Panzer MkIII's running, particularly across country, was due to the torsion-bar suspension, developed by Dr Ferdinand Porsche.

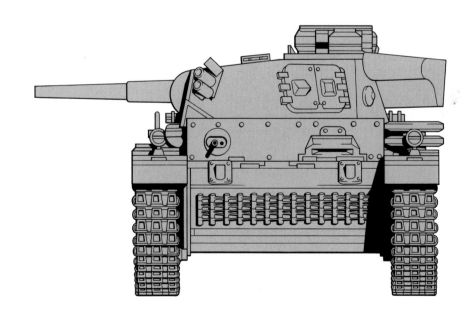

the south, the occupation of the Crimea and the industrial and coal region of the Donets, together with the isolation of the Russian oil region in the Caucasus; and, in the north, the encirclement of Leningrad and joining up with the Finns.'

By now, however, the Army, though still successful, was not having the campaign all its own way. The assaults on Leningrad were repulsed, and Leeb had to resort to siege tactics; meanwhile, Timoshenko launched heavy counter-attacks against Army Group Centre, which had been shorn of its armour. But in the south, the attack on Kiev was going well.

Against this background, the Führer had a change of heart about the 'secondary importance' of Moscow. A mere 16 days after Directive 34 came Directive 35, in which he called for Army Groups North and South to reinforce Army Group Centre, shatter Timoshenko's troublesome forces and storm the Russian capital.

At last the German generals were free to concentrate on what they had regarded all along as their principal objective, but Hitler had left his 'about face' too late for them to capitalize on it. By 30 September, when the offensive against Moscow opened, winter was not far away.

Three German armies, along with three armoured groups, moved east on a front 483km/300mls wide. The intention was for the Ninth and Fourth Armies, supported by the 3rd and 4th Armoured Groups on the left and right flanks respectively, to envelop Red Army formations around the town of Vyazma, about 200km/125mls southwest of the capital.

The Army excelled itself in this two-fold double envelopment and took 663,000 prisoners, 1,242 tanks and 5,412 guns. On 7 October Vyazma fell, Bryansk the next day, and on 14 October Hoth's tanks seized Kalinin. Then the German armour, followed by the infantry, rumbled off in the general direction of Moscow, where initial panic soon gave way to a resolution to defend the city at all costs.

Stalin, who on 12 October had transferred the government 805km/500mls southeast to Kuibyshev, remained in the Kremlin to direct operations. While the civilian population was set to work digging trenches and anti-tank ditches, changes were made in the Red Army hierarchy. Marshal Timoshenko was transferred to the Ukraine to replace the disastrous Budënny and to try to prevent the Caucasus and its precious oil from being overrun, while the Soviet troops in the Moscow area were entrusted to Marshal Georgi Zhukov, who was to prove himself an able tactician.

German tanks, *above*, advancing at speed into the Russian interior in early August 1941.

Enormous numbers of Russian troops were captured, even into early December, *right*, when the winter weather had set in. Those fit enough to walk were taken into captivity as slave labour. Few survived the harsh conditions and sparse diet.

German infantry, *right*, going forward in front of a Panzer MkIII in mid-December, when the snow had settled. German flags were tied on to the tanks so that they were easily identified by the Luftwaffe.

In the tracks of Napoleon

There were notable similarities between the German invasion of Russia in 1941 and Napoleon's in 1812. Both Napoleon and Hitler had failed to subdue Great Britain; both had won Russia's temporary co-operation and both felt it essential to attack Russia before she could attack them. And, tempting fate, Hitler's invasion started on 22 June, the same day as Napoleon's.

There, however, valid comparison ends, for Napoleon's hope of success lay principally in the superiority of his forces and in better leadership. His aim was to bring the Russian Army to battle and destroy it. Hitler needed to encircle, then eliminate, hundreds of thousands of Russia's finest troops, and in this he was at first dramatically successful. But his attack had to encompass the entire, vast front.

Hitler's armies were faced with continual fighting, whereas Napoleon's problem was to bring the enemy to battle, but Hitler had the element of surprise on his side.

Both Napoleon and Hitler fell victim in large measure not to Russia's military skill but to her limitless manpower and the severity of the winter weather.

On the March from Moscow by John Laslett Pott (1837–98) vividly depicts the misery of Napoleon's *Grande Armée* in the Russian winter of 1812.

Primitive propaganda

Both German and Russian propaganda was, in general, of the most primitive and distorted kind. For the most part, German propaganda for the home market portrayed their soldiers as crusaders against bestial, 'sub-human' people. Propaganda posters and leaflets designed for the occupied areas depicted the Germans as liberating Russians from Stalin's tyranny and the pernicious influence of his 'Bolshevik/Jewish lackeys'. This might have proved effective, notably in the Ukraine which had always sought independence from Moscow, had not the Germans sent in extermination squads to destroy all resistance, thus demonstrating in the harshest way the hollowness of their claims.

Soviet propaganda depicted the Germans, with some justice, as cruel, barbaric and murderous, but it was more subtle than German propaganda in one respect at least. Aware that Communism was detested by a great number of the people in the USSR, the Government called for maximum effort not on behalf of the Party, but for the nation as a whole, in the 'Great Patriotic War'. In this way, Russian propaganda was hugely successful in mobilizing a virtually limitless army and workforce.

Most general propaganda relied on visual impact. The German leaflet, *below*, however, was to serve as a deserter's passport. It reads in part: 'The person producing this does not want a senseless bloodbath in the interests of the Jews and the commissars. He is leaving the defeated Red Army and is coming over to the side of the German armed forces.'

As increasingly wet weather slowed and often bogged down the German advance, Zhukov made good use of the time to strengthen his command considerably by moving up from the depths of Siberia divisions that German Intelligence did not know existed. These troops were well-equipped, too, thanks to an all-out effort in Russian arms and munitions factories. Then, as German forward elements gradually crept closer to Moscow, snow flurries announced the imminent arrival of Zhukov's best ally—winter.

The first hard frosts came on the night of 3 November, firming roads and allowing German mechanized units to move in force again; but it also showed that the German Army was not properly clad to withstand the bitter cold. As temperatures plummeted over the next few days, so the number of cases of frost-bite soared.

Nevertheless, despite the misgivings of some senior officers, the German High Command, urged on by Hitler, planned a final push for Moscow, now only 64km/40mls away from their forward positions.

The panzers, as usual, made good progress, then found themselves out on a limb because Kluge's right flank had almost immediately been fought to a standstill by the Russians, and the advance of the remainder of the Fourth Army had been delayed until these battered troops were once more fit for action. Heavy fighting ensued when the offensive was renewed toward the end of November, and Kluge's mauled right wing was again halted. This time, the centre and left were ordered to press on and, on 2 December, some fighting patrols actually entered the suburbs of Moscow.

That was as far as the Germans ever reached. The infiltrators were beaten back and, in the face of a deadly combination of intense cold and fierce enemy resistance, the Fourth Army was obliged to abandon all hope of penetrating Zhukov's Moscow defences. The armoured columns exposed on the northern and southern flanks came to the same conclusion. It was now so cold that men, some still in summer uniforms, were freezing to death at their posts, vehicles would not start, aircraft were grounded and lubricants were solidifying in weapons. The Russian winter, perhaps more than the amazing tenacity of the Red Army, had thwarted Hitler's plans. General Guderian best summed it up in a letter to his wife: 'We have seriously underestimated the Russians, the extent of the country and the treachery of the climate. This is the revenge of reality.'

Now, then, was the time for Marshal Zhukov to spring his carefully nurtured

The German offensive

In June 1941, the German Army was probably the most efficient fighting force in history. But during November and December, the morale and fighting ability of the ordinary German soldier in Russia deteriorated to a marked degree. Soldiers did not have appropriate clothing for the icy winter conditions, nor even white smocks. In desperation, some men draped curtains and even tablecloths looted from peasants' homes over their uniforms. Many of their weapons became inoperable in the intense cold, and the Luftwaffe, on which the infantry relied heavily, was often grounded. German supply lines were so grossly extended that essential supplies either did not reach the front or took an excessively long time to do so.

Russian readiness

By the time the German forces neared Moscow, the Russian soldier had powerful advantages over his adversary. He was defending his homeland, he knew the terrain, was acclimatized to the weather, and his clothing and equipment were better suited to the terrible winter conditions. Russian supply lines were safer, transport was lighter, lessening the danger of its sinking into the snow, and all wheels were equipped with chains. All machinery was lubricated with oil that did not freeze. Such factors, compounded by a ferocious determination to rid his country of the invader, made the Russian soldier, untutored conscript though he was, into a formidable enemy. Then, too, the Russians possessed almost limitless manpower. As the German General Halder wrote on 11 August 1941: 'At the outset of war we reckoned on about 200 enemy divisions. By now we have counted up to 360.'

Moscow under siege

On 14 October 1941, Hoth's tanks captured Kalinin to the northwest of Moscow and broke the northern wing of the Russian front. For the Russians there now loomed the terrible spectre of encirclement as Guderian's five panzer divisions drove from the southwest in a pincer movement.

In Moscow, resolve was mixed with panic. The more able-bodied were formed into 'workers' battalions', while almost half a million others—the old, the young and the infirm—were drafted to the city's perimeter to labour, day and night, building defences and anti-tank traps. Government offices and staff were transferred to Kuibyshev, prompting flight by the more timorous party officials, their families and others who could escape. On 19 October, Moscow was declared to be in siege and seemed on the point of collapse.

Those building defences faced dreadful conditions: the temperature had dropped to minus 40°, and later fell further; there was light for only a few hours a day and the ground was frozen so hard it was almost impossible to dig. But the Russians had an inestimable advantage: they were used to, and completely at home in, these grim conditions.

For the Germans besieging the city it was the reverse. Lacking suitable clothing, any sentry who fell asleep on duty risked freezing to death; their automatic weapons were so frozen that they fired only single shots; their anti-tank ammunition would not fit into the breech because the packing grease was frozen solid; the engines of their tanks would not start. Butter, when there was any, had to be cut with a saw or severed with an axe, and boiling soup froze in less than 60 seconds. For a soldier to defecate in the open invited death.

The German troops were riddled with dysentry and there were more than 100,000 cases of frost-bite. Many committed suicide, most by holding a hand grenade—the only weapon certain to function in such conditions—against the stomach.

The plan

Von Bock's Army Group Centre began its last thrust toward Moscow on 16 November. The plan was for von Kluge's Fourth Army (1) to make a head-on attack, while Reinhardt's five panzer divisions (2) were to encircle the city to the north, and Hoepner's four panzer divisions (3) and Guderian's command, now called the 2nd Armoured (4), were to swing around from the south. The Germans aimed to surround Moscow, then starve the inhabitants into surrender.

According to plan, the panzer divisions advanced north under Reinhardt (1), those under Guderian (3) south, in an encircling movement. Von Kluge's 11 infantry divisions and Hoepner's panzers (2) in the centre attacked, but they failed to break through. During the night of 5–6 December, the Russians counter-attacked and the Germans were thrown on the defensive. Headlong flight might have followed had not Hitler forbidden retreat and ordered that the line must be stabilized.

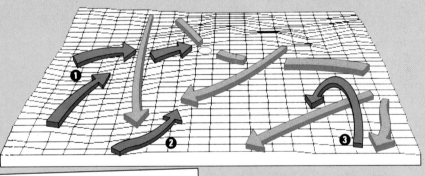

The reality

Muscovites—women, old men, the disabled and the young, in all some 500,000—laboured without cease to dig anti-tank ditches after fires had been lit to thaw the ground. Fortifications were erected and inner defence rings were built within the city.

counter-offensive. Using fresh Siberian divisions, specially clothed to withstand the rigours of winter warfare, he attacked along a 322-km/200-ml front with a ferocity that staggered the enemy.

On 18 December Hitler, who had just declared war on the United States, thereby ensuring that eventually Germany would have to fight on two major fronts, arrogantly took over command of the Army in place of Brauchitsch. Ignoring his generals' advice to withdraw to a defensive line west of Smolensk, Hitler demanded that his hard-pressed armies should stand and fight where they were. Officers who were forced to pull back were relieved of their commands, including Generals Guderian and Hoepner, whose armoured columns would have been exposed to encirclement and annihilation had they not been withdrawn.

Ultimately recognizing the necessity of protecting his dwindling forces from the severe weather, the Führer permitted a limited fallback into the fortified perimeters of forward supply bases. These all-round defensive positions were nicknamed 'hedgehogs' by German soldiers.

All the time, Russian counter-attacks continued, supplemented by partisan harassment operations in the German rear. Zhukhov's men took what hedgehogs they could and moved around those they could not. Even when the snow lay feet thick and temperatures plunged to minus 40°, white-uniformed Soviet troops on sledges and skis did not let up their pressure on the suffering German Army. Indeed, the Germans found that the Siberian troops could lie motionless in the snow all day, only to attack again at nightfall.

This was the pattern that prevailed until the spring thaw, which bogged down both sides in the mud and provided a breathing space before campaigning could begin again as the ground dried out. When

it did, the Germans found their power so blunted that only in the south could they contemplate an offensive.

When the casualties of Operation Barbarossa up to the end of March 1942 came to be calculated, the figures reflected the enormous scale of the fighting. The Germans reported 1,073,006 killed, wounded, missing, taken prisoner or victims of frostbite. The Russians have never announced their losses, but most well-informed estimates place them in excess of 2,000,000.

Commenting on the Führer's Soviet débâcle, the British Prime Minister, Winston Churchill, said with obvious relish, 'There is a winter, you know, in Russia. For a good many months the temperature is apt to fall very low. There is snow, there is frost, and all that. Hitler forgot about this Russian winter. He must have been very loosely educated. We heard all about it at school; but he forgot it. I have never made such a bad mistake as that.'

In early January 1942, German Army Group Centre, commanded by Field Marshal von Kluge (following von Bock's resignation), was recoiling before Russian counterattacks. Although the Red Army had suffered enormous losses during the previous six months, it still had huge reserves of manpower. This was evident when a new Russian offensive opened near Moscow on 10 January—165 Russian divisions were massed against von Kluge's 68.

Around the town of Volokolamsk, 97km/60mls northwest of the capital, lay the shivering German Third Army, under Colonel-General Georg-Hans Reinhardt, target of Major-General Andrei Vlasov's fresh and well-equipped Twentieth Army. The attack, supported by artillery, was made in temperatures well below freezing; but within three days, the German lines had been penetrated and they had been forced to retreat.

Russia reprieved

The Germans failed to capture Moscow, but they held a defensive line throughout the winter and frustrated all Russian attempts to encircle them. Great victories lay ahead for the Germans, notably their advance into the Caucasus in 1942, but they had been savaged at Moscow, and the Army's record of being able to achieve whatever objective it was set was broken. Had Moscow fallen, Russian resistance might have collapsed; as it was, its successful defence ensured that other great battles would be fought at Stalingrad and Kursk.

The temperature was exceptionally low, −60°C/−73°F, when Vlasov launched his attack. A blizzard was blowing, and the snow was deep, with drifting (1), but he did not think of postponing the offensive to await more favourable conditions.

The German positions (2) had come under intense artillery bombardment before the attack began, and they were under sporadic fire until their defences were breached three days later. Many buildings were set on fire in the suburbs of the town of Volokolamsk (3).

Five battalions of ski troops (4) were deployed in the fighting. Wearing white camouflage uniforms and armed with submachine-guns, they skied swiftly and easily across country to reach the scene of the action, then fought on foot.

Russian infantry (5), clad in thick quilted uniforms to insulate them against the freezing weather, pursued the Germans relentlessly. Heavy casualties seemed not to sap the morale of Red Army soldiers.

Broad-tracked T34 tanks (6) made slow progress through the deep snow, but did not sink. They gave the infantry invaluable support and, once the German line was broken, ranged far behind the enemy's rear positions.

Malta/*December 1941-July 1942*

The strategic importance of the British island of Malta appears to have been lost on Benito Mussolini when he declared war on the Allies on 10 June 1940. It was an oversight which would cost Italy and Germany dear, for Malta is critically situated in the Mediterranean between Sicily and North Africa.

In 1936 the Duce allied himself to Nazi Germany in the Rome-Berlin Axis, but despite his militaristic posing and successes in Abyssinia (Ethiopia), his forces were ill-prepared for a prolonged struggle. However, when France was on the point of collapse and Hitler's power was soaring, Mussolini could see opportunities for a share of the spoils at little cost.

Then the Duce began to get carried away by his role as warlord and decided to invade Greece and Albania and, from Italian-controlled Libya, to send in his divisions against the British in Egypt to seize the important Suez Canal and so open the gateway to the Arabian oilfields.

When Mussolini declared war, there were only 68 anti-aircraft guns, instead of the recommended 156, on Malta to protect the naval base at Valletta and three airfields. The air defences, also, were totally inadequate—9 obsolescent biplanes: 5 Fairey Swordfish torpedo bombers, and 4 Gloster Gladiator fighters, which on their own offered battle to the Italian raiders for almost three weeks. Britain was now preparing to increase the effectiveness of Malta in both offence and defence. Hawker Hurricane fighters and more Swordfish torpedo bombers were moved to the island and destroyers and submarines were to operate from Valletta against enemy shipping. In September the first convoy of merchant ships arrived with supplies to boost local stocks.

By the end of 1940, Mussolini's war effort was in tatters. In just six months his land forces had met with disaster in Greece and North Africa, and the Royal Navy had dealt a crippling blow to his fleet at Taranto. Hitler, therefore, decided to intervene to redress the balance, and immediately the conflict became tougher.

In December the Luftwaffe's 10 Fliegerkorps, commanded by Lieutenant-General Hans Geissler, arrived in Sicily—just 96km/60mls from Malta—his Messerschmitt fighters and Junkers bombers boosting Axis strength to about 400 aircraft. On Malta's three airfields—Luqa, Hal Far and Takali—the AOC, Air Vice-Marshal Hugh Lloyd, now had 16 Vickers Armstrong Wellington bombers, 12 Swordfish torpedo bombers, a handful of American-made Martin Maryland light bombers and just 16 Hurricane fighters,

Faith, Hope and Charity— a gallant trio

Malta's quota of fighter aircraft had been set at four squadrons of Hawker Hurricanes; but, when Italy declared war, there was still not a single fighter on the island. However, in May 1940, four obsolescent Gloster Gladiators had been found crated in a Fleet Air Arm store. By 4 June they had been hastily assembled, and, manned by scratch crews, they took on the Regia Aeronautica. One was quickly damaged beyond repair, but the remaining three, nicknamed Faith, Hope and Charity, continued the battle alone for 18 days until four Hurricanes arrived to assist them. The pilots became local heroes: they were cheered by the Maltese every time they took off and their photographs appeared in the windows of many shops. The skeletal remains of 'Faith' can still be seen in the Malta War Museum in Valletta.

The Commanders

Malta was fortunate in one respect at least: her senior commanders were all men of courage and ability. **Lieutenant-General Sir William Dobbie (1879–1964)**, the Governor and Commander-in-Chief at the opening of hostilities, faced daunting tasks with inadequate resources. He had to organize the protection of the airfields and harbours by whatever means he could; he had to provide troops with shelter against inevitable air attack and he had to transform the amiable islanders, used for centuries to a peaceful life, into a resolute fighting force. In dealing with his responsibilities, this dour Scot was fortified by an abiding faith (he was a Plymouth Brother), by an awareness of the perils ahead and by his friendliness and approachability. The arduous demands made on him eventually exhausted him physically and mentally, and on 8 May 1942 he was reluctantly replaced.

His successor **Lord Gort (1886–1946)** had much in common with Dobbie. A 'people's governor' and a man of great courage (he had been awarded the Victoria Cross in World War I and had seen the BEF safely out of Dunkirk in 1940), he too was a devout Christian. Both men were quiet in manner, straightforward and without vanity; and both shared the hardships of the civilian population. Gort used a bicycle whenever possible to save petrol and, being contemptuous of personal safety, did not allow air raids to disrupt his movements.

The air commanders were, likewise, well equipped for their onerous duties. **Air Vice-Marshal Hugh Pughe Lloyd (1894–1981)** worked, lived and slept on the airfields and was the idol of his men. He was responsible for the expansion of the airfield defences, the runways and dispersal pens—an unenviable task since there was solid rock beneath the shallow soil, hardly a flat surface anywhere and little modern construction equipment. Work began in June 1941 and within 6 months the dispersal area for aircraft had been increased ninefold. The Axis in Sicily took great interest in the work and sent escorted photographic planes over two or three times a week to observe progress.

Lloyd's successor, in July 1942, was **Air Vice-Marshal Sir Keith Park (1892–1975)** of Battle of Britain fame. As soon as he had sufficient fighters, he introduced the tactic of forward interception—attacking enemy bombers before they reached the island—so preventing much damage and loss of life among the people of Malta.

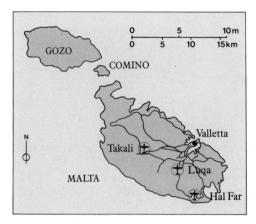

The three airfields on Malta—Takali, Luqa and Hal Far—presented exposed targets to enemy bombers. Other targets were the capital, Valletta, the great naval dockyard and all the facilities of Grand Harbour. Malta, in fact, presented an ideal target for massed bombers supported by heavy fighter cover.

On 18 November 1941, the British Eighth Army launched its second campaign in North Africa (1). Hitler was obliged to abandon the offensive against Moscow (2) on 5 December because of stiffening Russian resistance and the onset of winter. On 6 December Russia mounted a counter-attack. On 7 December, Japanese carrier-borne aircraft bombed Pearl Harbour (3) and the following day the Allies, excepting the USSR, declared war on her.

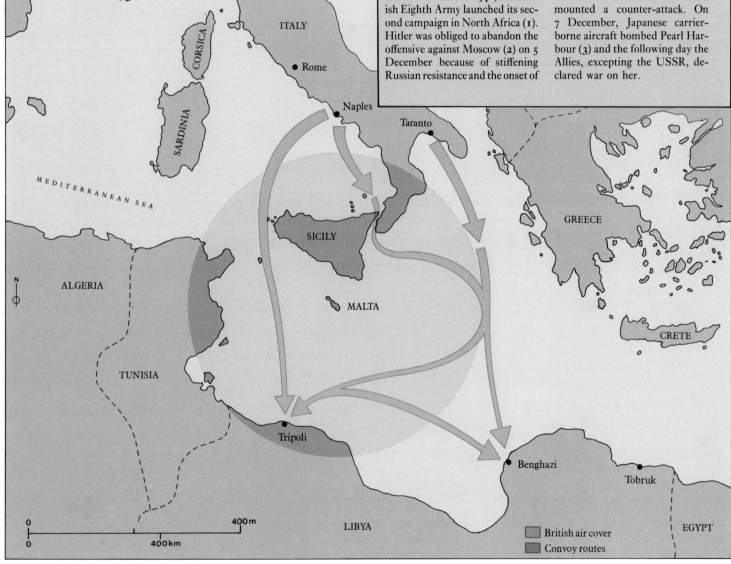

Malta lies almost exactly midway across the Mediterranean, with Alexandria, in 1941 the nearest Allied land base, 1,290km/800mls to the east, and the British naval bastion of Gibraltar some 1,610km/1,000mls to the west. Moreover, the island is situated south of Sicily and to the north of Tripolitania, thus dominating the central Mediterranean.

Malta's strategic importance in 1941 was, therefore, of the highest order, both in allowing the free passage of British convoys to Egypt and in preventing Axis reinforcements being safely transported to succour Rommel's Axis forces campaigning in North Africa.

Furthermore, the Germans' superior air force in the Mediterranean region, notably their Stukas, prevented British aircraft-carriers, based at Alexandria, from operating to full effect. But Malta was 'an unsinkable aircraft-carrier' and filled the role that the Navy would otherwise have had to play.

For these reasons, the island, threatened from north and south by enemy-held territory and to the southwest by hostile Tunisia, controlled by Vichy France, was heavily reinforced by the British.

with the prospect of a further 16 coming in with the next convoy. Geissler's objective was to achieve air superiority so that the newly formed Afrika Korps commanded by Lieutenant-General Erwin Rommel, its transport and equipment, could safely be shipped to Libya and kept supplied. He set about his task with a characteristic thoroughness, and in early January 1941 Malta began to feel the full weight of the Luftwaffe's presence.

Until then, convoys, though under attack by the Italians, had been getting through to replenish the island. Now this situation began to change dramatically because 10 Fliegerkorps had been trained in an anti-shipping role. On 10 January

Geissler's Ju 87 Stukas homed in on the new British aircraft-carrier *Illustrious*, which was on convoy escort duty, and severely damaged her. She struggled into Valletta's Grand Harbour, where attempts were made to repair her in the naval dockyard, but these were largely frustrated by dive-bombing raids, and *Illustrious*, roughly patched up, got away on the night of 23 January to begin a circuitous voyage to an American dockyard for repairs.

As preparations neared completion for the transfer of the Afrika Korps from Italian ports to Libya, Malta came under increased aerial bombardment and her meagre complement of aircraft took a

terrible pounding. At the end of February, the surviving Wellington bombers were withdrawn, and at the beginning of March the Hurricane fighter force was reduced to only eight serviceable machines. As a result, Rommel's new command and thousands of Italian reinforcements were shipped to North Africa almost without incident.

Although air raids on the island continued on and off for the next six months or so, their ferocity was diminished by the dispersal of Geissler's Fliegerkorps to provide air cover for German operations in the Balkans and the Western Desert. During this comparative lull, Malta's fighter defences were much strengthened,

Heavy flak, fired by anti-aircraft guns, reached high altitudes and, timed by fuse, exploded in deadly fragments of steel. In areas of dense flak, pilots flew as high as they could without compromising their bombing accuracy. (To bomb accurately entailed holding a steady course from the start of a bomb run to the point of bomb release, during which

time aircraft were highly vulnerable.) Usually individual aircraft were attacked, but ground defences around Valletta employed a new tactic. By concentrating anti-aircraft fire into a predetermined 'box' ahead of the bombers, with each battery firing at a fixed height and range, all incoming aircraft had to penetrate a wall of fire.

On 16 January 1941, at 13.55, Luftwaffe dive-bombers appeared over Malta for the first time. Around 70 Ju 87 Stukas attacked in waves, their main target being the carrier *Illustrious.* Six days earlier she had been nursed into Grand Harbour, Valletta, after being badly damaged on convoy escort duty,

and was now being hastily patched up in the naval dockyard in French Creek. Luftwaffe pilots made several unsuccessful attempts to sink the carrier, and under cover of darkness on 23 January the big ship slipped away to Alexandria.

A radical new anti-aircraft fire plan was put into operation during the 16 January attack. Guns of the Dockyard Defence Battery (4) joined others (1) all around Grand Harbour to create a curtain of fire

and swirling smoke through which the Stukas had to dive at French Creek.

Parlatorio Wharf (3) in the naval dockyard where *Illustrious* (5) was berthed was largely destroyed, but only one bomb hit the carrier, slightly

damaging her flight deck. All through the action her guns added their fire to those of the island's defences.

Route of
German
bombers.

Valletta

GRAND HARBOUR

French Creek

Historic buildings,
churches, homes and
shops were demolished
in Senglea (2),
Conspicua and
Vittoriosa, the 'Three
Cities' in the area of
French Creek. The
raid left 53 dead and
19 injured.

The Fulmar fighters
from *Illustrious* had
been flown off to land
bases, and they joined
the battle. One Fulmar
(6) chased a Stuka (7)
as it dropped its
bomb, then raced low
over the water, trying
to get away under the
anti-aircraft barrage. It
was shot down into
the sea just beyond the
breakwater. The
Germans lost at least
10 aircraft in the raid,
the British none.

the bombers returned, and the convoys continued to run the gauntlet, although in November 1941 Britain sustained a great loss when the aircraft-carrier *Ark Royal* was sunk.

On the face of it, the British, who were shipping supplies to Egypt via the Cape of Good Hope, were seriously disadvantaged by the fact that the Axis powers had to move their oil only 483km/300mls across the Mediterranean. Malta, however, tipped the scales in Britain's favour, for it was ideally placed for launching effective sea and air strikes against enemy convoys. More than 60 per cent of the Afrika Korps' supplies shipped from Italy went to the bottom. The fuel was the worst loss, and in November Rommel's operations were threatened with curtailment because of dwindling oil reserves. It was this dangerous situation which, more than anything else, brought the full force of Axis wrath down on Malta.

On the night of 4 December 1941, the enemy began a systematic bombing campaign which continued for five months in a concerted effort to crush opposition from the Royal Navy and the Royal Air Force. Sometimes as many as 300 bombers were overhead at one time. Plans were also made for 'Operation Hercules', a belated invasion of Malta.

The Luftwaffe, now represented by Field Marshal Albert Kesselring's Luftflotte 2, and the Regia Aeronautica together far outnumbered the British defenders. Losses of RAF planes on the ground and in the air climbed alarmingly—by mid-February 1942 only 11 Hurricanes were functional—and the naval base at Valletta was badly hit.

In March, the arrival on Malta of the first Supermarine Spitfires, flown in from aircraft-carriers, gave an initial boost to the weary defenders. But many of these fast, front-line fighters were destroyed on the ground during mass raids on the airfields. However, with the help of army units, the overworked RAF redoubled its efforts to keep all available aircraft armed and fuelled ready for instant take-off, to repair damaged runways and build dispersal pens to protect the precious fighters from bomb blast.

Throughout March the air battle over Malta intensified. Enemy attacks on 26 March were so heavy that the RAF's official situation report for that day stated that there had been too many combats to describe them individually.

The Maltese people exhibited tremendous courage. Their homes, churches, public and historic buildings had been reduced to rubble; civilian casualties

An island's heroic endurance

World War II was the first in which civilians were involved in action to an extent at times almost equal to that of the armed forces. In recognition of this, in September 1940 at the height of the Blitz on London, King George VI instituted the George Cross, an award for civilian gallantry to rank with the Victoria Cross, the highest award to the services.

On 15 April 1942, the King made the inspired gesture of awarding the George Cross to the island of Malta and its people. The cross was brought to the island by the new Governor, Lord Gort, and handed over to the people in a simple but solemn ceremony, watched by thousands, in Palace Square, Valletta.

There was jubilation when, on 20 June 1943, the King himself disembarked from HMS *Aurora* to meet the islanders, the garrison and its commanders to thank them personally for their heroic endurance.

Malta's cities were severely damaged by bombing, but many civilians sheltered in caves in the rock, so heavy casualties were avoided. After a raid whole streets could be blocked with rubble; electricity cables and gas pipes were often severed, and water supplies cut off for long periods. The Maltese were at least spared the added horror of fire because, since the 16th century, all their buildings had been made of stone.

The convoys: Malta's life-lines

All Malta's needs—fuel, ammunition and food—had to be brought in by convoys, which presented large targets for enemy bombers and submarines and sustained dreadful punishment. Convoys running from Alexandria in the east usually comprised a small number of fast merchantmen, heavily escorted. However, once the Germans had become involved in North Africa, as a result of the Italian collapse there, and had moved strong bomber and fighter units to within striking distance of Malta, the situation rapidly deteriorated. Many merchantmen were sunk *en route*, others when unloading, and many of the cargoes, although successfully landed and hastily dispersed, were later destroyed.

Larger convoys were therefore assembled, notably 'Operation Excess', during which *Illustrious* was hit, which left Gibraltar in the first week of January 1941;

'Operation Substance' in July, which brought in 65,000 tons of food and ammunition; and, in June 1942, 'Operation Harpoon' with 43,000 tons of stores.

By July, however, the islanders, subsisting on rations considerably less plentiful even than those available in Great Britain during the Battle of the Atlantic, were close to starvation. A rescue operation, far bigger than any before, was therefore mounted.

Codenamed 'Operation Pedestal', this great convoy sailed from northern England on 2 August. The 14 fully laden merchantmen were protected by Force Z, a naval escort comprising 2 battleships, 3 aircraft-carriers, 3 cruisers and 14 destroyers. Along with it, escorted by a further 8 destroyers, went the old carrier *Furious*, with more Spitfires to be flown off to Malta. Royal Navy submarines patrolled the route.

The fleet sailed through the Straits of

Gibraltar in early August, and the next day it was sighted by an Italian submarine. A running battle developed with enemy aircraft, torpedo boats and submarines. The aircraft-carrier *Eagle*, 2 cruisers, 1 destroyer and 9 cargo ships were sunk, and the carrier *Indomitable* was badly damaged. But from the five merchantmen that reached Valletta, including the battered oil-tanker *Ohio*, which arrived on 15 August lashed between two destroyers, 32,000 tons of general cargo were unloaded and 13,600 tons of fuel, sufficient to allow the island to continue the struggle. Cheering crowds welcomed the survivors of Pedestal into harbour on the feast of Santa Maria, the patron saint of Malta.

The islanders were now better able to withstand the siege, which was virtually lifted when, in November 1942, another great convoy got through with supplies.

Malta could be supplied by convoy from either the western or eastern end of the Mediterranean. In the early months of the war the route from Gibraltar was favoured, since convoys could travel far south of the enemy's European bases and were, therefore, menaced by submarines only.

Danger on the route from Alexandria varied with the changing fortunes of war in North Africa.

The aircraft-carrier HMS *Indomitable* and, behind her, HMS *Eagle*, photographed from HMS *Victorious* during the Pedestal convoy. An Albacore, a reconnaissance craft and torpedo bomber, has just taken off from *Indomitable* on anti-submarine patrol. In the foreground, on *Victorious*'s deck, are two of her five Sea Hurricanes, standing by in readiness to scramble.

mounted, and hardships were endured through acute shortages of food and other necessities. On 15 April 1942, King George VI awarded the George Cross to Malta 'to honour her brave people'.

A month later Kesselring formed the erroneous opinion that the island was no longer a threat, and many of his squadrons were redeployed on the Eastern Front in Russia and in support of Axis forces in North Africa. After 10 May the frequency and intensity of the air raids on Malta were much reduced, and soon aircraft-carriers were able to increase the island's fighter strength to 300 Spitfires, sufficient to meet and beat any enemy challenge.

In June, Malta received a further reprieve. Rommel, who had captured the huge British base at Tobruk, now had a valuable stockpile of fuel and other stores, so he persuaded his superiors that it was no longer necessary to invade Malta and asked that the troops selected to take part

in Operation Hercules be assigned to him to boost his forces in North Africa.

In the meantime, the convoys trying to keep the island supplied were taking a battering from enemy naval and air forces. Only a few merchantmen were managing to get through, and so desperate was the situation that even submarines were running in small quantities of vital stores. It was obvious that unless the best part of a big convoy could reach Valletta with supplies, Malta would be overcome.

In early August, the Royal Navy mounted 'Operation Pedestal', the biggest convoy ever sent to Malta, in an all-out attempt to bring relief to the island. In a running battle against enemy aircraft, torpedo boats and submarines, the aircraft-carrier *Eagle*, two cruisers, a destroyer and nine cargo ships were sunk. But five merchantmen reached Valletta, allowing the island to continue the struggle.

Though the disruption of the Axis

supply routes to North Africa resumed, and Rommel, overextended and again desperately short of fuel, met his match in General Bernard Montgomery at El Alamein, the grim prospect of starvation once more faced Malta. But on 19 November, with less than a fortnight's food stocks left on the island, a convoy of four ships got through. Never again was the population to suffer the privations of a siege.

For a short time in October, when efforts were being made to ship more fuel to the Afrika Korps, the blitz on Malta was resumed. But after eight days, during which the RAF shot down more than 100 enemy aircraft for the loss of 27, the skies over the island became quiet again. After the tide had turned against Rommel in November 1942 there were still some heavy raids on the island. These, however, gradually died away when the Axis forces were chased out of North Africa in May 1943. The battle had been won.

The Luftwaffe and the Italian Regia Aeronautica bombed Malta heavily in spring 1942, and fighters were desperately needed to take on the enemy aircraft.

In March and April the first Spitfires were flown in from aircraft-carriers to supplement the few Hurricanes then defending Malta. But many were destroyed on the ground, and burnt-out aircraft and bomb craters often made airfields unusable.

Between March and May, the RAF, assisted by the army, made immense efforts to improve the three airfields—43km/ 27mls of runways were laid—and to speed up the servicing of aircraft. By 9 May, when 64 new Spitfires were

expected, their base at Takali boasted blast-proof dispersal pens and a rapid, well-rehearsed routine for getting fighters airborne again. There were nine raids on 9 May; one of the worst took place at 11.14.

Each Spitfire, as it arrived, was directed to a pen, *left*; here it is of stone lined with sandbags, but some pens at Takali had been cut into cliff-faces. Aircraft were refuelled manually from 23-l/5-gal cans by the groundcrew, who worked as a team, with a pilot in the cockpit ready for take-off. One pilot wrote: 'One lives here only to destroy the Hun ... living conditions, sleep, food, have gone by the board. ... It makes the Battle of Britain seem like child's play.'

A stream of new Spitfires (4) was coming in to land, having taken off from the carrier USS *Wasp* some four hours earlier. The new aircraft had the latest armament of four wing-mounted cannon.

Spitfires of the resident fighter squadron (3) scrambled to provide cover for the incoming fighters, which were mostly without ammunition and running low on fuel.

Bombs were bursting all over the airfield (1) and some of the planes were damaged or destroyed as they came in to land.

Repair squads were busy all day, filling in bomb craters (2), so the airfield was never out of action.

Takali's main anti-aircraft defences were 40-mm Bofors guns (5), which kept up a rapid, effective fire from sandbagged positions on the edge of the airfield—inadvertently creating a further hazard for incoming planes.

Dispersal pens (6) had been built all around Takali to protect aircraft from attack. Made from earth-filled fuel cans, blocks of stone from bombed buildings and sandbags, each pen contained fuel, spares and ammunition, and a groundcrew of five who could service an aircraft in as few as six minutes. Many newly arrived pilots went straight into action against the aircraft that had come to bomb them.

By the spring of 1942, Japan had overrun most of the southern and western Pacific and needed to protect the oil and raw materials it had seized. To this end, the Commander-in-Chief of the Japanese Navy, Admiral Isoroku Yamamoto, conceived an intricate plot to ambush and destroy Admiral Chester Nimitz's Pacific Fleet at Midway atoll. This barren but strategically important outpost guarded the western approaches to the Hawaiian islands and the United States itself.

Yamamoto's plan called first for a decoy attack on islands in the Aleutian chain in the north Pacific. Bombardment of Midway by a powerful carrier striking force was to be followed by infantry landings; and a reserve force, commanded by himself, was to be positioned halfway between Midway and the Aleutians. Since he had no radar, submarine patrols were to warn of the anticipated approach of the American fleet, so as to give him time to concentrate his ships and spring the trap. Finally, as a *ruse de guerre*, signal traffic between shore establishments and a non-existent fleet was broadcast, while Yamamoto's vast armada put to sea and deployed under strict radio silence.

The Americans, however, had broken the Japanese code and knew that a major attack on one of their Pacific bases was imminent. They also resorted to stratagem, and their's paid higher dividends than Yamamoto's. Knowing that AF was the code for the Japanese target, US Naval Intelligence asked commanders in all positions likely to attract an enemy attack to report to HQ with some distinctive problem. Midway complained of a faulty seawater distillation plant and, sure enough, a little later a radio message from Japanese Intelligence was intercepted announcing that AF had this trouble.

Forewarned of the whole outline of Yamamoto's plan, Admiral Nimitz was able to make his dispositions accordingly. A task force was sent to the Aleutians area as a precaution, while in the central Pacific Nimitz split his forces into two strong carrier groups designed to surprise the would-be surprisers at Midway.

Task Force 16, the aircraft carriers *Hornet* and *Enterprise*, escorted by six cruisers and nine destroyers, went to sea commanded by Rear-Admiral Raymond Spruance. The carrier *Yorktown*, which had been damaged in the Coral Sea battle, was quickly patched up at Pearl Harbor, and, with two cruisers and five destroyers, formed Task Force 17 under the command of Rear-Admiral Frank Fletcher, who had tactical control of the ensuing operations. By 2 June, the two US task

Pearl Harbor: casualties and survivors

The magazine of the US destroyer *Shaw* exploding during the attack on Pearl Harbor.

USS *Lexington, above,* loa: 270m/888ft; maximum speed: 33kn; armament: eight 8-in guns (when sunk was not carrying them), 63 aircraft.

USS *Enterprise, above,* loa: 246m/809ft; maximum speed: 32kn; armament: eight 5-in guns; 96 aircraft.

USS *Saratoga, below,* loa: 246m/809ft; maximum speed: 33kn; armament: twelve 5-in AA guns, four 6-pound guns and eight AA machine-guns.

Japan was the first of the great powers to appreciate the potential of heavy aircraft-carriers in naval warfare; by 1941 she had built six and more were under construction. Yet when Japan launched, without warning, 360 bombers and covering fighters on Pearl Harbor at 08.25 on 7 December 1941, their prime target was the eight battleships of the US Pacific Fleet. Every ship in the harbour (more than 90 in all) except the *Pennsylvania*, which was in dry dock, was damaged or destroyed. The battleship *Arizona* blew up, the *West Virginia* and *California* sank and the *Oklahoma* capsized.

Despite immediate appearances—the

broken US Pacific Fleet lay under a pall of smoke—the Japanese had not achieved their aim. The two carriers based on Pearl Harbor, *Lexington* and *Enterprise*, together with their strong cruiser formations, were at sea, returning from delivering marine fighter planes to Wake and Midway Islands. Thus the Japanese, despite their absolute and justified faith in the invincibility of the aircraft-carrier, missed precisely the prize that they should have done everything in their power to seize. Four US carriers—*Lexington, Enterprise, Saratoga* and *Yorktown*—were, therefore, still operational in the Pacific.

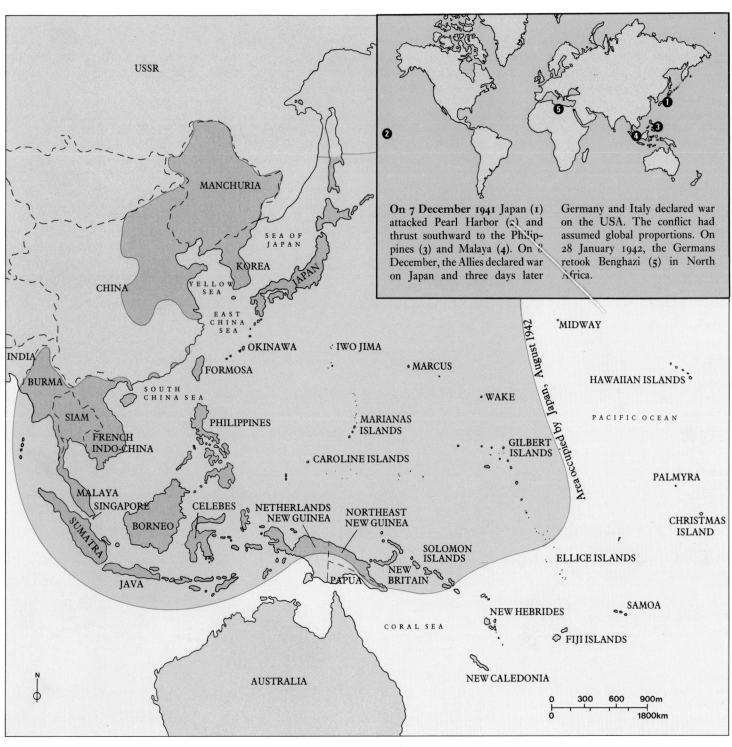

On 7 December 1941 Japan (1) attacked Pearl Harbor (2) and thrust southward to the Philippines (3) and Malaya (4). On 8 December, the Allies declared war on Japan and three days later Germany and Italy declared war on the USA. The conflict had assumed global proportions. On 28 January 1942, the Germans retook Benghazi (5) in North Africa.

Japan embarked on an imperialist policy of expansion as early as 1895 when she occupied Formosa (Taiwan). It was not until the 1930s, however, that American isolationism gave her a further chance at unimpeded encroachment in Asia; in 1931 she again invaded Manchuria and in 1937 attacked China. When Germany overran France and Holland in 1940, placing British, French and Dutch Far Eastern colonies at her mercy, Japan grasped her opportunity.

Following her attack on Pearl Harbor, Japan advanced in three directions: against the Dutch East Indies and the Philippines to seize war materials; into mainland Asia by way of Malaya and Burma, and into the Pacific Ocean toward Guam, New Guinea, the Bismarck Archipelago and the Solomon Islands.

Japanese successes were spectacular, but in April 1942, 16 B25 Mitchell bombers from the carrier *Hornet* under the command of Lieutenant-Colonel James Doolittle bombed Tokyo and three other mainland cities. The damage inflicted was slight but the psychological impact immense. Japan realized that, for mainland safety, she had to extend her conquests as well as safeguard those she already had. Consequently, in May 1942 the Japanese attempted to move troops into southern New Guinea to create a buffer zone between their newly acquired territories and Australia and a springboard for a possible future attack on Australia.

The Battle of the Coral Sea (4–8 May 1942) resulted from a bid to thwart this plan by two US aircraft-carrier forces and a strong supporting force of American and Australian warships.

forces on station some 400km/250mls northeast of Midway, were poised to do battle with the Japanese, who had left their bases between 25 and 27 May but had not been sighted since. However, the Japanese had not fixed the position of Fletcher's and Spruance's commands either, for their submarines had arrived in the patrol area after the US ships had passed.

The next day, as planned, the Japanese attacked the Aleutian islands of Attu and Kiska and were puzzled by the Americans' muted response. They were, in fact, after a bigger catch 3,220km/2,000mls to the south, where the first of the enemy shoal had been discovered by a long-range reconnaissance aircraft 1,125km/700mls southwest of Midway at about the same time as the Aleutian bombardment opened. These ships were identified as the troop transports of the invading forces.

When dawn broke on 4 June, TF16 and TF17 were 320km/200mls northeast of Midway. Unknown to them, Nagumo's command, which included the four big carriers *Akagi*, *Kaga*, *Soryu* and *Hiryu*, was some 400km/250mls to the west and already launching aircraft to attack Midway. An hour later, at 05.30, a US Catalina flying boat spotted the Japanese carriers and raised the alarm; at the same time Midway's radar picked up the incoming enemy aircraft 160km/100mls away.

Fletcher decided to attack, and while his flagship *Yorktown* quickly set about recovering her reconnaissance aircraft, Spruance and TF16 steamed at full speed toward Nagumo's carriers.

In the meantime, the Japanese first strike of 72 bombers escorted by 36 fighters, under the command of Lieutenant Joichi Tomonaga, was closing on

Midway when it was intercepted by 26 American Brewster Buffaloes and Grumman Wildcats. But they were no match for the Mitsubishi Zeros, then the finest fighters operating in the Pacific theatre of war.

From Nagumo's point of view the raid was not an unqualified success: although great damage had been inflicted the American airfields were still operational, as the appearance of torpedo bombers and Marauder bombers over his ships at 07.10 proved.

Suspecting that American warships might be in the area—though his reconnaissance patrols had so far reported none—the cautious Japanese admiral had kept his second strike standing by loaded with torpedoes and armour-piercing bombs to meet a possible naval attack. Now he ordered the aircraft to be rearmed

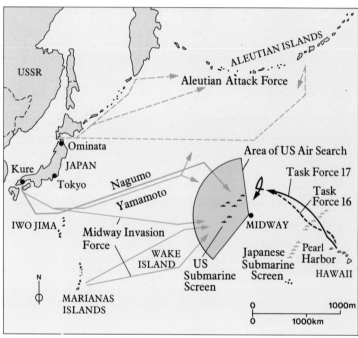

Admiral Yamamoto divided his Combined Fleet into five for the attack on Midway, with an advance group of submarines to probe ahead. The Americans, however, had broken the Japanese code, knew of their intentions and moved Task Force 16 (Spruance) and Task Force 17 (Fletcher) to Midway before the submarines reached their allotted station.

The Japanese made a diversionary raid with their Northern

Force and Second Carrier Striking Force on the Aleutian Islands to the north, which the Americans virtually ignored. Yamamoto's First Carrier Striking Force (Nagumo) moved northeast and then turned southeast for the attack on Midway. The Second Fleet Covering Group, the Transport and Support Groups, together with a minesweeping group, steamed eastward farther south.

Meanwhile, US Task Forces 16 and 17 had combined northeast of Midway.

US dive-bombers, which the Japanese had failed to detect, plunged from high altitude on three of Nagumo's four carriers at 10.20 on 4 June 1942. Weather conditions—smooth sea and good visibility—were ideal for dive-bombers.

Dauntless dive-bombers (3) from the *Enterprise* found the carriers at about 10.05. Fifteen minutes later, having manoeuvred into position, the bombers dived on both the *Akagi* (5) and the *Kaga* (2).

The first hit on the *Akagi* (5) exploded bombs that, in haste, had been stacked in the hangars during rearming. An instant later, following a second hit, the carrier was reduced to an inferno, repeatedly wracked with awesome explosions as further bombs detonated in the hangars below deck. About 45 minutes after the attack began, the *Akagi* was abandoned.

Plunging from a height of 14,000ft and then flying through concentrated anti-aircraft fire (4) from escorting Japanese warships, the Dauntlesses scored four direct hits in quick succession on the *Kaga* (2). She, too, was immediately engulfed in uncontrollable flames. Later in the day she was abandoned and sank shortly afterward.

An earlier attack on the *Soryu* (1) had been beaten off by Zeros (6). Then bombers from the US carrier *Yorktown* dived on her and scored three hits: petrol tanks and magazines exploded, swiftly reducing her to a blazing hulk. All three carriers sank within 16 hours of being attacked.

with incendiary and high-explosive bombs for a second raid on Midway.

Fifteen minutes later, while his flight-deck crews were working feverishly to swap the bombers' armament, Nagumo first learned from a reconnaissance pilot of the presence of 10 US warships 386km/ 240mls away and steering toward him. No mention was made of carriers, even though at that time TF16's *Hornet* and *Enterprise* were launching aircraft.

Nagumo was obliged to cancel the rearming process and order his aircraft, some still with torpedoes, others now with bombs, to prepare to attack the American fleet. Then, at 08.20, he received alarming news: the seaplane pilot reported a carrier bringing up the rear of the American force. Nagumo could not order an immediate launch, much though he needed to, since the flight decks had to be kept clear to receive Tomonaga's aircraft returning from Midway—all now low on fuel and many damaged. He therefore ordered that all aircraft should be taken below and that as many bombers as possible should be armed with torpedoes. Working at speed, the flight-deck crew of *Akagi* stacked the bombs they were replacing in the hangars, instead of returning them to the heavily armoured magazines—an expedient that was shortly to have most disastrous consequences.

At 09.30, while the Japanese carriers' decks were littered with Tomonaga's unfuelled, unarmed aircraft, the first of TF16's strike of 117 aircraft roared into view. An hour's flying time behind them were another 35 aircraft from TF17. But the American attack was uncoordinated. The formations from *Hornet* and *Enterprise*, comprising low-flying Douglas Devastator torpedo bombers with a fighter cover of Grumman Wildcats, as well as higher-flying, unprotected Douglas Dauntless dive-bombers, made their way toward Nagumo's fleet through layered cloud.

Fifteen Devastators from *Hornet*, unprotected by fighters, braved a 50-strong combat air patrol of Zeros and a concentrated barrage of anti-aircraft fire to make the first attack. Every one was shot down. Next, 14 Devastators from *Enterprise* winged in and 11 of them were lost. When the *Yorktown*'s 12 Devastators eventually arrived on the scene they too attacked, but only two survived. The slow Devastators had been savaged by the Zeros without damaging Nagumo's ships.

While the air battle raged above them, the Japanese flight-deck crews had been struggling to prepare aircraft for a strike against the American ships; 102 were

A6M2 Zero-Sen

Aichi D3A Val

Nakajima B5N Kate

Grumman F4F/FM Wildcat

Douglas SBD/A-24 Dauntless

Douglas TBD Devastator

| 0 | 5 | 10 | 15 ft |
| 0 | 2 | 4m | |

Carrier fighters

The single-seat 'Zero' was the first carrier-based aircraft to out-perform those that were land-based. Built by Mitsubishi, it had unequalled range and manoeuvrability and in 1942 was the most sophisticated fighter in the Pacific theatre.

The most accurate of Japanese dive-bombers, the two-seat 'Val' was the craft chosen for the bombing of Pearl Harbor. Sturdy and highly manoeuvrable, they made effective fighter aircraft once they had released their bombs.

First built in 1935, the original 'Kate' three-seat bomber was obsolescent by 1942. But 103 B5N1s, as well as 40 B5N2 torpedo bombers, had taken part in the Pearl Harbor attack, and the B5N2 was largely responsible for the damage to the *Yorktown*. Production ceased in 1944.

A compact single-seat naval fighter, the Wildcat was especially suitable for operating from small escort carriers and was engaged in thousands of actions. It was noted for its manoeuvrability.

A two-seat carrier-based or land-based dive-bomber, the Dauntless was the most effective American combat aircraft and sank more Japanese ships than any other weapon.

Manned by a crew of three, the Devastator torpedo bomber was used extensively at the beginning of the Pacific war. The torpedo was aimed by sighting through doors in the belly of the aircraft. Outdated by 1942, it was withdrawn after Midway.

Devastator torpedo bombers being prepared for take-off from the deck of *Enterprise*. Of the 14 craft from this ship that took part in the first strike against Nagumo's carriers, all but three were destroyed. The planes' wings, which were folded for stowage, are being secured in the horizontal position. Returning aircraft dropped hooks to claw the deck arrester cables (in the foreground) to reduce speed and prevent their over-shooting.

The Commanders

Spruance (*left*) and Nimitz

Nagumo

Yamamoto

Admiral Isoroku Yamamoto (1884–1943) knew the Americans well, for he had studied at Harvard and been naval attaché (1925–7) in Washington DC. He was appointed Commander-in-Chief of the Japanese Combined Fleet in 1939. Although he had opposed an alliance with Germany, he was a strong advocate of war against the Anglo-Saxons and was largely responsible for the attack on Pearl Harbor. His First Air Fleet commander, **Vice-Admiral Chuichi Nagumo (1887–1944)**, a gifted and energetic officer, had aged and become indecisive by the time of the Battle of Midway and too readily approved without comment plans submitted by his staff. Moreover, he was an unsuitable choice to command the First Air Fleet, since his

speciality was torpedo warfare. Nagumo, who was later appointed to the command of the Central Pacific Fleet and entrusted with the defence of the Mariana Islands, committed suicide when US forces successfully landed on Saipan.

Admiral Chester W. Nimitz (1885–1966), a highly gifted organizer and strategist, was appointed Commander-in-Chief of the US Pacific Fleet on 31 December 1941, shortly after the Japanese attack on Pearl Harbor. He retained all officers in their posts in the belief that the disaster 'could have happened to anybody' and that his confidence in them would help restore morale. Nimitz, the commander chiefly responsible for the victory at Midway and the ensuing destruction of Japanese naval

strength, was among those on the *Missouri* on 3 September 1945 who received Japan's formal surrender.

Admiral Raymond A. Spruance (1886–1969) of Task Force 16, a calm, decisive commander but one receptive to advice, possessed to a high degree the ability to anticipate an enemy's intentions while keeping them guessing as to his own. He so intensely disliked personal publicity that he gave no interviews until after his retirement. When Nagumo's fleet was sighted, Spruance's superior, Admiral Frank J. Fletcher, was recovering his aircraft, so he ordered Spruance to engage the enemy fleet first, thus allowing this very able commander to act independently, critically affecting the battle's outcome.

ft 000 | 40km/25mls | 80km/50mls | 120km/75mls | 160km/100mls | 200km/125mls

30

20

10

Radar coverage on the US aircraft carriers extended more than 125 nautical miles and reached upward in excess of 30,000ft. This gave a great advantage to the fighters of their combat air patrols, whose job it was to intercept attacking aircraft before they reached the flat-tops.

The radar beams formed 'fingers' and, far from being a drawback, the gaps were a help to radar operators. By marking the ranges at which an enemy formation vanished from the screen then appeared again, they could calculate the raiders' altitude accurately.

Attacking aircraft

Aircraft carrier emitting radar from control tower

reported ready for launch. By 10.15, nine minutes later, Nagumo, feeling that he had regained the initiative, gave permission for them to take off.

But just at that moment, 14,000 feet above the Japanese carrier group, whose combat air patrol was low in altitude as well as fuel and ammunition after routing the Devastators, there lurked an unseen menace. Unnoticed by Nagumo's sailors, who were still on the alert for torpedo attacks, the Douglas Dauntless dive-bombers from *Enterprise* and *Yorktown* had, by chance, arrived over the target at the same time.

Forming up, the 55 Dauntlesses screamed down on the unsuspecting Japanese, and, in little more time than it takes to boil an egg, they had changed the course of the war in the Pacific. Two bombs—one of 454kg/1,000lb and one of 227kg/500lb—struck *Akagi*, Nagumo's flagship; four 454-kg/1,000-lb bombs hit *Kaga* and later three ploughed into *Soryu*, sealing the fate of three of Japan's biggest carriers and their complement of around 200 aircraft.

The American raid was hardly over before the *Hiryu*, which had lost a third of her aircraft on the Midway raid, was ordered to launch a counter-strike with whatever planes she had available. At 11.00, 18 dive-bombers escorted by half a dozen Zeros climbed away on a direct course for Fletcher's command, the position of which was being monitored by a Japanese reconnaissance aircraft. Just eight dive-bombers managed to get through to *Yorktown*, and only one got away after the attack, but they were not unsuccessful in their desperate mission. Three 227-kg/500-lb bombs thudded into the carrier, causing serious damage.

Meanwhile, Admiral Spruance, who was cruising unhindered to the southeast, prepared to blow the troublesome *Hiryu* out of the water. Twenty-four Daunt-lesses from *Enterprise*, followed by a fur-ther 16 from *Hornet*, flew off to seek out the Japanese carrier and at 17.00 found it, sailing under an umbrella of six Zeros. The enemy fighters intercepted the lead-ing elements of the Dauntless strike, but those coming behind hit *Hiryu* four times. The last of Nagumo's carriers was reduced to a blazing hulk, which next morning would have her end hastened by torpedoes from her own destroyer escort.

As darkness fell on 4 June, Admiral Fletcher turned TF17 east to avoid an encounter with the survivors of Nagumo's command. At 02.55 on 5 June, however, appalled by his losses, Yamamoto cancel-led the invasion of Midway and withdrew.

Devastators about to dive on ships of the Japanese Fleet. Perforations on the trailing, or rear edge, of the wings of these bombers gave extra stability when pilots aimed as they came out of a dive.

The Japanese carrier *Hiryu*, *above*, zigzagging to avoid bomb attacks by American B-17s. This expedient was far more effective against torpedo attack, for submarines were less manoeuvrable than bombers, which could follow the target's changing course moment by moment.

Four bombs, exploding in quick succession, set fire to aircraft on the *Hiryu*'s flight deck, causing further explosions, *right*. The ship was finally sunk by torpedoes from her escorting destroyers. Both her captain and Admiral Yamaguchi, whose flagship she was, went down with her. The latter tied himself to the bridge to ensure that he perished.

The death of the *Yorktown*

The US carrier *Yorktown* had been in action since the opening of hostilities, but was badly damaged at the Battle of the Coral Sea. She managed to reach Pearl Harbor on 27 May, trailing a 16-km/10-ml oil slick, and was greeted by sirens and cheering sailors. The damage she had sustained would normally have taken three months to repair, but 1,400 dockyard workers made her fit to sail within 48 hours. On 30 May she left harbour to rejoin Admiral Fletcher's Task Force 17.

In the Battle of Midway she played a notable part. Her dive-bombers, with those from the *Enterprise*, were responsible for

the destruction of Nagumo's flagship *Akagi*, her sister carrier the *Kaga*, and the *Soryu*. The *Hiryu*, however, remained and launched 18 dive-bombers against the *Yorktown* in revenge.

Yorktown was recovering her Dauntlesses when the alarm sounded. She halted landings, stopped refuelling operations and purged the fuel supply system with inert carbon dioxide gas to reduce the risk of an explosion if the ship were hit.

The Japanese scored three bomb hits, causing great damage and fires, which were quickly brought under control. Two hours later she was attacked again; four Kates

launched their torpedoes at a mere 457m/ 500yds range. *Yorktown* managed to avoid two but, in turning sharply to do so, received a double hit amidships, which stopped her. When she began to list badly, and was thought to be in danger of capsizing, her entire crew was safely transferred to other ships.

Even then, the Americans hoped to save her, and she was taken in tow to Pearl Harbor, but on 6 June was detected by a Japanese submarine and hit by two of its torpedoes. At dawn the following day, the mauled carrier finally succumbed, capsizing and going to the bottom.

Every major ship of the US Navy had a badge, in the case of the *Yorktown* an American eagle perched on a cannon.

Aircraft-carrier squadrons often adopted unofficial, humorous emblems, such as Squadron VF-3's Felix the Cat.

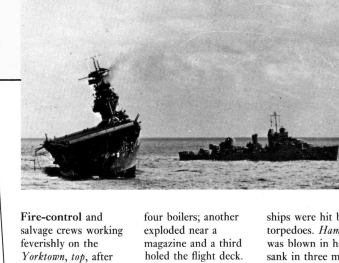

Fire-control and salvage crews working feverishly on the *Yorktown*, *top*, after she had been hit by three bombs in an attack by *Hiryu*'s aircraft. One bomb went down her stack, destroying three of her

four boilers; another exploded near a magazine and a third holed the flight deck.

The destroyer *Hamman*, *above*, turning to come alongside the crippled *Yorktown* to power her pumps. Later both

ships were hit by torpedoes. *Hamman* was blown in half and sank in three minutes. Her depth charges exploded underwater, killing 81 of her crew who had jumped or been thrown overboard by the explosion.

Guadalcanal/*August 1942-February 1943*

In the summer of 1942, the victorious Imperial Japanese Army was consolidating its huge gains in Southeast Asia, the East Indies and the Pacific Islands. At the same time, the English-language propaganda broadcasts by 'Tokyo Rose' were constantly and mockingly enquiring as to the whereabouts of the famous United States Marine Corps. On 7 August she found out: they were landing on Guadalcanal.

That remote, practically unheard-of island, one of the Solomons chain, had suddenly assumed enormous strategic importance when it was learned that the Japanese were building an airfield there. If enemy bombers were ever allowed to operate from it, then vital supply lines, stretching across the Pacific from the USA to fuel an Allied build-up in Australia and New Zealand, would be compromised.

Speed was paramount if this new threat were to be neutralized, so American planners, urged on by their Chief of Naval Operations, Admiral Ernest King, hurriedly cobbled together their first big land offensive of the war. On 2 July, the attack was ordered for 1 August; and since it was to be carried out by the Navy's ships, aircraft and troops, overall command of the operation was given to Vice-Admiral Robert L. Ghormley, Commander of the South Pacific Area, who had little faith in the venture.

The only adequate force available that was trained for amphibious landings was Major-General Alexander Vandegrift's 1st Division of the US Marine Corps, the leading elements of which had just arrived in New Zealand to begin a six-month course of battle practice. Vandegrift asked for more time to gather his forces, but Admiral King would agree to only a week's delay, so the date for this hastily contrived assault was moved to 7 August.

As a result, the 19,000-strong US 1st Marine Division sailed with only 60 days' supplies, enough ammunition for ten days of heavy fighting, and nothing like its full complement of transport. To add to their troubles, Rear-Admiral Frank Fletcher, commanding the naval task force, gave Vandegrift two days instead of his hoped-for five to complete the landing because he did not wish to over-expose his warships, particularly his three aircraft carriers, to enemy air attack.

After a three-hour preliminary bombardment by cruisers and destroyers, the Marines went in, protected by an air umbrella from Fletcher's carriers. The main body headed for the north coast of Guadalcanal east of Lunga Point, while a lesser force of 6,000 men made for the

The Marines

The Marines were allegedly the toughest troops in the US forces. Their training, of the most rigorous, brutal kind, taken to the point of recruits' exhaustion and often collapse, was designed to build them into efficient weapons of war by first destroying their individuality. Their heads were shaved, their names replaced by numbers and they had to eat sitting at attention. Corporal punishment—often for the most trivial misdemeanour—though officially banned, was commonplace: many a trainee, having dropped his rifle, was seen next by his comrades with a bloody nose, the work of his Drill Instructor.

In tandem with this debasement went a deliberate policy of welding the new group into a proud, self-contained unit. To this end the Marines, or 'sea soldiers', had evolved a language of their own. Thus, a latrine was called 'a head', information was 'dope' when speculative and 'the word' when confirmed; Marines did not go on leave, they were 'granted liberty'; they did not say 'Yes, Sir' to their officers but 'Aye, aye, Sir'. Marines prided themselves on their toughness, some thinking it manly to drink hair tonic rather than innocuous beer.

Having been turned into ruthless killers, they became pitiless, often sadistic, in conflict. Sometimes Marines would slip through enemy lines at night to search out two sleeping Japanese soldiers, then slit the throat of one and leave his comrade to find the corpse next day. Whatever may be thought of the dehumanizing training, it is doubtful whether any other US force could have endured and triumphed over the appalling conditions that obtained during the fighting on Guadalcanal.

The first wave of the 1st Marine Division, *left*, going ashore at 09:10 at 'Beach Red', 5,486m/6,000yds east of Lunga Point. The front, 1,463m/1,600yds wide, was deserted and the Japanese had omitted to lay mines, enabling the landing to be made without loss. The number of Marines landed was not great and this may have deceived the Japanese into underestimating their capability.

A navy boat, *left*, converted for use as a landing craft, bringing in Marines of the second wave. These vessels lacked movable bow ramps, so men had to manhandle equipment and weapons to the shore, an exhausting and often impossible task.

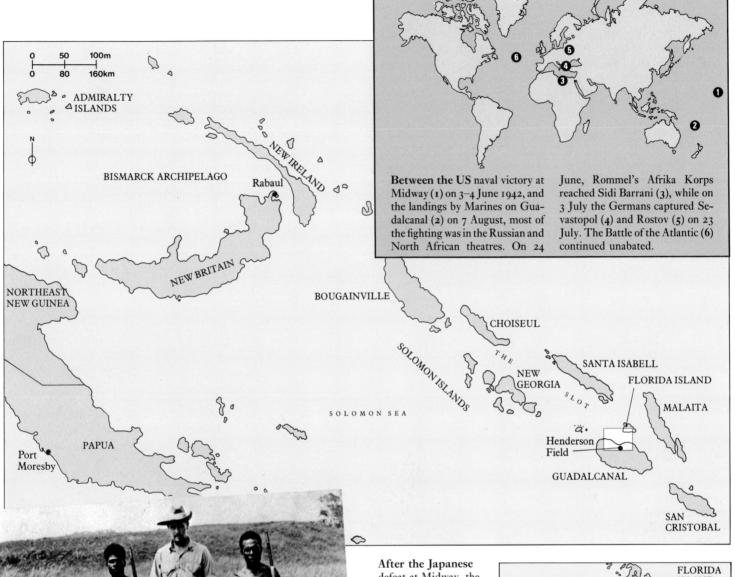

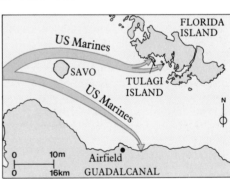

Between the US naval victory at Midway (1) on 3–4 June 1942, and the landings by Marines on Guadalcanal (2) on 7 August, most of the fighting was in the Russian and North African theatres. On 24 June, Rommel's Afrika Korps reached Sidi Barrani (3), while on 3 July the Germans captured Sevastopol (4) and Rostov (5) on 23 July. The Battle of the Atlantic (6) continued unabated.

After the Japanese defeat at Midway, the crucial sector of the Pacific War reverted to the southwest. To intensify their hold on captured areas, the Japanese planned to cross New Guinea from their bases on the north coast to capture the Allied base of Port Moresby and simultaneously to strengthen their position in the Solomons. The Americans, meanwhile, were planning an advance on Rabaul along the New Guinea coast and through the Solomon Islands. On 5 July 1942, however, reconnaissance aircraft confirmed reports from Australian Coastwatchers that the Japanese were already building an airstrip on Guadalcanal.

This island, 145km/ 90mls long and 40km/ 25mls wide, with a mountainous heartland, forests and swamps, lies near the southwest end of the chain; whoever held the island could dominate the area. If the Japanese were to complete the airfield, they could not only frustrate Allied attempts to recapture the Solomon Islands but could severely disrupt supply lines between the USA and Australia and New Zealand, where a build-up for future deployment was in progress.

The Allies were provided with details of enemy movements in occupied areas by the Australian Coastwatching Service. The Coastwatchers were mostly planters or local officials who knew the people and terrain well. They hid behind Japanese lines and radioed information as to troop, aircraft and ship movements to their HQ in Australia. Captain Martin Clemens, who had been British District Officer for Guadalcanal until the Japanese occupation, was one of the most effective. He operated from a cunningly camouflaged hideout in the jungle, with about 60 native scouts.

small island complex of Tulagi–Tanambogo–Gavutu, 32km/20mls away on the opposite side of Skylark Channel. The somewhat chaotic landings on Guadalcanal were virtually unopposed. The surprised Japanese soon recovered, however, and began to bomb the anchored transports and the beachhead, where a jumble of stores and equipment was being unmethodically dumped.

In the meantime, the Marines were fighting their way toward the unfinished airfield 4.8km/3mls inland, and secured it within 36 hours. But their situation had become precarious and Vandegrift had serious doubts as to whether Guadalcanal could be held. The deterioration began on the evening of 8 August when Admiral Fletcher decided to withdraw his carriers, a move which would leave the partially unloaded transports without air cover and

render their position untenable. If the carriers left, the transports would have to go too.

That night, the enemy took a hand as well. Vice-Admiral Gunichi Mikawa, with five heavy cruisers, two light cruisers and a destroyer, slipped undetected into Skylark Channel and within 40 minutes sank one cruiser of the Royal Australian Navy and three US cruisers.

On 9 August the unprotected transports followed Fletcher over the horizon. Aboard were 3,000 Marines who had not yet disembarked, half of the division's supplies, much of its reserve ammunition, and most of its barbed wire and heavy artillery. When, indeed if, these ships would return was not known, so it was understandable that Vandegrift and his depleted command should feel they had been abandoned by the navy.

Nevertheless, the Marines made the best of their unattractive situation, supplementing dwindling rations with Japanese food and whatever edible roots and berries they could find. Using captured weapons and ammunition, they strengthened their defences and with the enemy's undamaged engineering equipment rushed to complete the airfield as quickly as possible.

Meanwhile, the Japanese sneaked in fresh assault troops, and in the early hours of 20 August Colonel Kiyono Ichiki led the first big counter-attack on the Americans, fully expecting to overrun them. Hitting Vandegrift's left flank at the mouth of the Ilu river, the Japanese went in, in three separate waves, each of which was cut down by well-directed fire. This repulse, which cost 1,000 dead, was too much for Ichiki: he committed suicide.

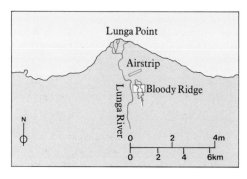

Major General Vandegrift's Marines, nearing exhaustion after holding the vital airfield sector of Guadalcanal for more than a month, were subjected to their greatest test when Major-General Kiyotaki Kawaguchi launched an attack by some 3,000 infantrymen on Henderson Field. They approached by way of an open ridge 1.6km/1ml long, which rose above the dense jungle to the south of the airstrip. Vandegrift entrusted the hill's defence to Lieutenant-Colonel Merritt Edson and the 700 men remaining from the 1st Raider Battalion and the 1st Parachute Battalion. The Japanese

opened the attack on the night of 12 September 1942, following a bombardment by their ships and aircraft. Fighting, often illuminated by the eerie glow of flares, continued all that night and throughout the next. Edson's troops were forced back to within 914m/1,000yds of Henderson Field, but Kawaguchi, having suffered dreadful losses, was ultimately forced to retreat from what the Marines came to call 'Bloody Ridge'.

Edson positioned his men on the western slope of the ridge (5), the eastern side (2) being held by paratroopers. Crouching in foxholes protected by barbed wire, they used rifles, machine-guns, mortars and grenades to repulse incessant Japanese attacks.

Men of the 1st Raider Battalion (6), positioned between the ridge and the Lunga river 731m/800yds to the west, clashed repeatedly with infiltrating Japanese patrols. When his men were in danger of being cut off, Edson ordered them back to the main defence line.

Kawaguchi's battalions, deployed on both sides of the ridge (3,4), time and again stormed up the open, grassy slope, only to be cut down by the concentrated fire of the Marines. More than 600 Japanese were killed in the two nights of fighting.

Strongly pressed, Edson gradually withdrew to the top of the ridge and by the end of the second night's fighting his men were dug in on the last knoll (1) above the airstrip. There the Japanese were finally halted and repulsed by the Marines, supported by artillery fire from batteries near Henderson Field and, after dawn, by air strikes.

75

Guadalcanal/3

Later that day, to the immense relief of General Vandegrift, the first US aircraft, 12 Douglas Dauntless dive-bombers and 19 Grumman Wildcat fighters, landed on what had become known as Henderson Field, in memory of a Marine pilot, Major Lofton Henderson, who had been killed at the Battle of Midway.

At last fully alert to the fact that the Marines meant to keep their foothold on Guadalcanal, the Japanese High Command, unused to reverses, moved swiftly to try to regain the initiative. It was now that the so-called 'Tokyo Express' came into its own. Fast convoys of troop-laden destroyers and transports made their way at night through the 'Slot' and deposited cargoes of soldiers close to the American defence zone.

As the opposing navies and air forces strove to upset each other's reinforcement programmes for Guadalcanal and suffered heavy losses in the process, the Marines grimly held on to their perimeter. Intense heat, tropical rain storms, insects, rats, poor diet, malaria, dysentry were all stoically endured by Vandegrift's men, as well as the wartime hazards of enemy shelling, bombing and ferocious infantry attacks launched suddenly from the dense surrounding jungle.

At the beginning of September, the Tokyo Express succeeded in landing several battalions under Major-General Kiyotaki Kawaguchi. Most of this force were moved inland to attack Henderson Field from the south, an area which the Japanese thought was not so heavily defended as the coastal perimeter.

On the nights of 12 and 13 September, Kawaguchi stormed the ridge which stood between him and the airstrip. But dug in on that hog's back were some of the toughest men in the US Marine Corps—a Raider battalion and a parachute battalion, jointly commanded by Colonel Merritt 'Red Mike' Edson. These front-line troops were supported by another Marine infantry battalion plus artillery.

Though the American line bent in the course of heavy and bitter fighting, it did not break. Dawn on the 14th revealed heaps of Japanese casualties littering the slopes, so earning the battlefield the name of 'Bloody Ridge'. It is estimated that 600 enemy soldiers were killed and another 600 wounded: the Marines lost 40 dead and 103 wounded from a force of 700 men.

Five days after Edson's epic stand, the first major reinforcements and shipments of supplies since the landing of 7 August began to arrive. At last some of the pressure could be taken off the magnificent 1st Marine Division and the equally

The landing

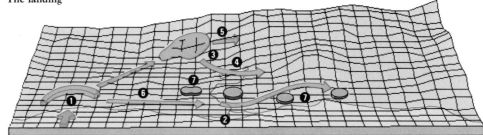

The six-month battle for the island of Guadalcanal fell into three distinct phases. In the first, though meeting heavy, often suicidal, opposition on Tulagi Island on the other side of the sound, the 1st Division of the US Marines (1) gained an immediate, almost unopposed, foothold on the north coast of Guadalcanal, east of Lunga Point (2). They achieved tactical surprise and within 36 hours a column (3) captured the main objective, an airfield under construction (4)—this was later named Henderson Field by the Marines—while a detachment (5) probed high ground farther inland. Another US force (6) moved along the coast to complete the encirclement of four Japanese camps (7). A perimeter curving inland from the towns of Kukum in the west and Tenaru in the east was established, and the Marines were then free to complete the airstrip and prepare it for use by US aircraft.

Bloody Ridge

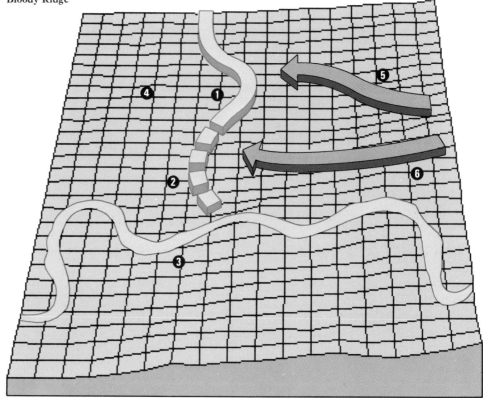

Colonel Merritt Edson's main position (1) was on the southern tip of the grassy ridge (4) that provided an easy approach to the vital, US-held airfield less than 3km/2mls to the north. Patrols (2) protected his flank in the jungle between the ridge and the nearby River Lunga (3). A strong Japanese force made an arduous march over rough terrain in a loop from its base on the coast to launch a two-pronged assault (5, 6) on the ridge on the night of 12 September. They intended to storm the ridge, then go on to recapture the airfield; but the attack, which was continued throughout the night of the 13th as well, was beaten off by the Marines and failed.

The Commanders

Vice-Admiral Robert L. Ghormley (1883–1958), US Commander, South Pacific, was in some ways an unfortunate choice for campaign commander since he was convinced the situation in the Solomon Islands was hopeless. Throughout the campaign he remained pessimistic of its outcome. Admiral Nimitz was disturbed by Ghormley's lack of confidence and, seeking a more agressive commander, replaced him on 18 October with Admiral William F. Halsey, one of the most experienced officers in the US Navy.

Ghormley was not the only pessimist during the Guadalcanal campaign. **Rear Admiral Raizo Tanaka (1892–1969)**, the

veteran Japanese destroyer commander who had led the Landing Force at Midway, was placed in command of the Guadalcanal Reinforcement Force. And 'Tanaka the tenacious', as he was known, was convinced that Guadalcanal was indefensible and that the army should be evacuated before it was destroyed. The High Command at first ignored his advice—unwisely, since its soundness was soon to be demonstrated by the ineffectiveness of the 'Tokyo Express'. For although his destroyers successfully and repeatedly reached their destinations, the men and supplies which they carried were never sufficient for the purpose. After six months of useless fighting, however, the

remnants of the Japanese forces were withdrawn from the island. Tanaka's sound but pessimistic appraisal of the military situation brought about his dismissal.

Lt.Colonel Merritt 'Red Mike' Edson (1897–1955), Marine commander at the Battle of 'Bloody Ridge', was the archetypal Marine, tough and taciturn. He was a strong advocate of his men living off the land—or, better still, the enemy. This they achieved in fine style on 7 September, when they carried out a sea-borne raid on a Japanese supply depot at Taivu and returned with their assault boats full of rice, tinned meat and vegetables, as well as plentiful supplies of beer and sake.

The Japanese retreat

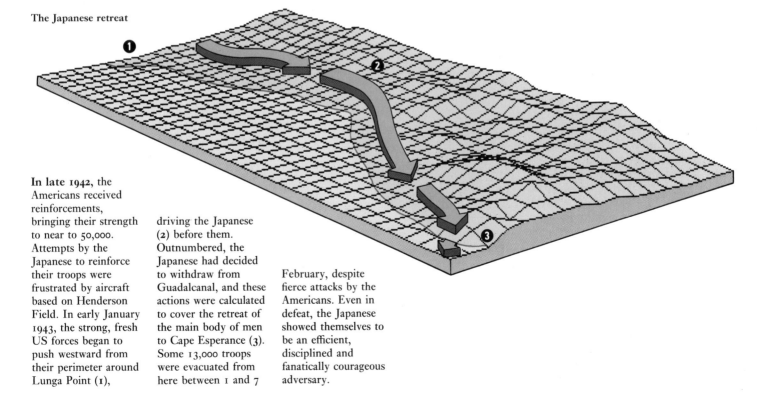

In late 1942, the Americans received reinforcements, bringing their strength to near to 50,000. Attempts by the Japanese to reinforce their troops were frustrated by aircraft based on Henderson Field. In early January 1943, the strong, fresh US forces began to push westward from their perimeter around Lunga Point (1),

driving the Japanese (2) before them. Outnumbered, the Japanese had decided to withdraw from Guadalcanal, and these actions were calculated to cover the retreat of the main body of men to Cape Esperance (3). Some 13,000 troops were evacuated from here between 1 and 7

February, despite fierce attacks by the Americans. Even in defeat, the Japanese showed themselves to be an efficient, disciplined and fanatically courageous adversary.

courageous crews of the motley collection of aircraft at Henderson Field.

But as the Americans increased their beachhead, built another fighter strip at Kukum and generally strengthened their positions, the Japanese also stepped up their commitment to push the US forces off the island. Enemy troops were concentrating mainly on the west bank of the Matanikau River near the mouth, directly opposite the American right flank; throughout the rest of September and into early October there were several bloody engagements in this sector.

On 9 October, Lieutenant-General Harukichi Hyakutake, the senior Japanese commander in the area, came to Guadalcanal to lead operations. Bringing with him reinforcements which would boost his strength to 20,000 men, plus additional batteries of artillery, he planned to strike a decisive blow within ten days. Meanwhile, on the other side of the barbed-wire entanglements, General Vandegrift had the Japanese outnumbered by some 3,000 men, thanks to the arrival of the first US Army troops to set foot on Guadalcanal, the 164th Infantry.

The Hyakutake plan, almost a carbon copy of the disastrous Kawaguchi effort a month earlier, called for 6,000 troops to hack their way inland and attack Henderson Field from the south, while 3,000 more launched a simultaneous assault on the American right flank. The date set for the attack, 19 October, came and went as the main Japanese column was still struggling through the thick jungle.

Hyakutake rescheduled the operation for 24 October but, due to a misunderstanding, the smaller flanking attack went in 24 hours early and was shot to pieces. Bloody Ridge then became the object of two concentrated Japanese attacks on the nights of 24 and 25 October, both of which were repulsed with enormous loss of life. The enemy continued to pour in more reserves, and the war of attrition wore on in the same unrelenting fashion.

In the meantime, there had been a change in command on the American side. Ghormley was relieved and the South Pacific area got a new, aggressive leader, Vice-Admiral William Halsey, who began a huge build-up of American troops on Guadalcanal. And on 9 December came yet another change in command, when General Vandegrift was ordered to withdraw his weary 1st Marine Division and to hand over to Major-General Alexander Patch. While this was going on, more and more aircraft and battalions were arriving on the island and, as 1942 turned to 1943, Patch had air superiority and 50,000

troops at his disposal. Hyakutake, on the other hand, had only half that number, a lengthening sick list, a shortage of supplies and little prospect of their replenishment, thanks to US air and naval patrols.

Using three divisions, Patch mounted a major offensive westward against the main Japanese positions that lay beyond the Matanikau River. The enemy fought stubbornly, but sheer weight of numbers and strength of firepower drove them back. On 23 January, Hyakutake's headquarters at Kokumbona was overrun. But on the same day, news of the approach of a large Japanese naval force caused Patch briefly to check his advance in case it was an invasion fleet and he had to redeploy.

A similar false alarm on the 30th also served to delay the mopping-up process. In fact, the ships sighted on each occasion were a force of Japanese destroyers which

were standing by ready to take off their infantry. On the night of 8 February, these ships moved in close to Cape Esperance and began evacuating troops. After six long and bloody months the Battle of Guadalcanal was over.

American casualties amounted to some 5,600, of whom more than 1,500 had been killed, compared to Japanese losses of 24,000 dead. In the fierce naval and air battles, both sides suffered huge losses, but the Japanese could less afford to lose ships, aircraft and trained aircrew.

The victory at Guadalcanal provided the US land forces with their first real stepping-stone on the road to Tokyo. Indeed, Admiral Tanaka, who by running convoys through the Slot had done so much to prolong the campaign, believed that 'Japan's doom was sealed with the closing of the struggle for Guadalcanal'.

The badge of the 'Seabees', *above*, as the Construction Battalions were called. These combat troops, trained as specialist engineers, extended and repaired the landing strips at Henderson Field.

The 1st Marine Division's badge, *above right*, commemorated their first campaign in World War II.

Marines, laden with ammunition, packs, mortars and machine-guns, searched out Japanese holed up in the jungle. The weight of their equipment added to the misery of struggling through the dense, fetid undergrowth. Each man needed two canteens of water daily, but had to make do with one; and there were not enough salt tablets to mitigate the effect of the jungle heat.

Sea battles of Guadalcanal

Crucial to the outcome of the fighting on Guadalcanal were the naval engagements, four major and many lesser encounters that took place in the waters near the island.

On the night of 8–9 August, a strong force of Japanese cruisers and destroyers surprised the US naval force guarding the approach to the site where troops and supplies were still being landed on Guadalcanal. In little more than half an hour, three US heavy cruisers were sunk, together with the Australian cruiser *Canberra*. The Japanese suffered no losses but missed a valuable opportunity: had they continued eastward they might have sunk all the American transports landing troops and supplies and gained control of the island.

On 23 August, in the Eastern Solomons, an attempt to bring supplies to the Japanese was intercepted and the following day the Japanese lost the aircraft-carrier *Ryujo* and the destroyer *Mutsuki*.

Then, on the night of 11–12 October, the two fleets again engaged, this time off Cape Esperance. During a confused action, the Americans lost the destroyer *Duncan* and the Japanese a cruiser and a destroyer.

Toward the end of that month, General Maruyama launched a major offensive against Henderson Field with aircraft of the Japanese Combined Fleet. However, the US aircraft-carriers *Enterprise* and *Hornet* had been ordered to intercept this force in the waters around the Santa Cruz Islands.

In the battle that followed, the Japanese sustained severe damage but lost no ships, while the US aircraft-carrier *Hornet* was so badly damaged that she had to be abandoned; later she was sunk by Japanese torpedoes.

In all, the Americans lost 2 aircraft-carriers, 7 cruisers and 14 destroyers; the Japanese lost 1 aircraft-carrier, 2 battleships, 4 cruisers and 11 destroyers. The losses sustained by both sides were not unequal, but there was a crucial distinction: America had vast reserves of ships and crews, whereas the Japanese, exhausted and depleted by endless battles, notably those at Midway and the Coral Sea, had sustained losses they could not replace.

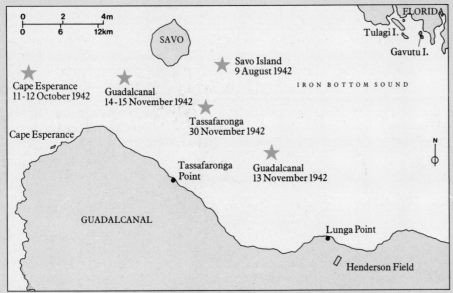

Japan's losses at sea did not, however, make the Marines secure, for Japanese reinforcements were available on the Shortland Islands; the problem was how to get them to Guadalcanal. The large, heavy barges used at first proved vulnerable to air attack, so Admiral Raizo Tanaka, knowing the US fleet was less skilled at night-fighting than his own, decided to move men under cover of darkness. Using fast destroyers, he organized a series of night dashes—dubbed the 'Tokyo Express' by the Marines— through the 'Slot'. This narrow but navigable channel between the two lines of islands that made up the Solomons ran down to Ironbottom Sound, so named because of the many wrecks of both Allied and Japanese ships that had been lost there. These destroyer-transports landed troops and supplies on either side of the US beachhead in the area of Tenaru and Kukum.

The Marines' landing on Guadalcanal was covered by fire from the big guns on US and Australian battleships and cruisers, *above*. The troops ashore also had medium artillery with them.

While on convoy escort duty off Guadalcanal on 15 September 1942, the American carrier *Wasp, far left,* was hit by three torpedoes from a Japanese submarine, which gashed her side and fractured fuel lines. These ignited and the ship was torn apart by huge explosions, killing 193 men. *Wasp* was abandoned and was eventually sunk by torpedoes fired by the USS *Lansdowne*. All but one of her aircraft were landed on the carrier *Hornet*.

El Alamein/*October-November 1942*

Mussolini already had a million-strong army in Libya when he declared war on the Allies on 10 June 1940. In neighbouring Egypt, guarding major British bases, the Suez Canal and the gateway to the Arabian oilfields, there was a force of just on 36,000 men. The Duce desperately wanted to conquer Egypt to prove to Adolf Hitler that Fascist Italy, too, was capable of significant victories.

On 13 September, five Italian divisions under Marshall Graziani began a rapid advance into Egypt, where they dug in in front of the main British defences at Mersa Matruh. Then, on 9 December, General Archibald Wavell launched 'Operation Compass', a British counter-offensive; the Italians suffered heavy casualties and were pushed back more than 800km/500mls.

Mussolini's defeats in North Africa in 1940 so alarmed Hitler that he felt obliged to send help to the demoralized Italians. In January 1941, therefore, General Erwin Rommel, an astute panzer commander, was sent to the desert at the head of a specially raised armoured group, the Deutsches Afrika Korps. Though theoretically subordinate to the Italian Commander-in-Chief in Libya, General Italo Gariboldi, Rommel assumed front-line command immediately. The war in North Africa, sometimes described as 'a

gentleman's war' because it was fought fairly between soldiers in an area virtually devoid of civilians and property, now took on a tougher complexion.

Rommel mounted his first attack on 24 March 1941 and at once exhibited a flair for desert warfare. By early April he had chased the British out of Libya, except for the garrison defending the port of Tobruk. Wavell's riposte, 'Operation Battleaxe', was halted at Halfaya Pass, Libya, on 17 June; and less than three weeks later a new British commander, General Sir Claude Auchinleck, was appointed.

On 18 November, he opened his first offensive, 'Operation Crusader', with the newly created Eighth Army. Meanwhile, Rommel, who had laid siege to Tobruk, had run short of supplies and was forced to retreat. By early January 1942, Auchinleck had penetrated as far west as Wavell had done, and it was now the British whose supply lines were overextended. Rommel quickly turned on his attackers and by 4 February had reached Derna. He won Tobruk on 21 June and by July was a mere 113km/70mls from Alexandria.

The British Prime Minister, Winston Churchill, despairing about what he called 'a serious and quite unexpected crisis', made the long journey to the desert front to judge the situation for himself.

Although General Auchinleck, as G.O.C. Middle East, had taken direct command of the flagging Eighth Army and had begun reorganizing it into self-contained battle groups, which managed to halt Rommel's latest and longest advance, Churchill decided that changes in command were required. The Prime Minister wanted the action in North Africa brought to a quick end to clear the way for an invasion of Italy, which he knew would pay high dividends for the Allied cause.

Overall charge of British and Commonwealth land forces in the Middle East went to General Sir Harold Alexander, while the command of the Eighth Army defending Egypt was given to General W.H.E. Gott. But Gott was killed in an air crash before he could take over, and the second choice for this formidable command, Lieutenant-General Bernard Montgomery, was ordered out from England. His arrival in the desert in early August marked the beginning of a dramatic and permanent change in British fortunes.

Meanwhile, Axis excitement at finding their forward elements so far inside Egypt began to wane as their supply situation worsened. Convoys from Benghazi, using the single highway running along the North African coast, were taking seven days to reach the front, and from the other

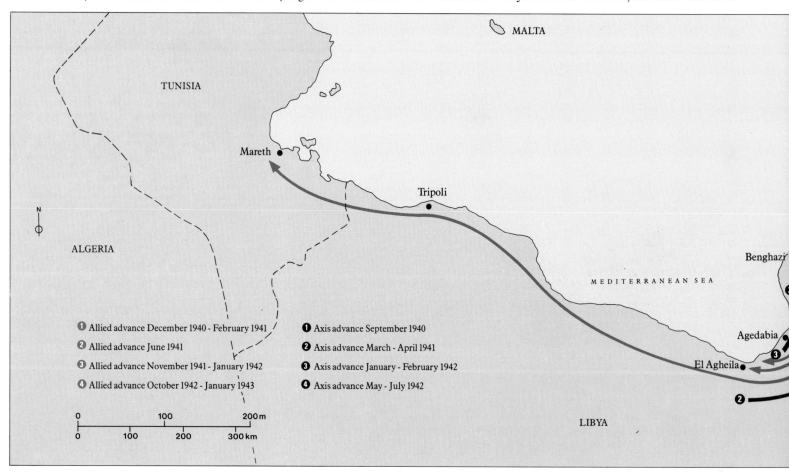

Allied advance December 1940 - February 1941
Allied advance June 1941
Allied advance November 1941 - January 1942
Allied advance October 1942 - January 1943

Axis advance September 1940
Axis advance March - April 1941
Axis advance January - February 1942
Axis advance May - July 1942

Desert warfare

Hostile conditions aggravated supply problems and made every-day life for the soldiers in the desert a disorientating experience. Transport columns had to navigate by compass or rely on native tracks. Few were as fortunate as this convoy, delivering supplies to the front, which had the landmark of a railway track by which to pinpoint its position. The dangers of warfare were increased by the lack of natural features, for the terrain offered soldiers little protection from attack, and trenches, such as the one on the right of this picture, could be seen by enemy aircraft. Men also suffered from lack of shelter from the burning sun and cold desert nights.

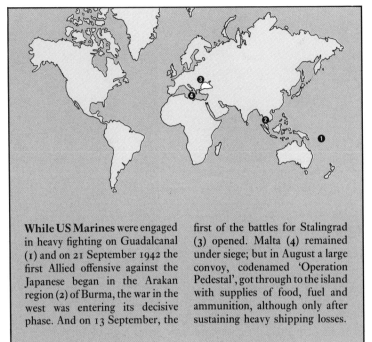

While US Marines were engaged in heavy fighting on Guadalcanal (1) and on 21 September 1942 the first Allied offensive against the Japanese began in the Arakan region (2) of Burma, the war in the west was entering its decisive phase. And on 13 September, the first of the battles for Stalingrad (3) opened. Malta (4) remained under siege; but in August a large convoy, codenamed 'Operation Pedestal', got through to the island with supplies of food, fuel and ammunition, although only after sustaining heavy shipping losses.

Between September 1940 and October 1942 the war in the desert developed into a series of running campaigns, *see map below*, in which first the Axis forces and then the British took the initiative, each advancing long distances until supply problems proved too great and they were obliged to fall back toward their main bases once again.

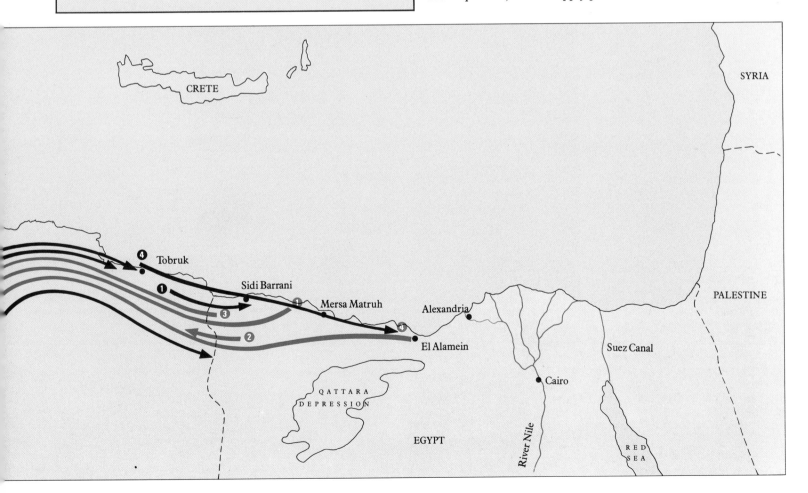

El Alamein/2

main base at Tripoli, 12 days. And when they finally arrived they were often much depleted, thanks to the attentions of the Allies' Desert Air Force, which had virtually complete control of the sky. Reinforcements, requested by Rommel to help in the next phase of his attack, did not please him either: they were Italian. 'What I need here are not still more Italian divisions ...' he said, 'but the German soldiers and the German equipment with which alone I am going ultimately to have to carry through my offensive.'

These difficulties notwithstanding, the Desert Fox, as he had been nicknamed, decided to make a desperate attempt to capitalize on his outstanding victories. However, his gamble did not pay off: when Rommel attacked at Alam el Halfa on 30 August, Montgomery was prepared for him. By 2 September, Axis forces had to withdraw beyond the area that stretched from El Alamein on the coast 64km/40mls south to the impassable Qattara Depression, a bottleneck with secure flanks that the British had already realized was of immense strategic importance. Defended in depth, it would effectively bar any further advance into Egypt, and it would also serve as an excellent jumping-off position for a counteroffensive.

With the Axis forces on the defensive and still short of supplies, Montgomery confidently pressed ahead behind his Alamein line with the task of welding the Eighth Army into a strong, superbly equipped force capable of dealing Rommel a crushing defeat. He built on Auchinleck's foundations, improved the morale immeasurably, and stockpiled vast quantities of weapons and ammunition to make certain that his command possessed overwhelming firepower.

Churchill, delighted that the British had seized the initiative at Alam el Halfa, was eager that the pace should be maintained. He pressed Montgomery to follow up the victory by exploiting the September full-moon period two weeks ahead, when there would be sufficient light to allow infantry and armour to operate safely in the desert at night. The Eighth Army's new commander refused; his men, he knew, would not be ready by then for a large-scale, hammer-blow attack of the kind he envisaged. The Prime Minister would have to curb his impatience until the October full moon, by which time Montgomery's meticulous preparations would be complete.

Montgomery's plan, 'Operation Lightfoot', hinged on the element of surprise. It was essential that Rommel should not

Camouflage was the only cover for aircraft flying over the flat, barren desert landscape. Its leopard-like markings enable this Messerschmitt Bf 109 to disappear against the small rocks and red-yellow sand.

Versatile halftracks were the most useful vehicles in this terrain. The German SdKfz personnel carrier (*right*) could be adapted for many uses, including that of a weapons platform, but the symbol on this car indicates that it was used for towing. Maximum vision, provided by the low bonnet, made it ideal for reconnaissance, and the steering could be switched from moving the front wheels to controlling the track over uneven surfaces.

The Commanders

Rommel

Montgomery

Field Marshal Erwin Rommel (1891–1944) was a dashing, handsome man who had won the Iron Cross and Prussia's highest award, the *Pour le Mérite*, during World War I. He was made a general in 1939 and took part in several campaigns, proving himself a master of blitzkrieg tactics.

A great commander in the field, Rommel thrived on the challenge of desert warfare, and his string of victories soon mesmerized his own troops and those of the Allies alike—it is significant that the Eighth

Army's attack at El Alamein was opened in his absence. On his return to Africa, Rommel rallied his forces to present such stiff opposition that some British commanders urged retreat. But his talents were unsuited to a war of attrition, and it was Rommel who retreated.

Both Rommel and his opponent in the Western Desert, **Lieutenant-General Bernard Montgomery (1897–1976)**, were quick to appreciate the value of combat propaganda, and both created a cult around themselves.

Montgomery served in France during World War I, and then in India and Palestine. At the outbreak of World War II he was posted to the BEF and was at Dunkirk. In 1942 he was appointed as Churchill's 'new broom' commander of the Eighth Army at a time when defeats and harsh conditions had sapped its morale and it seemed incapable of victory.

A remarkable self-publicist, with a deep belief in the value of strong, central command, Montgomery deliberately set out to promote his image as a leader. At the same time, by discipline and training, he encouraged self-confidence and a sense of identity in his demoralized troops. He was, however, prepared to adapt his plans, as was shown by his rapid development of Operation Supercharge after the break-in. While Rommel showed more flair and a feeling for battle, Montgomery's great merit lay in his unwavering determination to achieve his goal.

Following the victory in North Africa, Montgomery led the Eighth Army in Sicily and Italy before returning to the United Kingdom to take part in the imminent Normandy landings. He was promoted to Field Marshal in 1944.

51st Highland Division

8th Armoured Division

7th Armoured Division

Afrika Korps

Shoulder flashes worn by Allied divisions, and the insignia of the Afrika Korps, personalized the uniforms and equipment of the men fighting the desert war. Perhaps the most famous of these morale-boosting badges was the jerboa, *above right*. This little animal is perfectly suited to life in the desert, and its adoption by the men of 7th Armoured Division as their symbol earned them the nickname of the 'Desert Rats'.

Montgomery himself wore either a tank corps beret with two badges or an Australian slouch hat covered in badges. And, always conscious of the importance of *ésprit de corps*, he capitalized on the divisions' individuality by matching their specific capabilities to the job to be done.

be able to predict accurately either the time of the attack or the direction from which it would come. Although it would be impossible to pretend that no attack was being prepared, the British and Commonwealth troops camouflaged the main sites of unit and equipment concentrations in the north and constructed huge dummy staging areas in the south, in an attempt to throw the Desert Fox off the scent. These fake installations were built at a rate calculated to make Rommel think that no attack would be launched until early November.

In mid-October, on the eve of the British offensive, the Eighth Army totalled 195,000 men, 1,351 tanks, including 285 of the new American Shermans, and 1,900 pieces of artillery, ranging from 2-pounder anti-tank guns to medium weapons. The Axis forces comprised 100,000 men, 510 tanks, of which 300 were inferior Italian models, and 1,325 guns.

Amid the frenetic pre-attack activity in the Eighth Army, Montgomery was displaying a theatrical streak that was a gift to the Press. This usually austere senior officer wore distinctly casual uniform, topped with either an unconventional two-badged tank beret or an Australian slouch hat decorated with regimental insignia. He mingled freely with his troops, delivering morale-boosting, fighting speeches of the 'no withdrawal, no surrender' variety. The men loved it. The son of a bishop, Monty revealed his staunch faith in his eve-of-attack message, when he prayed for the support of 'the Lord mighty in battle' in the coming fight.

On 23 October, in an effort to ensure that secrecy was maintained right up to the last minute, the assault troops of the Eighth Army were confined to their slit trenches: they could not abandon cover even to use the latrines. But such precautions had the desired effect. The Axis forces first realized that a major attack was imminent at 21.40 in the evening, when the biggest artillery barrage since World War I opened up.

While 1,000 guns pounded at German and Italian positions in prelude to the main assault, the Eighth Army's commander was in bed. Montgomery had made painstaking plans for this night attack and it was now up to his fighting units to execute them. He took the view that nothing could be gained by his staying up. He would serve his troops better by getting a good night's sleep and being fresh to take charge of the situation the next morning.

Unfortunately for the Axis troops, their inspired—and inspiring—leader, Field

EIGHTH ARMY

PERSONAL MESSAGE
from the
ARMY COMMANDER

(To be read out to all Troops)

1. When I assumed command of the Eighth Army I said that the mandate was to destroy ROMMEL and his Army, and that it would be done as soon as we were ready.

2. We are ready NOW.

The battle which is now about to begin will be one of the decisive battles of history. It will be the turning point of the war. The eyes of the whole world will be on us, watching anxiously which way the battle will swing.

We can give them their answer at once: "It will swing our way."

3. We have first-class equipment; good tanks; good anti-tank guns; plenty of artillery and plenty of ammunition; and we are backed up by the finest air striking force in the world.

All that is necessary is that each one of us, every officer and man, should enter this battle with the determination to see it through — to fight and to kill — and finally, to win.

If we all do this there can be only one result — together we will hit the enemy for "six," right out of North Africa.

4. The sooner we win this battle, which will be the turning point of the war, the sooner we shall all get back home to our families.

5. Therefore, let every officer and man enter the battle with a stout heart, and the determination to do his duty so long as he has breath in his body.

AND LET NO MAN SURRENDER SO LONG AS HE IS UNWOUNDED AND CAN FIGHT.

Let us all pray that "the Lord mighty in battle" will give us the victory.

B. L. Montgomery
Lieutenant-General, G.O.C.-in-C., Eighth Army.

23-10-42
Middle East Forces.

Montgomery's message, issued to the officers and men of the Eighth Army on the eve of Operation Lightfoot, epitomised his belief that 'the morale of the soldier is the greatest single factor in war.' Montgomery realized that to ensure a lasting victory the fighting spirit of the troops must be at its peak.

More substantial addresses to the commanders stressed how essential a positive attitude was, for he feared they might have no stomach for the days of brutal 'dogfighting' he knew would follow the initial attack.

Deception and trickery

In a landscape devoid of natural cover, camouflage and deception played a major part in battle tactics. Forces on both sides were soon receiving sand-yellow equipment, which afforded them some concealment. More devious was the use of fake minefields in the middle of which live mines were laid; this economized on munitions and unsuspecting men were enticed into danger.

During the prelude to Operation Lightfoot, a deception on a large scale was carried out to persuade the Axis forces that an attack was due in the south. The real concentration of Allied supplies in the north was disguised, while the secondary forces in the south were supplemented with dummy tanks, *above*, trucks, guns, and even a fake oil pipeline. Just before the battle, operational guns and tanks, hidden under hessian covers painted as lorries, were moved up from the south. Codenamed 'Operation Bertram', this elaborate scheme, which succeeded in duping enemy air reconnaissance, was made possible by the expert camouflage units which had been established by General Wavell at the beginning of the campaign in the desert.

Mines and minefields

Mines played a dominant role in desert warfare, creating artificial obstacles where there were no natural defences. They were used as strategic support in an attack or to form a defensive perimeter, and the variety of mines and methods of deployment became increasingly sophisticated and specialized during the campaign.

Teller, or plate, mines often had anti-tank fuses only, which allow forward companies of infantry to walk over them with impunity, inducing the tanks to follow to their destruction. Anti-personnel mines could inflict dozens of different injuries; the German S-mine was especially feared. When trodden on, its three-pronged detonator was triggered and the mine flew into the air, where it exploded at waist height, spewing out hundreds of ball bearings.

Mines were laid in enormous quantities after February 1942. Both sides linked many old fields with belts of new mines, so forming vast 'marshes'. At El Alamein, a major problem was the clearance of gaps through such fields on the night of 23–24 October, although the new mine detectors relieved men of the need to crawl along the ground, prodding it with their bayonets.

Once cleared, the path through a minefield was marked by white cones and tape. At night the path was made clearer by the addition of poles supporting a hurricane lamp at each end of a cross-bar. These lamps were placed in empty fuel cans with a hole cut out of the side facing the advance so that no light was visible to the enemy. Green glass was used to indicate the clear side of the line, amber the dangerous side. Red lights warned of uncleared minefields.

Anti-tank mines.

Dummy minefield.

S-mines shot out lethal steel balls at waist level.

Trip-wire mines.

Aircraft bombs attached by fuse wire to manual detonators.

Barbed wire fence.

Piles of stones or petrol cans marking boundaries.

Gaps in minefields.

Defensive positions.

Polish mine detectors, shaped like upright vacuum cleaners, were swept across the sand in front of the operator; the presence of a mine created a high-pitched whine in the sapper's earphones. The only drawback to these detectors was that it needed great courage to stand upright under fire.

'**Devil's Garden**' minefields were used extensively by Rommel during the campaign. The diagram, *above*, based on a map captured by the Allies, shows their fatal ingenuity. A variety of mines was used strategically for maximum effect. By leaving paths through the minefield, the Germans lured British units into a killing ground.

Even though Allied soldiers were trained in the dangerous work of clearing such fields by October 1942, booby traps and trick wires meant that luck played a large part in their survival.

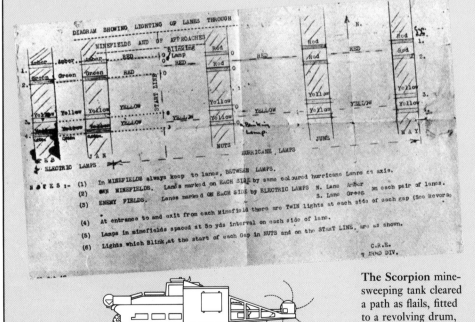

The diagram, *left*, is based on a document issued by the 7th Armoured Division which took part in the southern diversionary attack of Operation Lightfoot. It shows how the minefields held by the Allies were lit and the beginning of the enemy minefields, 'January' and 'February', which were breached by 44th Division on the night of 23 October.

The Scorpion mine-sweeping tank cleared a path as flails, fitted to a revolving drum, exploded mines in front of the vehicle. Sappers would detonate any mines missed by the tank. 'Snail' lorries marked the safe track with diesel oil.

El Alamein/4

Marshal Rommel, was on sick leave in Austria when the Eighth Army struck. To add to their troubles, General Georg Stumme, the officer appointed by Hitler temporarily to relieve Rommel, died of a heart attack while on reconnaissance on the morning of 24 October. Hitler immediately telephoned the Desert Fox to tell him to return to Egypt. Meanwhile, General Ritter von Thoma, who now commanded the Afrika Korps, had to manage the whole Axis army as best he could in the face of a major offensive.

The Eighth Army soon found that the minefields were far deeper than they had calculated (they stretched for 8km/5mls in some places). Moreover, they met extremely stiff resistance, particularly from the Germans. By the end of two days of heavy fighting, the attack was beginning to lose impetus. Thousands of men had been killed or wounded and the remainder of the assault units were exhausted, so Montgomery reversed his intention to continue the battle until the Axis defences were pierced in the north by the 1st and 10th Armoured Divisions and in the south by the 7th Armoured Division. He then made fresh plans for a breakthrough to take place a few days later.

After Rommel returned, he launched a strong counter-attack on the bulge in the British line around Kidney Ridge on 27 October, which was vigorously repulsed with heavy casualties. Then Montgomery went over to the offensive again on the night of 28–29 October, sending the 9th Australian Division northward to threaten the coast road. The Australians created a salient in the enemy positions, which they held against repeated German counter-attacks. In the meantime, guessing that Montgomery was softening him up for an attack along the highway, Rommel decided to break up the 'corsetted' deployment of Axis troops, whereby German units were sandwiched with Italian forces, who were regarded as being generally unreliable. He brought up all German formations from his southern flank in preparation for a final, desperate attempt to hold his positions in the area of the vital road. Realizing that the odds were stacked against him, however, he was also

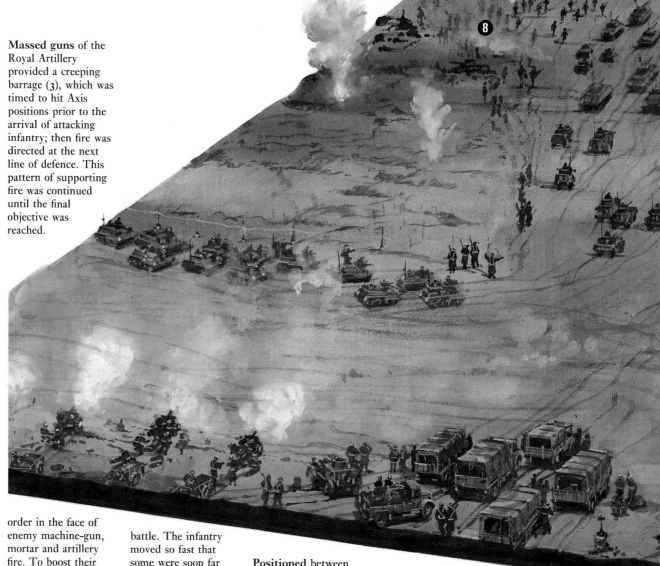

During the opening hours of 'Operation Lightfoot', infantrymen of the 51st Highland Division had to overrun Axis strongpoints in their advance to their heavily defended objective, the Miteiriya Ridge. Although this was a small part of the operation, the Highlanders' night action was typical of much of the fighting along the entire front. The view is of the Highlanders' left flank, when the 7th Black Watch 'leapfrogged' the 5th Camerons at the half-way mark of the advance.

Axis strongpoints (2), protected by minefields, dotted the plain below Miteiriya Ridge (1) to a depth of 5km/3mls. The Scots gave these positions the names of Scottish towns; they had to be overrun, one by one, in the dust and darkness.

Men of the 7th Battalion, the Argyll and Sutherland Highlanders (4), advanced in open

Massed guns of the Royal Artillery provided a creeping barrage (3), which was timed to hit Axis positions prior to the arrival of attacking infantry; then fire was directed at the next line of defence. This pattern of supporting fire was continued until the final objective was reached.

order in the face of enemy machine-gun, mortar and artillery fire. To boost their already high morale, the commander brought up the regimental pipers to march ahead and play their comrades into

battle. The infantry moved so fast that some were soon far ahead of the parties of Royal Engineers, whose task was to clear paths for them through the ubiquitous minefields.

Positioned between the Scottish units, to support them in their dash for the ridge, was an armoured column (5) of Valentines of the 50th Royal Tank

Regiment. Mines, gunfire, soft ground, dust, darkness and wrecked vehicles, however, combined to slow down the tanks

so much that the infantry far outdistanced them as the assault developed.

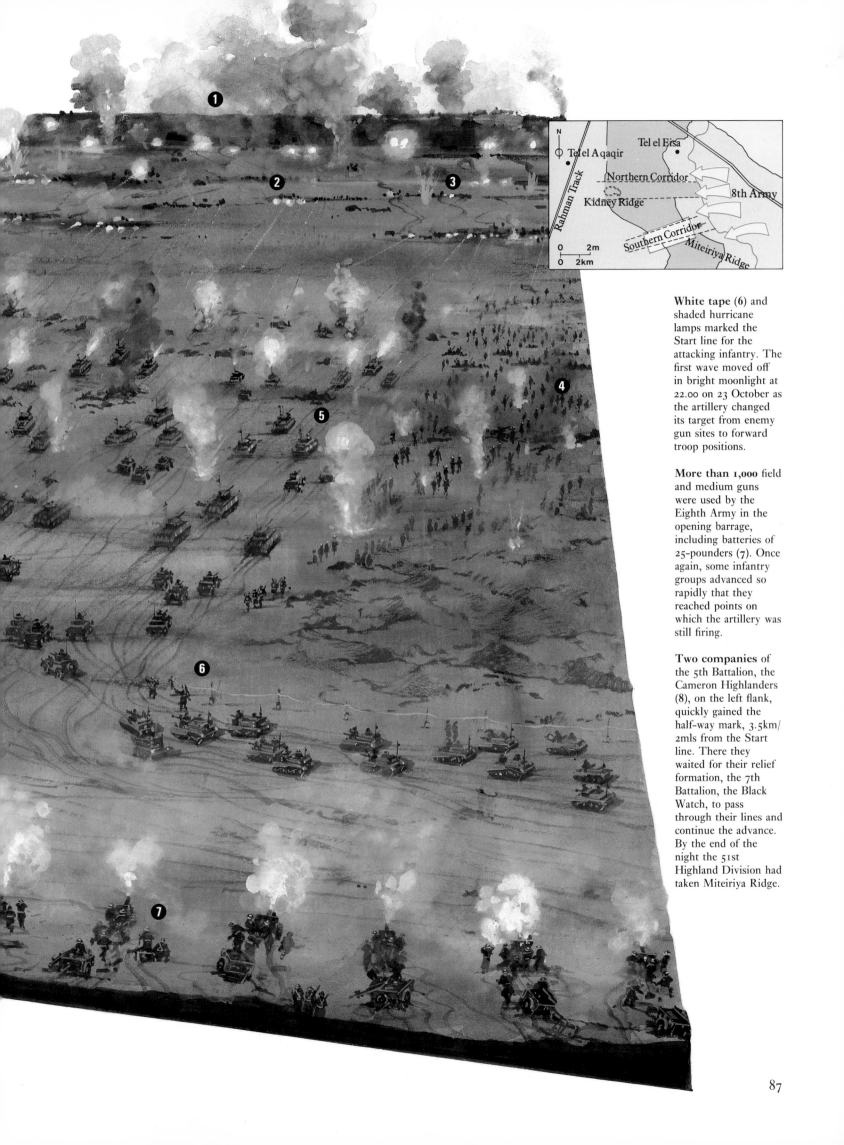

White tape (6) and shaded hurricane lamps marked the Start line for the attacking infantry. The first wave moved off in bright moonlight at 22.00 on 23 October as the artillery changed its target from enemy gun sites to forward troop positions.

More than 1,000 field and medium guns were used by the Eighth Army in the opening barrage, including batteries of 25-pounders (7). Once again, some infantry groups advanced so rapidly that they reached points on which the artillery was still firing.

Two companies of the 5th Battalion, the Cameron Highlanders (8), on the left flank, quickly gained the half-way mark, 3.5km/2mls from the Start line. There they waited for their relief formation, the 7th Battalion, the Black Watch, to pass through their lines and continue the advance. By the end of the night the 51st Highland Division had taken Miteiriya Ridge.

making prudent contingency plans for a possible withdrawal along that highway to Fuka, some 97km/60mls to the west.

Back in Britain, Winston Churchill was astonished at the Eighth Army's apparent inability to mount a prolonged offensive. He felt that a vital opportunity was being missed and accused Montgomery of fighting 'a half-hearted battle'. Montgomery, however, remained unaffected by such harsh criticism. He carried on making preparations and redeploying troops for a new operation, codenamed 'Supercharge' to be launched in the Kidney Ridge area, to the south of Rommel's main concentrations of German forces.

This second—and final—phase of the Battle of El Alamein began on the night of 1–2 November. Initially the enemy were caught unawares, but resistance soon stiffened. Rommel, however, knew that he could not hold out much longer. Short of almost everything it takes to sustain an army in an escalating battle, he decided to order a withdrawal.

On 3 November, following a break in the fighting, the battered Axis forces began to retreat, only to have their orders countermanded by the Führer himself. In a grandiloquent order, divorced from reality, Hitler told his unimpressed Field Marshal: '... there can be no other thought but to stand fast, yield not a yard of ground and throw every gun and every man into the battle.'

Montgomery's longed-for breakout occurred early the following day. While the British 1st Armoured Division and the remnants of the Afrika Korps were heavily engaged around Tel el Aqaqir, the 7th Armoured Division exploited a gap created by the infantry in the lightly held Axis line south of Kidney Ridge. Rommel knew that the only way to avoid encirclement would be to retreat to Fuka. For this he required Hitler's permission, which was reluctantly given. Then he began a general withdrawal to try to save as much of his shattered army as possible. But only mobile forces stood any chance of getting away: large numbers of infantry—mostly Italian—were taken prisoner.

The Eighth Army began its pursuit at daybreak on 5 November, but the only significant part of the Afrika Korps to be cut off was the remains of the 20th Mobile Corps. Progress by the 7th Armoured Division and the 2nd New Zealand Infantry Division, hoping to deliver a 'left hook' to the retreating enemy, was slowed down by a dummy minefield, subsequently found to be British, just south of Fuka; then they ran out of fuel. In the meantime, Rommel was preparing to fall back a

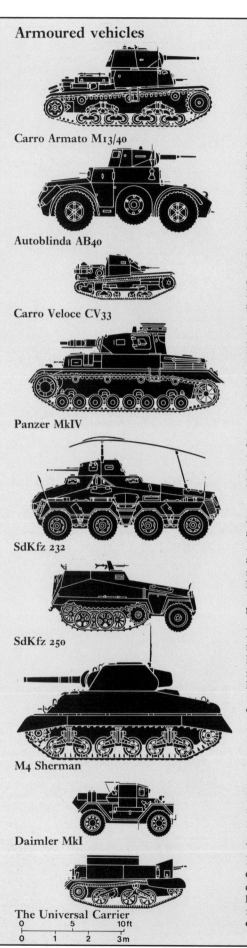

Armoured vehicles

Carro Armato M13/40

Autoblinda AB40

Carro Veloce CV33

Panzer MkIV

SdKfz 232

SdKfz 250

M4 Sherman

Daimler MkI

The Universal Carrier

0   5   10ft
0   1   2   3m

Carro Armato M13/40 Medium Tank Due to frequent breakdowns, the M13/40 was soon replaced by the M14/41; its powerful 108Kw/145hp engine was fitted with filters.
Road speed: 32kmh/20mph; range 200km/125mls; armament: one 47-mm gun, three 8-mm machine-guns, one 8-mm anti-aircraft gun.

Autoblinda AB40 Armoured Car Both front and rear wheels on the AB40 could be steered and all four were powered, giving it remarkable mobility as a reconnaissance vehicle.
Road speed: 76kmh/47mph; range: 400km/250mls; armament: three 8-mm machine-guns.

Carro Veloce CV33 Tankette Until 1943, when production ceased, the CV33 was widely used in North Africa as a flame-thrower, a radio vehicle or to tow a tracked trailer with supplies or ammunition.
Road speed: 42kmh/26mph; range 125km/78mls; armament: twin 8-mm machine-guns.

Panzer MkIV By mid-1941 this reliable medium tank was sometimes fitted with a long-barrelled 75-mm gun; it was the mainstay of the Afrika Korps.
Road speed: 40kmh/25mph; range 200km/125mls; armament: one 75-mm gun and two 7.92-mm machine-guns.

SdKfz 232 The 8-wheeled SdKfz armoured car, used by German forces throughout the war, was the most advanced cross-country vehicle at the time and particularly suited to the desert.
Road speed: 85kmh/53mph; range: 270km/170mls; armament: one 20-mm gun.

SdKfz 250 Introduced in 1940, this light armoured halftrack served throughout the war. It appeared in 13 variants, mostly open-topped, and was used by many corps, including engineers and signals.
Road speed: 60kmh/37mph; range: 300km/186mls; armament: varied, from light machine-guns to an anti-tank gun.

M4 Sherman The most widely produced medium tank of WWII, the Sherman was fast, hardy and reliable. Its rubber-block tracks made it mobile and effective in the desert.
Road speed: 42kmh/26mph; range: 160km/100mls; armament: one 75-mm gun, two 3-in, one 5-in machine-guns, one 2-in smoke mortar.

Daimler MkI Armoured Car The British Army's standard armoured car from 1941, the Daimler had power steering, disc brakes and restricted 4-wheel drive; it was used for reconnaissance.
Road speed: 80kmh/50mph; range: 328km/205mls with auxiliary tanks; armament: one 2-pounder gun, one 7.92-mm machine-gun.

The Universal Carrier Usually called the Bren Gun Carrier, this versatile vehicle could carry both men and light weapons and had controls identical to a truck's.
Road speed: 51kmh/32mph; range 256km/160mls; armament: one Bren light machine-gun or one Boys anti-tank rifle.

Montgomery's plans: 'Lightfoot' and 'Supercharge'

'Operation Lightfoot' was a carefully planned strategy, dependent on several factors, including the success of the 'Bertram' deception plot and swift minefield clearance. Montgomery decided on a two-pronged attack, with the main thrust in the north. After a prolonged artillery barrage, an infantry advance by 30th Corps was to be made through strongly defended minefields. Once a gap had been cleared, the armour of 10th Corps was to move forward. Such a difficult operation could only be carried out at full moon, and the night of 23–24 October was chosen.

The secondary attack in the south was far smaller than Rommel had expected, for the huge build-up of dummy forces had tricked Luftwaffe reconnaissance. The object of 13th Corps' advance was to prevent relief forces reaching the northern sector and to

enable a light, mobile force to pass behind the Axis positions and cut them off.

Strong defences prevented the first attack from achieving its objective, a line just beyond Miteiriya Ridge. But later the Allies consolidated a position deeper into Axis lines. From this base they began a 'crumbling' operation, attacking enemy infantry divisions and so drawing armoured divisions into battle at places of the Eighth Army's choosing.

The thrust in the north by the 9th Australian Division and the crumbling process had another unforeseen result which aided the Allies: German troops were brought up to reinforce the northern sector, isolating the unreliable Italians in the south.

By 30 October, the infantry on both sides had been worn down by a series of

dogfights, and many Allied commanders urged withdrawal. But Montgomery was confident that, by a change of plan, victory could be achieved.

He exploited the concentration of German armour and, with 'Operation Supercharge', drove a wedge between the Germans and the Italians. Once more, after a barrage on the night of 1–2 November, an infantry attack was made. Since there were no complex minefields to be cleared, the British 9th Armoured Brigade was able to move rapidly to capture a hastily deserted German headquarters and the Rahman Track—the main Axis supply route—for Rommel had expected an attack from the north. Now, cut off from their supply lines and relief troops, the Germans were forced into retreat, and this time they were unable to rally and strike back.

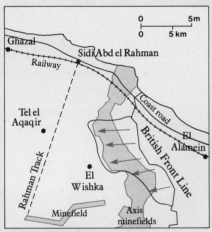

Extent of 'Lightfoot' advance

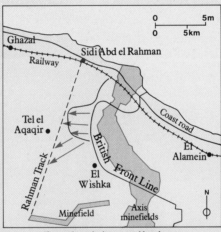

'Supercharge' advance and break out

The battle was fought in an area which all British commanders had recognized as of strategic importance. The Qattara Depression, an impassable salt marsh about 64km/40mls inland, formed the southern limit of the battlefield. Miteiriya Ridge and Kidney Ridge, natural obstacles in the west, were held by the Axis. South of El Alamein, the Allies had two vantage points on high ground.

Minefields in front of Miteiriya Ridge slowed down Operation Lightfoot, *far left*. During the course of Operation Supercharge, however, the relatively clear area west of this ridge enabled the Eighth Army rapidly to seize the Rahman Track and an enemy HQ near Tel el Aqaqir.

A daylight patrol launches a lightning attack with fixed bayonets.

Gunners, too, relied on surprise – an advantage lost when they fired their guns at night, so illuminating their positions.

further 129km/80mls to Mersa Matruh. At noon on 6 November, a sudden rain storm turned the desert into a quagmire and completely halted British movement. All chance of cutting off what remained of Rommel's army was lost. Meanwhile, the Desert Fox, who later criticized Montgomery for not pressing on with the chase, capitalized on the time gained by the bad weather. He rallied all that remained of the Afrika Korps—now down to about 20 tanks—and sent them back along the coast road as fast as they could go. Most of all, he wanted distance between his retreating columns and the Eighth Army.

On 7 November, under cover of darkness, Rommel managed to reach the Egypt-Libya border at Sollum. The next day he learned of 'Operation Torch', an Allied invasion of Morocco and Algeria commanded by the US General Dwight D. Eisenhower. This was the first Anglo-American joint venture and the first Allied seaborne landing. The depleted Axis army in North Africa was now to be squeezed into submission on two fronts.

In the course of the 12-day conflict at El Alamein, the Eighth Army inflicted grievous losses on the Germans and the Italians. Half of Rommel's 100,000-strong army were killed, wounded or taken prisoner, and 450 tanks and about 1,000 guns were taken or destroyed. (The Desert War, from start to finish, cost the Axis almost one million men killed or taken prisoner.) British and Commonwealth forces suffered 13,500 casualties at El Alamein. Five hundred of their tanks were knocked out in the fighting, but only 150 were beyond repair; in all, 100 guns were destroyed.

When Churchill learned of the final outcome of events at El Alamein, he was overjoyed and ordered that church bells all over Britain should break the silence maintained since war broke out in 1939 and ring in celebration. Later, the Prime Minister would claim, 'Before Alamein we never had a victory, after Alamein we never had a defeat.'

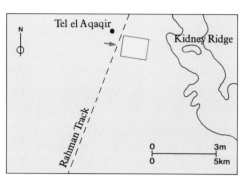

The scene at 09.00 on 4 November 1942, a sunny day with a clear blue sky, when tanks of the 22nd Armoured Brigade finally broke through Rommel's defences in strength. They also severed the Rahman Track, the main supply line from the coast into the desert, which the enemy used to move anti-tank guns from one threatened sector to another.

The infantry battalions of the 5th Indian Brigade—one each from the Rajputana Rifles, the Baluchi Regiment and the Essex Regiment—dug in (2) after successfully completing a 6.4-km/4-ml advance the previous night to open a gap for the tanks. The Brigade gave an exemplary display of an infantry night attack, taking out anti-tank guns and strong points. Then, protected by a sustained artillery barrage, they waited in their trenches until the tanks passed through.

Dense clouds of dust (1) indicated the main body of 22nd Armoured Brigade's tanks, moving forward in support of the advance units.

The leading tanks, both Shermans (3) and Crusaders (4), moved forward between the 5th Indian Brigade's trenches and made for the destroyed and burning Axis positions. As the first few tanks were followed through the gaps by more and more, the stream became a torrent and soon a huge concentration of armour was manoeuvring in unmined areas behind the German tanks, forcing them to withdraw.

The Axis anti-tank screen (5) in the less heavily defended area south of the main fighting was quickly eliminated by artillery fire and by the advancing infantry brigade.

Brightly coloured pennants (6), flown from the aerials of armoured vehicles, identified units and the rank of each vehicle's commander. These and other pennants could also be used to signal general orders, such as 'Rally' and 'Disperse'.

When outnumbered by British tanks, those of the Afrika Korps would often turn and retreat, expecting the British to follow, as they usually did. The Germans would lead their enemy straight on to well-sited and camouflaged anti-tank guns, which then opened up at point-blank range.

The German 50-mm Pak 38 anti-tank gun was most effective, especially when firing tungsten-cored bullets. Because the tungsten was so heavy, lightweight metal was used to build them up to the required calibre. Such bullets had high muzzle velocity but soon lost speed in flight. By fitting the gun with a tapered bore, which compressed the bullet, it became a heavy, small-calibre shot, with great speed in flight.

Springboard into Italy

Although the European war could not be won or lost in the desert, the British triumph at El Alamein had disastrous consequences for the Germans. As the Allied 'Torch' forces advanced from the west and the Eighth Army from the east, Rommel found himself trapped, and he was forced to evacuate North Africa, leaving it clear for use as a springboard for an Allied invasion of Sicily and then Italy. Hitler, when speaking of Germany's defeat in World War I, had repeatedly said that his country must never again fight simultaneously on two fronts. Soon his deteriorating fortunes would oblige him to fight on three: in Russia, in Italy, and, after June 1944, in western Europe.

Stalingrad/*November 1942-January 1943*

The German Army's huge losses and frightful hardships in Russia since the beginning of 'Operation Barbarossa' in June 1941 did not dismay Hitler. On the contrary, he initiated a major summer offensive in 1942 that was designed to destroy the Soviets' ability to resist. The Führer, supreme operational commander of the 1,600-km/1,000-ml Eastern Front, erroneously believed that the Red Army had used up much of its manpower and *matériel* in the winter fighting, so he hurried reinforcements eastward. By drawing on Romania, Hungary and Italy, he managed to field a numerically strong force; it was well equipped but contained elements whose fighting prowess was highly suspect.

The main German thrust was to be delivered against the industrial and oil-producing regions in the south; in the north, efforts to take Leningrad were to continue; the central front was to hold fast. The offensive opened in June, took the Russians by surprise, and began to record successes in the old blitzkrieg style, which made Hitler overly optimistic. On 23 July, the Führer issued Directive 49 abandoning the step-by-step conquest of the south, starting with Stalingrad. He now intended to carry out two simultaneous and diverging attacks on Stalingrad and the Caucasus. Hitler was unmoved by his generals' warnings that their forces were not strong enough to carry both objectives at the same time.

Stalingrad was the ultimate goal of the Sixth Army, led by Colonel-General Friedrich Paulus, and the Fourth Panzer Army, under Colonel-General Hermann Hoth, as they pushed southeastward in June and early July. And, but for the Führer's interference, it might have been taken without a fight. By detaching Hoth's armour and sending it south to the Caucasus, Hitler let slip the opportunity to enter the city before the Soviets could organize its defence.

A fortnight later, Hitler ordered the Fourth Panzer Army to turn northeast and drive again for Stalingrad. But he had lost his chance, and, by 9 August, Hoth was halted by lack of supplies 160km/100mls from the city. In the meantime, Paulus's Sixth Army had fought its way across the River Don and, on 23 August, was on the right bank of the Volga north of Stalingrad and moving into the suburbs. While opposition from the Russian Sixty-second and Sixty-fourth Armies in Stalingrad stiffened, Paulus gained control of the gap between the Don and the Volga, established air and supply bases there and, on 2 September, made contact with Hoth.

Allied aid to the USSR

The Russian motorized infantry shown here are using American-made armoured cars. All British and US markings were removed by the Russians from the tanks, other vehicles and weapons supplied to them, so that their troops would believe them to be of home manufacture. Between 1 October 1941, less than four months after the German invasion of Russia, and the end of June 1943, the USA dispatched to the USSR under lease-lend agreements all types of supplies, worth approximately $2,444 million. Despite heavy British shipping losses in transit, the flood later increased, as tanks and other equipment, originally earmarked for Great Britain, were diverted to Russia. Between July 1942 and January 1943, the USA allocated 1,200 tanks a month to Great Britain and Russia, rising to 2,000 a month and, later, 2,500. In addition, between July 1942 and July 1943, the USA provided 3,600 front-line aircraft.

Stalingrad before the German attack, *above*, was a large, modern city. In the foreground is the square dedicated to the fallen of the the Bolshevik Revolution. The city was reduced to a dead shell during the battle, as the later picture of the same square, *below*, shows, although some of its features are still discernable amid the devastation.

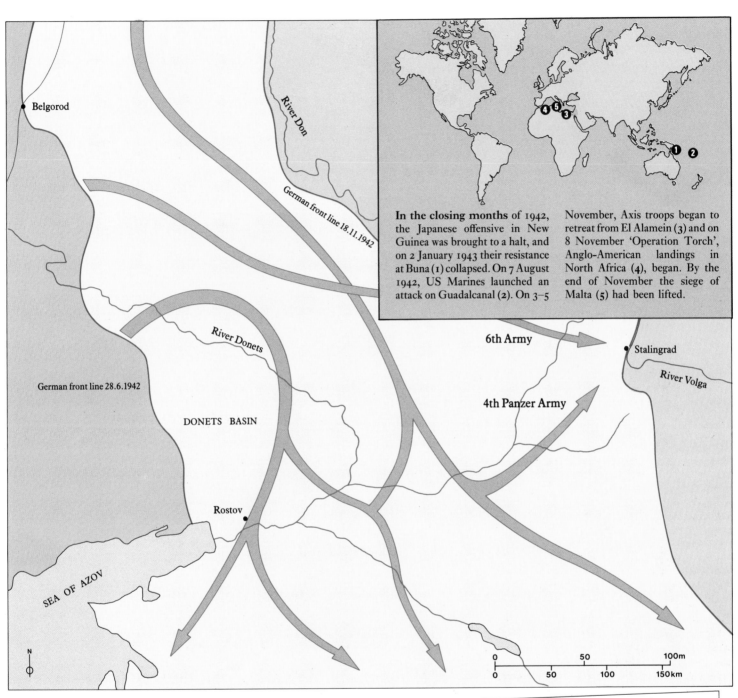

Belgorod

River Don

German front line 18.11.1942

German front line 28.6.1942

River Donets

DONETS BASIN

Rostov

SEA OF AZOV

N

In the closing months of 1942, the Japanese offensive in New Guinea was brought to a halt, and on 2 January 1943 their resistance at Buna (1) collapsed. On 7 August 1942, US Marines launched an attack on Guadalcanal (2). On 3–5 November, Axis troops began to retreat from El Alamein (3) and on 8 November 'Operation Torch', Anglo-American landings in North Africa (4), began. By the end of November the siege of Malta (5) had been lifted.

6th Army

Stalingrad

River Volga

4th Panzer Army

0   50   100m
0   50   100   150km

In the spring of 1942, Hitler issued directives for the Russian campaign. In essence, the northern and central fronts were to remain static, while all available forces were to be launched southeastward to seize the Caucasian oilfields. Army Group South was ordered first to capture the Crimea, then Voronezh was to be taken by striking east from the Orel-Kursk area. This accomplished, German armies from Voronezh and Dnepropetrovsk were to converge on Stalingrad. Once that city was taken, the way to the Caucasus would be open. German success was at first absolute, and by 23 July, when they captured Rostov, the Russian position could not have been worse. Astonishingly, Hitler then withdrew the Fourth Panzer Army from the Caucasian front and diverted it northeast to join the Sixth Army in capturing Stalingrad. At the same time, artillery formations were detached to reinforce the siege of Leningrad. This greatly weakened Army Group South, limiting any further advance on the Caucasian oilfields. The delay in investing Stalingrad enabled the Russians to reinforce it; and it remained untaken.

Stalingrad/2

Despite several days of heavy fighting and many bombing raids, the Russians, under Lieutenant-General Vasili Chuikov, clung on to the battered city. The German Army High Command, concerned about the inadequacy of the forces supposedly protecting the Sixth Army's left flank along the Don, advised withdrawal from Stalingrad to consolidate the line and prevent any chance of Paulus's being cut off by an enemy breakthrough. Instead Hitler transferred units from the weak Don sector to the Sixth Army and ordered it to capture the city.

Backed by bombers of Luftflotte 4, German infantry and armour commenced a mass assault through the fast-crumbling streets. Every metre of the way was contested by the Russians in fierce close-quarter fighting, from house to house, cellar to cellar, and even through the sewers; this determination was to characterize the prolonged and bloody struggle. The infantry dominated the battle because mountains of rubble made it difficult for tanks to operate effectively. After a week of intense fighting, the Germans managed to reach the city centre. A few days later, Paulus's troops fought their way into the industrial sector in the north also, but on 29 September Chuikov threw them out.

Regrouped, reinforced and supported by tanks and dive-bombers, the Germans tried again on 14 October and for ten days hammered at the Russian defences. Though the Russians were at first greatly outnumbered and obliged to give ground, they were able to ferry fresh troops and much-needed supplies across the wide Volga under cover of darkness. By 24 October, the Sixth Army had fought itself to a standstill in the north of Stalingrad without ejecting its stubborn enemy.

Not much was now left of this city which had once housed nearly half a million people. Hitler had deprived the Russians of its industrial output, but the south–north communications had not been severed because a railway line east of the Volga was still operating. The battle had degenerated into a conflict of egos: Stalin insisted on holding the city named after him; Hitler wanted to seize it for its symbolism and propaganda value. So the Germans prepared to launch a big assault in the southern district.

Then came news which obliged Hitler to send reinforcements south, not east. On 5 November, Rommel had been defeated at El Alamein and on the 8th, the Allies had landed in Morocco and Algeria,

In October 1942, General Vasili Chuikov's Sixty-second Army, defending Stalingrad, came under intense pressure from the German Sixth Army. Pushed back through the northern industrial suburbs, Chuikov had to rely for supplies on ferry runs by night from the east shore, such as this on 16 October. The ships, mostly ferryboats and launches crammed with reinforcements and munitions crossed under heavy fire.

Guided by the glow of candle flares (1), the Germans kept the Russian positions along Stalingrad's ruined waterfront (2) under constant fire from their six-barrelled Nebelwerfer mortars.

Soviet casualties would have been greater but for the protection afforded by deep ravines (4), which cut into the west bank of the Volga and led up to the fiercely contested factory district.

Tunnels were dug into the sides of the ravines for use as amunition stores and first aid posts, and General Chuikov's headquarters was sited in one of them. Some housed Katyusha rocket launchers, which could quickly emerge, fire and retreat to safety before enemy guns could be ranged on them.

Facilities for treating wounded Russian soldiers in Stalingrad were inadequate, so casualties were kept in the ravines until nightfall and then ferried back to the east bank in the boats (3) that had completed supply runs. Many of the wounded were hit again as these boats came under German shellfire.

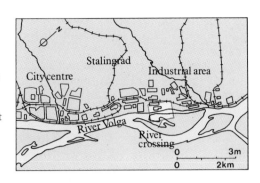

The Russians stationed their heavy and medium artillery on the heavily wooded east bank, invisible to the Germans. Their anti-aircraft guns (5), however, were mainly sited on the islands in the middle of the Volga. These gave the infantry some defence from attacks by enemy bombers.

A darkened ferry boat (6), its decks crammed with reinforcement troops, making its way through heavy fire toward the west bank of the Volga. There the Sixty-second Army was holding off German attacks not far from the water's edge. Chuikov relied on these vessels for his army's every need, and priority was given to ammunition, supplies and replacements.

Stalingrad/3

threatening the Axis forces in a dangerous pincer grip. This setback came as a bonus for Marshal Georgi Zhukov, who had been preparing a Russian counter-offensive against the Germans in the south. Having secretly built up vast reserves, he was poised to unleash them with the arrival of Russia's traditional ally: winter.

On 19 November, a massive Russian attack surprised and overran the Romanian Third Army northwest of Stalingrad, exposing the left flank of the Sixth Army as the German generals had foreseen in the summer. Twenty-four hours later, 160km/100mls to the south, the Soviets routed a mixed German and Romanian force guarding Paulus's other flank; the two Russian assault groups joined up within four days. General Paulus and his Sixth Army, comprising 200,000 fighting men and some 70,000 non-combatants, were cut off.

The Army High Command begged Hitler to permit the Sixth Army to make a break westward while the Russian ring was still not firmly established. But the Luftwaffe chief, Herman Goering, although he had absolutely no foundation for doing so, claimed his aircraft could fly in 500 tons of supplies a day to the surrounded Sixth Army, sufficient to keep it going as a fighting force. Hitler grabbed at this offer of a lifeline to Paulus and on 24 November ordered him to fortify his positions and await a relief column.

Three days later Field Marshal Erich von Manstein was placed at the head of a hodge-podge of units, Army Group Don, and briefed to relieve Stalingrad. He was not, however, to create a situation which would allow Paulus to withdraw; he was to go in and stabilize the German front line in the beleaguered city. Manstein set out on his unenviable mission on 12 December and arrived 48km/30mls outside Stalingrad on the 21st. Knowing that the Russians were closing in on him and that he would be unable to hold his advanced position for long, Manstein took it upon himself to order Paulus to break out and link up with him before it was too late. But Paulus decided that in the absence of a direct order from Hitler to evacuate Stalingrad he must stay where he was.

The relieving force fell back, fighting, and the last tragic phase of the Battle of Stalingrad began for the doomed Sixth Army. Squeezed in an ever-tightening vice by the surrounding Russian armies, deprived of proper clothing to withstand sub-zero temperatures and running low on all essentials due to the inadequacy of Goering's promised daily airlift, Paulus's rapidly dwindling command continued its

Hand-to hand fighting

At Stalingrad the Germans were forced to abandon the blitzkreig and encirclement tactics of which they were undisputed masters and engage in house-to-house fighting, in which the Russians, with their knowledge of the city, had the advantage.

The fiercest battle began on 4 October, when Paulus siezed the tractor factory and other industrial complexes in the north of the city. Fighting room by room, each littered with rubble and corpses, soldiers on both sides hurled grenades through windows and doorways, then sprayed the area with machine-gun fire. Soon they were so close that they attacked with rifle butts, spades and pieces of broken furniture.

Occasionally exhaustion induced a lull in the fighting; then the sniper came into his own. The Russians excelled at sharpshooting and, to redress the balance, Heinz Thorwald, head of the German snipers' school at Zossen, was flown into Stalingrad. There followed a stalking duel of nearly four days' duration between the German and a crack Russian sniper. For most of that time the German lay in no man's land, hidden by a sheet of iron and some rubble. His position finally detected, the Russian sniper's aide slightly raised his helmet by hand; the German fired, then briefly lifted his head to see if he had hit his target, only to be shot dead instantly.

Russian troops used the PPSh Model 1941. It was the most common submachinegun in the Red Army—more than 5 million were produced during the war—and could fire 900 rounds a minute. Mud, water, snow and ice had no effect on this 7.62-mm gun and the chromed barrel meant it did not need regular cleaning.

These German NCOs are carrying the 9-mm Mp 40 submachinegun. It was designed for easy factory processing, which permitted subcontractors to mass produce sections of the gun for later assembly, a revolutionary concept in the 1940s. Its sole drawback was its weight: more than 5.4kg/12lb when loaded.

When fighting house to house, the Russians employed small bodies of soldiers who gave each other close support. Their essential weapons were grenades and submachineguns. Soldiers threw grenades into all corners of a room and swept it with machine-gun fire before moving on.

The Commanders

Paulus

Von Manstein

Chuikov

General Friedrich Paulus (1890–1957) was an experienced and capable staff officer but he proved only an average field commander who was intimidated by his superiors and who grossly underestimated Russian strength at Stalingrad. Paulus had been a member of the German staff during the invasions of Poland in 1939 and of France in 1940. In September of that year he was appointed Quartermaster General of the General Staff.

During the siege of Stalingrad, Hitler decorated Paulus with the oak leaf to the Knight's Cross of the Iron Cross and promoted him Field Marshal, for no German of that rank had ever been taken prisoner. The Führer was disgusted at Paulus's surrender and astonished that he had not in preference shot himself; 'That's the last field marshal I promote in this war', Hitler told his staff. At the end of hostilities, Paulus, by then sympathetic to Communism, retired to East Germany.

In contrast, the Russian **Marshal Vasili Chuikov (1900–82)** was an independent-minded, imaginative commander (he had been demoted in the opening phases of the war for just that independence), who loved his men. He lived with his soldiers and endured their perils at the front. Moreover, he knew that the way to beat the Germans was to engage them at close quarters so that their artillery and the Luftwaffe could not operate for fear of hitting their own troops. Chuikov not only saved Stalingrad he destroyed for ever the legend of the German Army's invincibility.

After the German disaster at Stalingrad, the German front was stabilized, largely through the military genius of **Field Marshal Erich von Manstein (1887–1973)**, arguably the greatest strategist to emerge during the war and the man whose plan for the invasion of France in 1940 had been rewarded with unqualified success.

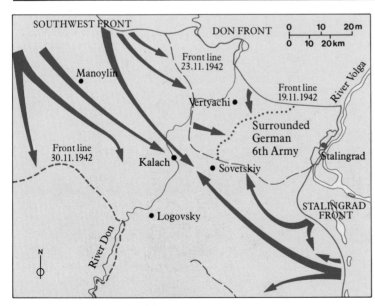

The Germans had no option but to use inferior, less well-equipped Romanian troops to protect the flanks of the Sixth Army at Stalingrad. On 19 November, when tanks could again operate after intense cold had frozen the water-logged ground, the Russians north of the city, under General Rokossovsky, struck westward and overwhelmed the Romanians. The next day, General Yeremenko's force attacked to the south and also smashed through the Romanian lines. On the 22nd, the two forces joined up near Kalach. Some 250,000 German troops were thus surrounded.

Paulus wanted to hold Stalingrad if adequate supplies could be flown in or, failing this, to attempt a breakout. Hitler might have reluctantly agreed to the withdrawal of the Sixth Army to stabilize the front; but he decided against this when Goering promised that the Luftwaffe could fly in up to 500 tons of *matériel* a day. The task was, however, quite beyond its ability. On the first two days of the airlift, the Luftwaffe brought in a mere 75 tons; later the quantity increased until, on 30 November, it reached 100 tons—still wholly inadequate for an army of 250,000. Then the airfields within the German perimeter were overrun or destroyed, making landing impossible, and the German position became untentable.

grim struggle. At the end of December, when Paulus saw that some of his starving men were reduced to devouring raw horse brains, he flew out a personal emissary to give the Führer a first-hand account of the deplorable condition of the Sixth Army. Hitler merely ordered him to hold out.

On 8 January, Lieutenant-General Konstantin Rokossovsky issued an ultimatum to Paulus, but he refused to surrender, and two days later the Soviets commenced a full-scale assault on his positions. As the enemy closed around his exhausted and dispirited troops, Paulus radioed to Hitler that his situation was hopeless. In testimony given after the war, Paulus said the Führer replied, 'Capitulation is impossible. The Sixth Army will do its historic duty at Stalingrad until the last man . . .'.

The end was not long in coming. By 25 January the Russians had overrun the last German airfield, preventing any supplies getting in and ending mercy flights out of the sick and wounded. Over the radio, which was the survivors' only link with the outside world, news came on 31 January that Hitler had been pleased to promote Colonel-General Paulus to Field Marshal. Later that day, the Sixth Army made its final broadcast, announcing the arrival of the enemy outside the headquarters command post.

The new Field Marshal, himself exhausted, had been obliged to surrender most of what remained of his command to General Mikhail Shumilov of the Soviet Sixty-fourth Army. Two days later, the German 11th Corps, which had been holding out in pockets in the north of the stricken city, also capitulated. As nearly a million men marched off to harsh captivity (from which it is estimated that as few as 5,000 returned after the war), Hitler raved about the disaster and threatened to court-martial Paulus. Ultimately, however, he accepted responsibility for the sacrifice of the Sixth Army. Nearly 150,000 Germans had died—three times as many as the Russians admitted they lost—all Paulus's guns, motor vehicles and equipment had been captured and the Luftwaffe had lost 500 transport aircraft.

The German Army, though far from being a broken force in early 1943, never recovered from the loss of an entire army, on top of casualties in excess of a million already sustained on the Eastern Front. All its great blitzkrieg victories were behind it. Hitler had overstretched Germany before the full might of the Allies could be assembled against him, and he would pay the price for such folly.

On 31 January 1943, the German Sixth Army surrendered to the Russians. In the tractor factory in Stalingrad's northern industrial area, however, General Karl Strecker and the remnants of his 11th Corps still held out. For two more days they held off all Russian attacks until, on 2 February, surrounded and without ammunition, their positions were overrun.

Taking cover amid the rubble, wrecked machinery and vehicles in the tractor factory's fitting shop (1), General Strecker's troops put up a desperate resistance, exacting many Russian casualties.

The German defenders (2) lacked heavy weapons and repelled Russian attacks with whatever remained—rifles, pistols and grenades. Some men had nothing but bayonets, spades and pieces of broken machinery to wield in the violent hand-to-hand fighting.

Corpses and the injured (3) lay where they fell, for there was neither time nor place to tend them in the devastated fitting shop.

Strecker's men had one remaining radio set (4). On this they listened to Hitler's exhortations to them to hold out to the end. And on this, at 08.40 on 2 February, as the Russians closed in, they transmitted their last message to the outside world, telling Germany and their leader that they had done their duty.

King George VI, in a felicitous gesture, initiated the design and making of a Sword of Honour to commemorate the defence of Stalingrad. Made of polished steel, with an ornate scabbard, it was, at the King's command, given by Churchill to Stalin during the Yalta Conference in February 1945. Stalin raised it, kissed the scabbard, and solemnly passed it to Marshal Voroshilov, the Inspector General of the Soviet Army, who promptly dropped it. The sword was then escorted from the room by a Russian guard of honour.

In addition to attacking the fitting shop with infantry, the Russians moved up tanks (5) and fired through broken-down sections of the wall. At 09.00 all German resistance ceased.

Kursk/*July-August 1943*

At the end of a second fearsome winter in Russia, still reeling from the loss of the entire Sixth Army at Stalingrad, the German troops took stock of their reduced circumstances. But, at the same time, Hitler was preparing a gamble of such magnitude that he would later say the very thought of it made his stomach turn over.

From the summer of 1941, when 'Operation Barbarossa' began, until the early spring of 1943, events on the Eastern Front had absorbed Hitler's interest more than those in any other theatre of war. Even taking into account the massive casualties already suffered by the Army, Waffen SS and Luftwaffe in this brutal campaign, by far the biggest concentrations of German forces were still to be found along the battle line which stretched from the Gulf of Finland to the Black Sea, across more than 1,600km/1,000mls of Soviet territory.

With the prospect of an early Allied attack on Italy, followed by a full-scale invasion of Western Europe, probably via France, the Führer realized that this imbalance of Nazi strength would have to be adjusted in order to reinforce these new danger areas. But recent reverses at the hands of the resilient Red Army had made it evident that he could not simply thin out his combat-hardened units in Russia to provide the additional seasoned troops required without endangering his position. The Soviets would have to be dealt a swift, crushing blow.

Impressed by the successful encirclement of a bulge in the Russian line at Izyum on the River Donets the previous spring, Hitler decided that there was only one place suitable for his proposed containing action—the 160-km/100-ml wide Kursk salient that jutted into the German positions between Orel in the north and Belgorod in the south. This loop, though defended by an increasing number of first-rate enemy units, seemed to Hitler ideal for a pincer attack. Codenamed 'Operation Citadel', it would have the double benefit of destroying a major part of the Red Army while straightening and shortening the German line.

It was the need to assemble the most powerful force possible, at speed, against a background of mounting danger that caused the Führer most anxiety. A strategic withdrawal and a general shortening of his lines would have released troops for duty elsewhere and provided a less stressful answer to his dilemma, but Hitler could never bring himself to give up conquered Russian soil.

When the Germans were finally ready, they had gathered almost 50 Army and

The war industry

The output of the German war industry had been stable between the Fall of France in 1940 and 1942. When it became apparent in that year that the war in the east would not be won quickly, if at all, production was dramatically increased, despite Allied bombing of German industrial centres.

In 1942 Germany produced 5,700 medium and heavy tanks; in the following year the number was roughly doubled. Production of aircraft of all descriptions increased from 14,700 to 25,200. For every gun and mortar manufactured in 1942, two came off the assembly lines in 1943, and ammunition production kept pace. Moreover, many of the vehicles and weapons produced in 1943 were of a new, more sophisticated and deadly design. Thus the Germans could replace machinery and weapons lost in battle and equip new formations, but much of this was destined for the defence of western Europe.

The Russians possessed an even greater manufacturing capacity. With virtually limitless manpower, they had been able to build and man hundreds of giant factories in the interior which, by 1943, were producing an ever-growing quantity of tanks, aircraft and arms of all kinds. To this were added huge consignments of war material from the USA and Britain.

The Soviets were also able to replenish their battle losses quicker than the Germans, ensuring that they were virtually always numerically a far superior force when fighting broke out.

Russian T34s, *top*,
and German Panther tanks, *above*, being mass produced.

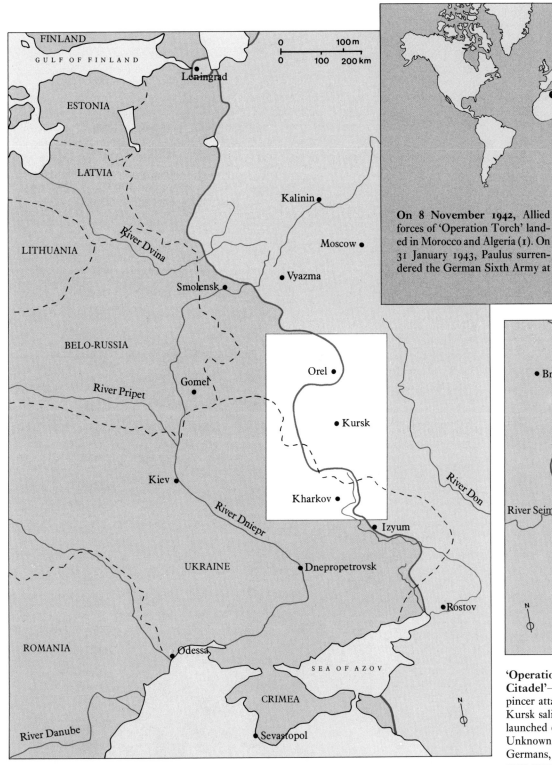

On 8 November 1942, Allied forces of 'Operation Torch' landed in Morocco and Algeria (1). On 31 January 1943, Paulus surrendered the German Sixth Army at Stalingrad (2). Wingate's Chindits made their first penetration into Burma (3) on 8 February, and on 13 May the Axis forces capitulated in Tunisia (4).

'Operation Citadel'—the German pincer attack on the Kursk salient—was launched on 5 July. Unknown to the Germans, the Russians were superior not only in manpower but in weaponry and were strongly positioned behind new anti-tank defences. In the north, Model's Ninth Army advanced only 19km/12mls, at great cost; while in the south the Fourth Panzer Army, though initially more successful, was brought to a halt after a mere 32-km/20-ml advance in 10 days.

On 15 July, the heavily reinforced Russians counterattacked, ultimately eliminating the salient by closing in behind the Germans. General Walter Warlimont of the Operations Staff later wrote: 'Operation Citadel was more than a battle lost; it handed the Russians the initiative and we never recovered it again right up to the end of the war.'

After the capitulation of the Sixth Army at Stalingrad, the German front was stabilized (largely through the strategy of Field Marshal von Manstein) on a line from Leningrad in the north to Rostov on the Sea of Azov. In the centre-south section, however, there remained a gigantic Russian salient, bulging out to the west of Kursk between Orel and Belgorod. If the Russians were to exploit this situation, German forces on either side would risk encirclement. The Germans therefore planned to liquidate the salient by thrusts from the north and south, thereby shortening their line and allowing troops to be transferred to other fronts. But the Russians were fully informed of German intentions by the so-called 'Lucy Ring', an espionage network operating via Switzerland and reporting direct to Moscow. This advance information gave the Russians time to build eight lines of formidable anti-tank defences in the salient.

Kursk/2

Waffen SS divisions, more than 2,000 tanks, some 1,000 assault guns and 1,800 aircraft.

The attack southward across the neck of the Kursk salient would be delivered by troops from Field Marshal Gunther Hans von Kluge's Army Group Centre, spearheaded by the Ninth Army, under Colonel-General Walther Model, with almost 1,000 tanks. Air support would be provided by Luftflotte 6. A simultaneous punch northward was to come from Army Group South, Field Marshal Erich von Manstein's command, assisted by aircraft from Luftflotte 4. Colonel-General Hermann Hoth's Fourth Panzer Army comprising around 1,200 tanks would be the driving wedge. The rest of the salient would be held by seven infantry divisions.

By the time the Germans were at last poised to strike their blows, the Russians were, however, more than ready to receive them. They had known since early April of the enemy's plans to try to pinch out the Kursk salient, partly by observing their preparations but mostly from a stream of reports sent by a spy in the German High Command.

Under the overall direction of Marshal Georgi Zhukov, the Chief of the General Staff, the Soviets decided to let the Germans exhaust themselves against their defences, then launch a massive counter-attack. But even if Citadel were cancelled for any reason, there was still to be a major Soviet offensive in the summer of 1943, breaking the Red Army's established pattern of assaulting only when the severity of the Russian winter was on its side.

Inside the Kursk salient, the northern sector was occupied by General Konstantin Rokossovsky's Central Front (a front being roughly equal to a small army group) and the southern sector by General Nikolai Vatutin's Voronezh Front. To the rear lay General Ivan Koniev's Steppe Front as a back-up.

Imprecise as Russian admissions of strength have always been, it seems probable that there were as many as 75 divisions and more than 3,500 tanks in the salient, supported by around 3,000 aircraft, many of which were faster and of a more modern design than any previously seen in the skies over the Eastern Front. And Koniev had another 1,500 tanks in reserve. But that was not all.

The Soviets, out to blunt the expected German thrusts before starting their own offensive, had prepared defences up to 40km/25mls deep in places involving hundreds of thousands of land mines, 20,000 pieces of artillery, 6,000 anti-tank guns and 1,000 Katyusha rocket launchers.

The Russians deployed so many of their T34 tanks during the Battle of Kursk that the Germans had increasingly to call on the Luftwaffe for support. One of their most successful air commando units comprised new Stuka Ju 87Gs, specially adapted for use against tanks. These proved deadly, but the Germans possessed too few to make a significant impact on the huge concentrations of Russian armour in the Kursk salient.

Hauptman Hans-Ulrich Rudel, the outstanding Stuka pilot of the war, developed an almost foolproof method of destroying enemy tanks by coming in from behind (1) and aiming at the rear of a T34 (2), where the engine was mounted and the armour-plating thinnest. In addition, ventilation holes had been cut in the metal to allow heat from the engine to escape, thereby further weakening it.

A T34 blows up (3) after being hit by cannon shells from a Stuka (6), which has dived on it from the rear. It was important for pilots not to dive so close to the target that they risked being brought down by flying fragments of metal. A single Stuka Ju 87G could, if enemy fighters were not present, pick off one tank after another in a column by making repeated dives and always going for the rear tank.

Stuka Ju 87Gs (5) were the direct descendants of models that had proved deadly in Poland and France. The diving siren, dive brakes and bomb racks were removed from these aircraft, which were then equipped with two powerful 37-mm cannon(4), mounted singly in a pod under each wing.

Kursk/3

Then a German deserter gave them the date and time of the attack. Armed with this last piece of information about the German assault, the Red Army artillery pre-empted it by bombarding the German forming-up points a few minutes before the waiting troops were due to move forward. Thus the curtain was raised on a great, sprawling, fragmented, convulsive battle, made even more difficult by the onset of heavy rain which transformed the soft, corn-growing fields around Kursk into a morass.

Hitler had expected a lightning armoured offensive in which the assaulting columns from Army Groups South and Centre would bulldoze their way through the Russians on their respective fronts to make a triumphant junction in open country, 'bagging' the huge Soviet forces trapped within the salient. It was not to be. Manstein's northward lunge, ably supported by waves of Stuka dive-bombers, was the more promising of the two attacks, though initial progress was slowed by soft ground, minefields, air strikes and determined opposition from tanks, artillery and infantry.

After 48 hours of fierce fighting, the Germans had penetrated just 11km/7mls into three isolated sections of the Soviet defence system. Then, with a mighty push, Hoth's Fourth Panzer Army suddenly surged forward in a style which alarmed Vatutin and had Stalin himself intervening to rush in tank reinforcements. For a fleeting moment it seemed that Hitler's gamble might pay off.

But in a series of fierce armoured engagements, in which the Soviets' utilitarian and ubiquitous T34 medium tank amply demonstrated its ability to knock out all the latest panzers, Hoth's advance was halted. By 9 July the German spearhead in the south was, at most, 32km/20mls from its starting point. Casualties had been heavy and the surviving troops were battle fatigued. Kursk was beyond their reach, even though at that stage Manstein refused to believe it.

In the north, Model's Ninth Army had done less well; 10km/6mls were covered on the first day, as far as many units ever got. Four days later some of his panzers were 19km/12mls inside the Russian lines, but even their valiant efforts against such savage resistance were hardly the stuff that blitzkrieg was made of.

While his Operation Citadel was foundering amid the Soviets' cunningly constructed defences, Hitler learned on 10 July that British and American forces had landed in Sicily and that the collapse of Italy, including the Italian-garrisoned

The tanks at Kursk

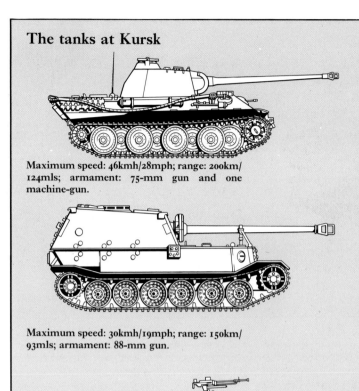

Maximum speed: 46kmh/28mph; range: 200km/124mls; armament: 75-mm gun and one machine-gun.

Maximum speed: 30kmh/19mph; range: 150km/93mls; armament: 88-mm gun.

Maximum speed: 36kmh/22mph; range: 209km/130mls; armament: 76-mm gun and three machine-guns.

Maximum speed: 37kmh/23mph; range: 240km/150mls; armament: 152-mm gun and one machine-gun.

The German Panther V, modelled on the Russian T34, was first used at Kursk. Insufficiently tested and prematurely rushed to the front, most broke down on the journey from the railhead.

The Elefant self-propelled tank destroyer carried a powerful, limited-traverse 88-mm gun; its lack of any other armament, however, made it vulnerable to attacks from infantry who could attack it with impunity.

The SU152 was built on the chassis of the JS I heavy tank.

Following its hugely successful deployment at Kursk, the Russians nicknamed it the 'Conquering beast'.

The Russian KV-I heavy tank was first produced in 1939. At that time, the USSR was the only country to manufacture heavy tanks.

Tanks and self-propelled guns dominated all the battles on the Eastern Front. In the early months, the Panzer IIIs and IVs were overwhelmingly successful; then they met growing opposition from Russian tanks, notably the heavy KV–Is and the highly effective medium T34s.

As the Panzers came into increased contact with large concentrations of Soviet armour, the need for a powerful tank destroyer became evident. The Germans had experimented with a vehicle for just such a role before the war, using an anti-tank gun mounted on a tank chassis; now the concept was quickly revived. Captured Russian 76.2-mm guns were fitted on top of turretless Panzer IIs, inaugurating a long line of innovations with self-propelled guns. One of the biggest to be produced was

the 60-ton Jagdpanzer Tiger, nicknamed the 'Elefant', which mounted an 88-mm gun with a limited traverse. Several of these were rushed into combat at Kursk, where their lack of machine-gun protection from close-quarter infantry attack proved disastrous. German tank manufacturers resorted to experimentation with a great variety of different vehicles. Two promising tanks, the MkVI Tiger and the MkV Panther, were developed, but they went into battle at Kursk before they were ready.

The Russians also produced a range of self-propelled guns, mainly mounted on the T34 chassis. The last of these, the SU85, with an 85-mm gun, fought at Kursk, as did the SU152, a 50-ton assault gun with a powerful 152-mm howitzer mounted on a heavy JS I tank chassis.

The Commanders

Hoth

Model

Vatutin

Colonel-General Hermann Hoth (1885–1971), silver-haired and physically slight, was affectionately known to his men as 'Papa Hoth'. Originally an infantryman, he was posted to the Supreme General Staff as a captain in World War I. From 1935 onward, promotion came rapidly and in the Polish campaign he led the 15th Panzer Corps. Hoth also distinguished himself during the invasion of France in 1940, his Panzer Corps troops being the first to cross the River Meuse on 13 May. Hoth, almost always to be found at the front with his men, commanded Panzer Group 3 in the attack on the USSR and, with Guderian's and Hoepner's panzer groups, was responsible for the big encirclements of the summer and autumn of 1941.

Field Marshal Walther Model (1891–1945) served at Verdun in World War I, where he was wounded and decorated for bravery. After the war he remained in the army and in March 1938 was promoted to Major-General. He served in both the Polish and French campaigns; in October 1939 he broke through the Maginot line and captured Verdun, thus returning to the scene of his earlier valour. In the attack on the USSR, his 3rd Panzer Division formed the spearhead in the thrust to the River Dnieper. He earned the nickname 'The Führer's fireman' because Hitler repeatedly ordered him to take command in troublespots. In 1945, when his troops were surrounded in the Ruhr, he shot himself.

General Nikolai Vatutin (1901–44) distinguished himself as commander on many sectors during the war, notably at Stalingrad and Kursk and in the campaigns to liberate the Ukraine and recapture Kiev. He died in 1944 in an ambush by Ukrainian Nationalist partisans.

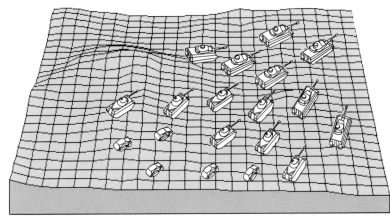

At Kursk the Germans were obliged to forgo their usual, hugely successful tactic of striking the enemy's lines with tanks in a narrow, pointed formation, which could then fan out in an encircling manoeuvre, for the Russians, with their enhanced firepower, were now capable of destroying these spear-like thrusts. Instead, the Germans evolved a tactic of formation in the shape of an axe, *panzerkeile*, with Tigers close-grouped at the front and the new Panthers and Mark IVs behind in fan formation. Infantry, armed with rifles and grenades, followed the tanks closely, and behind them came mortars and their crews in tracked carriers. The object was to punch a hole in the enemy's defences that was sufficiently strong and wide to withstand counter-attacks from the flanks.

The screaming sound generated by the discharge of the Russian Katyusha rocket-launcher and its great fire power had a demoralizing effect on German troops. Each of the eight launching ramps located at the back of the truck held two 13.2-cm calibre rockets, one on top of the other; all 16 were fired simultaneously. Elevation was variable and, since the ramps faced forward over the driver's cabin, aiming merely entailed facing the truck in the right direction. Katyusha rockets had a range of 8,000–8,500m/8,749–9,296yds. Reloading took five to ten minutes. The Russians often deployed hundreds of these launcher trucks in rows.

105

Balkans, was a distinct and imminent possibility. To add to the Führer's anxiety, Marshal Zhukov two days later triggered the first phase of his long-planned summer offensive—an attack around Orel to the north of the Kursk salient which threatened to take Model's Ninth Army in the rear. After a week of heavy fighting and no breakthrough on either front, it appears that Hitler considered writing off Citadel and transferring troops to the new fronts in southern Europe.

While Model was trying to extricate himself from the Russian trap in the north, Manstein persuaded the Führer to let him continue attacking in the south in the belief that he would soon force a way through Vatutin's defences. It was a forlorn hope, recognized as such by Hitler on 25 July when he finally shut down the doomed Citadel offensive. The fact that he had just heard that Mussolini had been deposed also had a bearing on his decision.

Successive Soviet counter-attacks pinned down, then pushed back, the survivors of this ill-fated campaign, in which perhaps as many as 100,000 men, more than 1,000 tanks and about the same number of aircraft had been wasted. Elsewhere on the Eastern Front, in the following weeks, the same relentless pressure was applied by the Red Army. To German astonishment, it was now better led, better equipped and more confident than ever.

By November the major centres of Kharkov, Smolensk and Kiev had all been retaken by the Russians, who had succeeded in driving the enemy back more than 322km/200mls—beyond even the inadequate protection of the so-called East Wall. This largely earthwork barricade had been hastily and inefficiently constructed when it became obvious that the German forces, short of replacements, armoured vehicles, aircraft and fuel, and with their extended supply lines under constant guerrilla attack, would have to retreat and regroup. Much was made of this East Wall by the Nazi propaganda machine. It was hailed as the bastion on which the forces of Communism would perish, but in fact it was virtually useless in the context of modern warfare.

Hitler's disastrous gamble at Kursk—the biggest tank battle ever fought—coupled with the weight and ferocity of Zhukov's subsequent counter-offensive guaranteed Germany's eventual defeat.

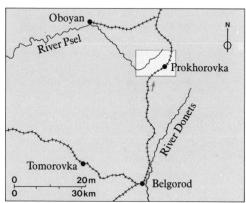

The map shows: Oboyan, River Psel, Prokhorovka, River Donets, Tomorovka, Belgorod. Scale 0–20m / 0–30km. N.

The Luftwaffe and the Red Air Force fought overhead, dropping bombs (2) whenever they could identify an enemy formation. These raids were called off when German and Russian tanks became so tightly interlocked that they no longer presented separate targets.

In the turmoil of bombs bursting, guns firing, and tanks churning up the dry ground, such a dense cloud of dust and smoke (1) was produced that some tanks collided (3).

On 12 July, a day of intense heat, 600 German tanks—all that General Hoth could assemble—moved across the dry, dusty steppe toward the town of Prokhorovka, where he hoped to penetrate a weakened section of the Russian front. For success, this design depended on a flank attack on approaching Soviet armoured reserves by three Panzer divisions from Army Detachment Kempf. Their advance, however, was slowed to a crawl by Shumilov's Seventh Guards Army, dug in behind cunningly sited minefields. Hoth's overworked tanks, manned by exhausted crews, had, therefore, to fight the ensuing eight-hour battle without support. They faced 850 armoured vehicles operated by the fresh, combat-ready crews of the Fifth Guards Tank Army. Nearly 1,500 tanks fired at each other point-blank in the most ferocious armoured clash in history. Each side lost some 300 tanks. The Russians could readily replace both their tanks and crews; the Germans could not.

Although the Russian Fifth Guards Tank Army possessed some new, powerful SU85 and SU152 self-propelled guns, their mainstay at Prokhorovka, as in all their battles, was the robust T34 tank (4), armed at that time with a 76.2-mm gun.

MkVI Tigers (5)
with 88-mm main
armament, and MkV
Panthers (6), mounting
long 75-mm guns,
were in the van of the
Fourth Panzer Army.
These latest examples
of German armour,
though formidable,
were badly in need of
servicing after a week
of hard fighting. And
the long-range
penetrating power of
their weapons was of
no advantage in close,
tank-to-tank fighting.

The Russian tank
commanders found
that their T34s were
more than a match for
the heavier, more
powerful German
tanks. They could
easily knock the
Panthers out (7),
provided they closed
with them quickly.

Anzio/Cassino/*January-May 1944*

Four months after landing in Italy in September 1943, the Allied forces came to a standstill 121km/75mls south of Rome. Their advance had been getting progressively slower in the face of exceptionally hard weather and a determined enemy, and blocking the way was the formidable Gustav Line, which at that moment marked the frontier of German-occupied Italy. The Rome-Berlin Axis had been dissolved by Italy's capitulation on 8 September, but the forces of the Third Reich, competently deployed by Field Marshal Albert Kesselring, meant to hold on to as much of their former ally's country as their fairly limited resources would allow.

The well-sited chain of fortifications that made up the Gustav Line stretched from Ortona on the Adriatic coast, across the Abruzzi Mountains, along the River Rapido to the mouth of the River Gargliano on the Tyrrhenian Sea. Its strongest and most important feature was Monte Cassino, which rose 518m/1,700ft above the Liri Valley and dominated the main road to Rome.

By 2 January 1944, Lieutenant-General Mark Clark's US Fifth Army had steadily fought its way up the west coast after a near-disastrous landing at Salerno. It had also already tried and failed to work around Cassino and isolate it, thereby avoiding a direct and expensive assault up its steep slopes.

After a series of inconclusive clashes with General Heinrich von Vietinghoff's Tenth Army, Clark rested and regrouped his forces for, with the approval of General Sir Harold Alexander, Commander-in-Chief of the Allied forces in Italy, he was scheduled to begin another attempt to bypass Cassino on 12 January. But this time there was a new dimension to the plan. It was intended that the US 2nd Corps, and the British 10th Corps supported by the French Expeditionary Corps, would launch an attack strong enough to ensure that the enemy would transfer reserves held around Rome to the battlefront. Meanwhile, preparations were also being completed for a surprise amphibious landing 89km/55mls up the west coast behind the Gustav Line, in an area then expected to be lightly held. Major-General John Lucas's US 6th Corps was picked for this seaborne operation, codenamed 'Shingle', for which the British Prime Minister, Winston Churchill, had been pressing. It needed the consent of the US President, however, since it involved delaying the transfer of 56 American LSTs (Landing Ships, Tanks) from the Mediterranean as part of the

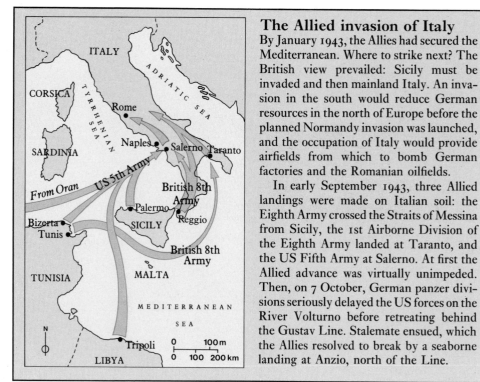

The Allied invasion of Italy

By January 1943, the Allies had secured the Mediterranean. Where to strike next? The British view prevailed: Sicily must be invaded and then mainland Italy. An invasion in the south would reduce German resources in the north of Europe before the planned Normandy invasion was launched, and the occupation of Italy would provide airfields from which to bomb German factories and the Romanian oilfields.

In early September 1943, three Allied landings were made on Italian soil: the Eighth Army crossed the Straits of Messina from Sicily, the 1st Airborne Division of the Eighth Army landed at Taranto, and the US Fifth Army at Salerno. At first the Allied advance was virtually unimpeded. Then, on 7 October, German panzer divisions seriously delayed the US forces on the River Volturno before retreating behind the Gustav Line. Stalemate ensued, which the Allies resolved to break by a seaborne landing at Anzio, north of the Line.

On 22 January 1944, men of the US 3rd Division landed south of Anzio. DUKWs, seen here both on land (1) and approaching the shore (2), carried troops, supplies or ammunition and were essential amphibious vehicles for any seaborne landing.

Unloading at the buffalo, or pontoon, (6) is a Landing Ship, Tanks (5), with another (10) to the right. Others farther out to sea (3,7,9) await their turn to use the buffaloes. The LSTs carried up to 60 tanks or trucks and were capable of an ocean-crossing.

Landing Craft, Tanks (11) were self-propelled barges with doors in the bows. LCTs carried three to five tanks and British versions could come close in, landing tanks in as little as 0.9m/3ft of water.

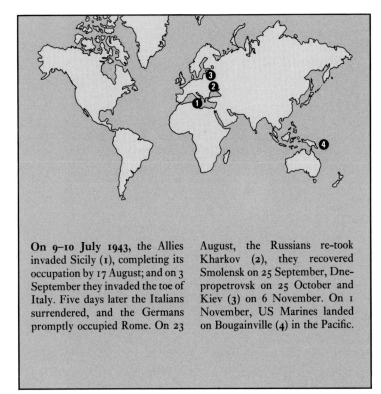

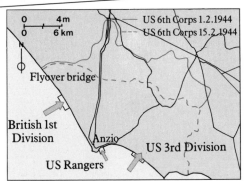

Troop transports at the north beach, with men of the British 2nd Infantry Division coming ashore *above*. Posts linked by tape indicated the routes that had been cleared of mines. Large markers at each pontoon ensured that ships landed their complement of troops at the prearranged point.

On 9–10 July 1943, the Allies invaded Sicily (1), completing its occupation by 17 August; and on 3 September they invaded the toe of Italy. Five days later the Italians surrendered, and the Germans promptly occupied Rome. On 23 August, the Russians re-took Kharkov (2), they recovered Smolensk on 25 September, Dne-propetrovsk on 25 October and Kiev (3) on 6 November. On 1 November, US Marines landed on Bougainville (4) in the Pacific.

Warships, standing well offshore, were used to 'soften up' the enemy by first bombarding coastal areas and then, after the landings had begun, positions farther inland.

The infantry were ferried ashore from troop ships either by Landing Craft, Infantry (8) or by Landing Craft, Assault (4). LCIs were large vessels, from which troops disembarked down ramps on each side of the bows. LCAs were smaller and could be carried on merchantmen and troop carriers; they were lowered into the sea by davits.

build-up for the invasion of Normandy, preparations for which were now well underway.

Alexander told Clark that the object of the landing at Anzio, which began at 02.00 on 22 January, was to sever the Germans' main communications in the Alban Hills southeast of Rome and to threaten the rear of enemy troops in the Gustav Line. But in his orders to Lucas, Clark diluted the aim to seizing and securing a beachhead around Anzio, then advancing on the Alban Hills. As a result, there has been continuing argument about the priorities of this operation.

Shingle, however, got off to a promising start: the landing was unopposed, the few Germans in the area being caught completely off-guard. But then Lucas concentrated all his efforts on getting his

command—the US 3rd Infantry Division (Major-General Lucian Truscott) and the British 1st Infantry Division (Major-General William Penney)—and its supplies and equipment ashore, and securing his position. Six days later his beachhead line reached only 16km/10mls inland from Anzio at its farthest point—as far as it would go for months. In London, Prime Minister Churchill fumed.

By their own admission, the Germans had no forces of any significance anywhere near Anzio on either 22 or 23 January. In fact, practically nothing lay between the Anglo-American assault group and Rome, 60km/37mls away, for the reserves stationed there had indeed been rushed south to support the Tenth Army around Cassino. But by the end of those 48 hours of dangerous exposure, the first units of

strong German reinforcements began to arrive. Colonel-General Eberhardt von Mackensen, commander of the Fourteenth Army in northern Italy, was charged with driving Lucas back. He soon had more than eight divisions, some of them armoured, converging on the pancake-flat plain behind Anzio, as well as considerable artillery support directed from vantage points in the surrounding hills. Shells began to reach virtually all corners of the beachhead, while infantry and armour vigorously patrolled and probed along the 6th Corps' perimeter. Positions changed hands frequently, and in one dreadful night engagement only six men from a force of 767 US Rangers regained the safety of their lines.

General Clark sent in another two divisions to reinforce Anzio, and all

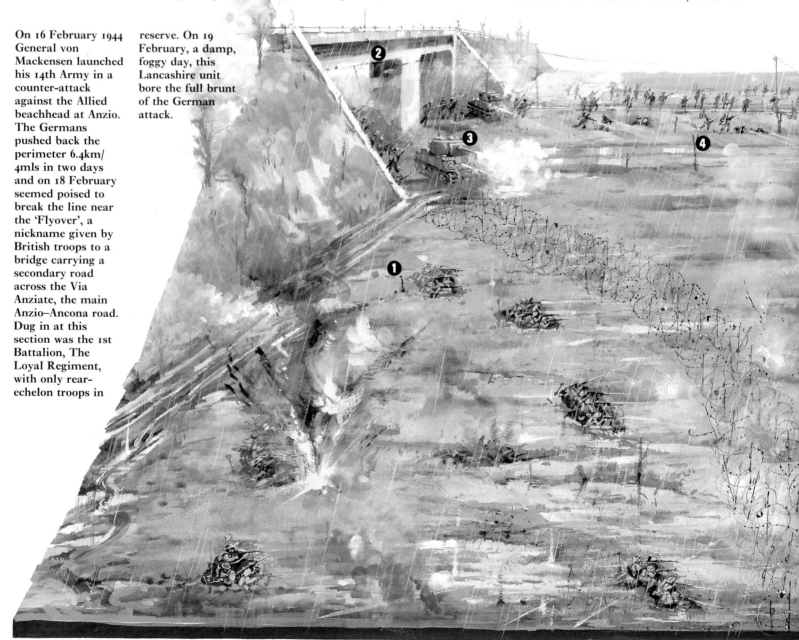

On 16 February 1944 General von Mackensen launched his 14th Army in a counter-attack against the Allied beachhead at Anzio. The Germans pushed back the perimeter 6.4km/4mls in two days and on 18 February seemed poised to break the line near the 'Flyover', a nickname given by British troops to a bridge carrying a secondary road across the Via Anziate, the main Anzio–Ancona road. Dug in at this section was the 1st Battalion, The Loyal Regiment, with only rear-echelon troops in reserve. On 19 February, a damp, foggy day, this Lancashire unit bore the full brunt of the German attack.

'A' Company of The Loyal Regiment (1) held positions covering the east side of the Flyover (2), with the rest of the battalion deployed on their right flank. Precisely at 05.00 on 19 February they came under heavy bombardment, followed by a German infantry attack. One of the Loyals' forward platoons was immediately overwhelmed.

Allied artillery officers used the Flyover as an observation post, since it gave a good view of German positions on the plain to the north. German gunners soon found its range, however, and made it untenable.

American Sherman tanks (3) came up the Via Anziate to support the hard-pressed Loyals; further timely help came from a company of Gordon Highlanders (4), positioned west of the Flyover.

In a scene reminiscent of the Western Front in WWI, heavily armed spearhead units (5) of a German infantry battalion raced for 'A' Company's positions under cover of an artillery barrage. When the Germans penetrated the minefields and wire protecting their slit trenches, the remaining platoons of the Loyals repulsed them in hand-to-hand fighting, despite having lost at least half their men.

Further waves of German troops (6) surged out of the cover of dead ground where, undetected by the Loyals, they had formed up for an assault. Although they fought stubbornly, the German infantrymen were now battle weary and lacked the impetus to break through the British line.

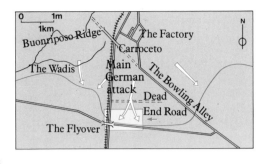

through February the fighting doubled in intensity as the Germans launched a series of counter-attacks. Mackensen's main thrust was made on 16 February; two days later his leading elements were only 10km/6mls from the shore, their way barred—though they did not know it—by only a slim line of infantry supported by rear-echelon troops. Fortunately for the Allies, these German units had fought themselves to a standstill and were incapable of exploiting their success.

Elsewhere along the Anglo-American perimeter pressure was maintained by the Germans despite heavy losses, particularly those inflicted by the Allied Air Force which outnumbered the Luftwaffe by about ten to one. The 6th Corps artillery, too, had a much more plentiful supply of ammunition than its opponents and was using it to good effect.

In the midst of this bitter fighting, in which some battalions on both sides were reduced to fewer than 100 men, Clark decided to relieve Lucas of command of the 6th Corps on the grounds of ill-health and replace him with the more forceful General Lucian Truscott.

On 1 March, Mackensen reluctantly reported to Field Marshal Kesselring that his forces were not strong enough to overcome the Allies, and all further offensive operations were cancelled. By the same token, Truscott was not strong enough to break out of his perimeter, so a long period of stalemate set in. It was to be a grim time, strongly reminiscent of the Western Front in World War I, during which combat-weary soldiers had to endure the miseries of freezing cold, wet and mud while fighting frequent fierce local actions across a narrow strip of shell-pocked no man's land. Territorial gains and losses by both sides were never greater than a few metres.

Churchill, who had been so critical of 6th Corps in the early days of the landing, later wrote a fitting epitaph for Operation Shingle: 'Anzio was a story of high opportunity and shattered hopes, of skilful inception on our part and swift recovery by the enemy, of valour shared by both.'

While Shingle was being prepared in early January, the Fifth Army had been hammering at the Gustav Line, with many casualties and without much success. On 25 January, two days after 6th Corps landed at Anzio, Clark decided on an action he had been trying to avoid—a head-on attack on the Cassino massif. This was defended by Lieutenant-General Fridolin von Senger und Etterlin's 14th Panzer Corps, which included some of the best units remaining in

German paratroops, although trained primarily for an airborne role, were regarded as an élite infantry fighting unit. But they were seldom given adequate artillery support. At Anzio they used a variety of vehicles, including SdKfz 232 armoured cars, to move up to the beachhead.

This Mark IV tank, backed into a partly demolished house, was used as an anti-tank gun, a common practice by this time, when the Germany Army was on the defensive. By 1944 the Allies had achieved overwhelming air superiority and, for protection, the Germans hid or camouflaged all tanks and artillery.

A German 280–mm railway gun, captured in northern Italy, being inspected by British gunners. One of these huge guns, with a range of up to 61km/38mls, was concealed in a tunnel near Anzio, from which it trundled out to fire 250-kg/551-lb shells into the Allied lines. It was nicknamed 'Anzio Annie'.

The type of artillery fire employed is determined by the type of target, its range, and whether or not it is visible from the gun position.

A howitzer lobs a powerful shell in a high arc and is ideal for indirect fire: bombarding an unseen target at a range of several miles.

An anti-tank gun is normally used against armour when it comes into sight. The gun fires a high-velocity round on a flat trajectory directly at its target.

A mortar, firing at a steep angle at short range, can drop its projectile into a trench and is used to clear weapon pits or to bombard areas where troops might be concealed.

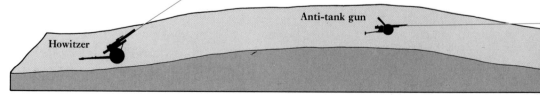

The Commanders

Kesselring

Freyberg

Clark

Major-General John P. Lucas (1890–1949) was overcautious and an unsuitable choice for a command that demanded the ability to improvise. Instead of breaking out of the Anzio perimeter, he awaited reinforcements. Churchill later wrote, 'I had hoped that we were hurling a wild cat on the shore, but all we had got was a stranded whale.'

Lucas was shortly replaced by **General Lucian Truscott (1895–1965)**, a brusque and confident man known to his troops as 'Old Gravel Mouth'. Another vigorous man was **General Mark Clark (1896–1984)**,

commander of the US Fifth Army, who had led the assault on Salerno, was a determined officer faulted by his critics for his love of publicity. He rarely travelled without an entourage of journalists and photographers.

Lieutenant-General Sir Bernard Freyberg VC (1889–1963), a man of exceptional courage served as a field commander in both World Wars. He cared for his New Zealand troops like a father.

During the Battle of Britain, **Field Marshal Albert Kesselring (1885–1960)** had commanded Luftflotte 2; in 1943 he

was appointed Commander-in-Chief of the Army in southern Europe. A gifted and experienced officer, it was he who convinced Hitler that Italy must be defended on a line south of Rome.

The commander of the 14th Panzer Corps, **General Fridolin von Senger und Etterlin (1891–1963)**, who masterminded the defence of Cassino, was, ironically, a lay member of the Benedictine Order. Though a loyal officer, he was anti-Nazi, and his efforts during the siege went largely unrecognized and unreported by the German authorities.

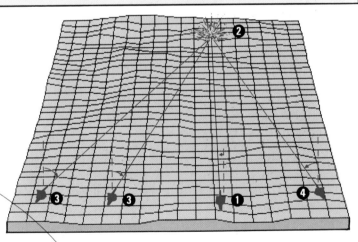

Each gun in a battery is laid on the centre of its arc of fire. The gun position officer calculates the range and bearing of the given target and orders one gun (1) to fire a ranging shot (2). Depending on the fall of the shot, corrections are made to achieve accuracy, then range and bearing are issued to the battery. Guns to the left of the ranging piece traverse precisely to the right of the arc of fire (3), those to the right traverse to the

Light aircraft, such as this Auster III, acted as aerial observation posts during a bombardment. The pilot would watch the fall of shot and pass back corrections to the gun position officer.

left (4) to bring converging fire to bear on the target.

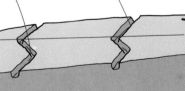

Mortar

the German Army. This commanding position was situated in the most difficult terrain and protected by minefields, barbed-wire entanglements and several cunningly sited reinforced concrete strongpoints with a wide field of fire. Against it was pitted the Fifth Army's freshest infantry division, the US 34th commanded by Major-General Charles Ryder. Against the better judgement of General Alphonse Juin, who saw no future in a direct attack on Cassino, his French Expeditionary Corps was to mount a simultaneous assault on the right flank to divert enemy forces from the 34th's front.

Thus began a prolonged nightmare for tens of thousands of soldiers, both Allied and German, who wallowed in mud by day and froze by night against the non-stop clatter of small-arms fire and the crump of explosions. It was an experience which tested men's endurance to the limit. Despite a valiant and superbly fought action by Juin's North African troops to relieve pressure on Ryder, by 11 February the 34th Division had been reduced to a shadow, but again without making any appreciable gains.

Although he had by now used up his last remaining fresh troops, it was with bad grace that Clark accepted General Alexander's offer of his Army Group Reserve to take over the battle for Cassino. This force comprised Lieutenant-General Bernard Freyberg's New Zealand Corps—the 2nd New Zealand, 4th Indian and 78th British Divisions—taken from the British Eighth Army on the east coast, where the fighting was not so heavy. Apparently the Fifth Army commander did not want British forces to reap the glory of capturing the heights on which so much American blood had been spilled. Nevertheless, of necessity, Clark agreed, although with reluctance.

However, before Freyberg would renew the assault he made a request, which at the time, and later, caused considerable controversy. Because it was assumed—wrongly, it would seem—that the Germans were using the fourteenth-century Benedictine monastery crowning Monte Cassino as an artillery observation post, he wanted it bombed. Neither Alexander nor Clark had previously considered the ancient building a legitimate target, but they bowed to this demand on the grounds that the commander on the spot regarded it as militarily desirable to save the lives of his men. And so, on the morning of 15 February, 222 bombers flew over in two waves and dropped nearly 450 tons of bombs on the historic abbey. As the dust settled and outraged condemnation began

A **German leaflet** dropped on Allied troops at Anzio.

'Get out, Germans!' This poster, put up initially in Sicily, was calculated to swing Italian support to the Allies as liberators.

Propaganda war

Propaganda was used by both sides to sap the morale of enemy troops. German propaganda included leaflets scattered over the Allied forward positions. Many were aimed at undermining Anglo-American relations. Those dropped on British troops often depicted better-paid US soldiers seducing British girls back home, while those directed at American lines always made the villain the fat, rich Jew, enjoying an opulent lifestyle in the USA.

An exhausted Allied soldier struggling to dig a 4.5-in gun out of deep mud, formed in the low-lying areas south of Cassino by constant rain in spring 1944. Because of the mud, the conflict here and at Anzio developed into a war of attrition – precisely what that landing had been designed to overcome.

The monastery

Monte Cassino, situated mid-way between Naples and Rome, dominated the Liri Valley and Route 6, the only inland route suitable for motorized vehicles. The summit of Monte Cassino, 518m/1,700ft above sea level, had for centuries been regarded as a holy place: during the classical period it was the site of a temple to Apollo, and St Benedict chose it in AD 524 as the site for the first monastery of his Order.

Because of its strategic position, the monastery of Monte Cassino was often overrun. It was sacked by the Lombards in 581, plundered and burnt by the Saracens in 883, rebuilt, and again destroyed by the Normans in 1030. In 1349, it was virtually destroyed by an earthquake, and in 1799 it was plundered by troops of revolutionary France.

But each time the monastery was rebuilt, restored and further embellished. A massive complex of buildings, formed around five great courtyards and looking more like an enormous castle than a place of prayer and contemplation, the monastery remained much as it had been designed by Pope Urban V (r. 1362–70) until it was totally destroyed in the fighting of 1944.

A place of pilgrimage for hundreds of thousands in the Middle Ages, it housed, after centuries of acquisitions, one of the most important libraries in the world, comprising more than 40,000 manuscripts and much of the extant writings of the authors of Antiquity. Behind the grim façade, endless labour had been expended over the years in making the interior both beautiful and lavish; the church itself was transformed in the 18th century into a baroque masterpiece.

This was the building—sacred, ancient and incomparably designed and decorated—that happened to be situated on the German Gustav Line, a serious obstacle in the Allies' path in the winter of 1943–4.

The Abbot at Monte Cassino, Gregorio Diamare, an unworldly man in his eighties, was visited on 14 October 1943 by German officers: the monastery would soon be in the front line and they wished to take all its moveable works of art to safety. The Abbot argued strenuously against this, but two days later the officers returned with trucks loaded with packing cases. German propaganda made much of the rescue operation.

Photographs showed art works from the monastery in German safe-keeping, *top*, and they were portrayed as the guardians of civilization in the face of Allied vandalism. In fact, they surrendered the packing cases to the Vatican only after strong pressure.

The Abbot, five monks and a caretaker party remained in the monastery. Later, on 15 February 1944, as Allied bombs destroyed the entire building, *right*, they were obliged to flee. Carrying a large wooden crucifix, the old man led the way toward the German lines.

General von Senger, the area commander, had the Abbot driven to his headquarters, where he stayed the night. The Abbot had earlier signed a document confirming that at no time had there been any German soldiers inside the monastery; now he was required to broadcast a statement praising German troops for their restraint. The next morning the General himself assisted the Abbot into a car, *left*, to take him to sanctuary with the Benedictine Order in Rome. But the old monk's ordeals were not over. His car was waylaid by agents of Goebbels, the German Propaganda Minister, and he was forced to make another broadcast. Shortly afterwards, von Ribbentrop, the Foreign Minister, ordered his agents to get yet another statement. At this the exhausted Abbot broke down and refused to cooperate, since he realized he was no longer a protected guest, but a prisoner.

to pour in from around the world, the Germans moved into the rubble and started to fortify it.

On 16 February, the 4th Indian Division opened its attack from the northeast, choosing the same line of advance as that previously taken by the shattered US 34th Division. It achieved similar disappointing results. Assaults could only be made on narrow fronts through the rocky defiles of the massif, the problems of supplying forward troops up tortuous, rain-washed mountain paths were enormous, and all movements were made under the guns of a resolute, well-entrenched enemy.

The 2nd New Zealand Division, attacking to the west of Cassino town at the foot of the monastery hill, made no impression either. After three days, therefore, General Freyberg decided to shut down this phase of the battle for the heights and to make new plans.

Meanwhile, on the other side of the lines, the 14th Panzer Corps, despite the successful defence of its vital sector, was becoming increasingly worried about the losses and lack of reserves, some of which had been transferred to the Anzio front. Fears were expressed that in some places the defences were not strong enough to beat off a concerted attack.

Just then, however, both hard-pressed sides earned a breathing space, for a bout of particularly bad weather suspended operations. More than three weeks were to pass before Freyberg was in a position to make a second effort to carry the German stronghold. This time, the 4th Indian Division would tackle the eastern slopes of Monastery Hill while the 2nd New Zealand Division, supported by the 4th New Zealand Armoured Brigade, would attack through Cassino. But first the town was to be bombed and shelled.

On 15 March, more than 1,000 tons of bombs were dropped on Cassino's narrow streets; then the area was saturated with a massive barrage from nearly 900 guns. Freyberg began moving forward in the early afternoon, but his tanks could not negotiate the rubble and craters left by the bombardment, and it was the infantry who had to face the 100 or so survivors of a garrison from the crack German 1st Parachute Division. They were emerging from the ruins, dazed but fighting-fit. To aid his veterans in their struggle, von Senger und Etterlin concentrated every artillery piece and as much ammunition as he could find on their assailants, while urgently requesting reinforcements.

Once again the attacking fronts proved too narrow to overwhelm the defenders. Both sides suffered heavy casualties and

Troops of the Polish 2nd Corps, seen here hurling grenades at enemy positions, really hated the Germans. Given the task of capturing the heights of Monte Cassino, General Anders undertook it feeling that 'victory would give new courage to the resistance movement in Poland and would cover Polish arms with glory.' The Polish and British flags were raised on the monastery on 18 May after the Germans had withdrawn.

In the ruins of Cassino, this young New Zealand officer is trying to locate his position with the aid of an aerial photograph. The destruction of all landmarks and the thick cloud of dust and smoke made it impossible for men to establish where they were as they moved into the town. Despite their superficial disregard for military discipline, the New Zealanders showed a tough professionalism in the fighting.

British infantrymen, one armed with a Thompson sub-machinegun, the others with Lee-Enfield rifles, moving through the devastated town of Cassino. It took weeks to clear the determined German snipers out of the ruins, for the rubble and wrecked buildings provided them with perfect cover.

The four battles for Monte Cassino

The struggle to break through the Gustav Line, in which Monte Cassino was the linch-pin, began on 12 January 1944. On the Allied right flank, the French Expeditionary Corps crossed the River Rapido, then turned south in a bid to outflank Monte Cassino. Simultaneously, the British 10th Corps on the left flank managed to get across the River Garigliano and establish a bridgehead; but in the centre of the front the US 2nd Corps, facing Monte Cassino itself, was halted by stiff German resistance. This point then became the crucial sector of the front.

The attacks upon Monte Cassino fell into four distinct phases. In the first, the US 34th Division, supported to their right by a regiment of the US 36th Division and beyond them the French, advanced to within 366m/400yds of the monastery, where they were halted. They were relieved by fresh units—the 2nd New Zealand and 4th Indian Divisions.

Following the massive bombing of the monastery, the second phase was opened by the Indians who tried to take it from the rear while the New Zealanders attacked from the south. Both offensives were repulsed. On 15 March the third phase opened with a bombardment of Cassino.

The New Zealand 2nd Division attacked the ruined town while the Indians advanced in the hills; both formations were again halted.

Finally, the Allies assembled their maximum strength—14 divisions, with the 6th South African Armoured Division in reserve. The US 2nd Corps crossed the River Garigliano on the left flank, while the French broke through on their right. The Canadian 1st Corps and the British 13th Corps, farther east, broke into the Liri Valley, building up such pressure that the Germans had finally to withdraw from their positions on the Cassino massif.

The first battle for Monte Cassino

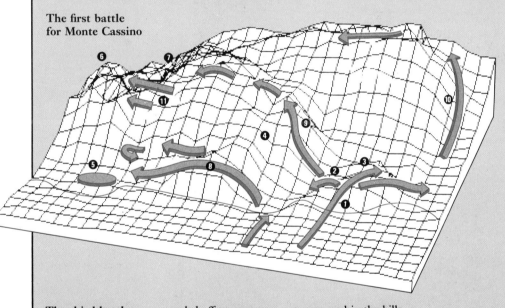

Having penetrated the German line (1) on the west bank of the River Rapido by the end of January 1944, the US 34th Division (2) with one regiment of the US 36th Division (3) was in the foothills of the massif (4), poised to wheel south to try to drive the enemy from its main positions in Cassino town (5) and the monastery (6) and on the surrounding peaks (7).

Three columns fanned out for the offensive; one regiment of the 34th (8) made for the town, while the rest pushed along the ridge (9). The 36th (10) swung out to cover the right flank. The force was too weak to overcome the enemy, but their vigorous attack took one battalion (11) to 366m/400yds of the monastery before it was beaten back.

When the action was brought to an end by bad weather on 12 February, the Allies had acquired a bridgehead on the massif that extended to about 1.2km/¾ml from the monastery.

The third battle

The third battle opened on 15 March with a devastating air and artillery attack on the town (1). At 02.00, men of the 2nd NZ Division, supported by tanks of the 4th NZ Armoured Brigade, moved toward the town to mop up survivors of the 1st German Parachute Battalion defending it, to scale the eastern slopes of the massif (2) and then to take the monastery (3) and other well-fortified peaks (4,5). Three companies of the 25th NZ Battalion (6,7,8) advanced into the town, a fourth, (9) peeled off to occupy Castle Hill (10), which dominated the eastern approach to the monastery.

That night, more NZ troops and men of the 4th Indian Division moved into the town, but the Germans had also reinforced their positions and close-quarter fighting developed, particularly around a German strongpoint to the west (11). The farthest point the Allies reached was Hangman's Hill (12). The Germans counterattacked strongly, pinning down the NZ troops, and in the hills the rest of the Indian Division sustained heavy losses without significant gains. Five days after the start of the battle, General Freyberg decided to close it down.

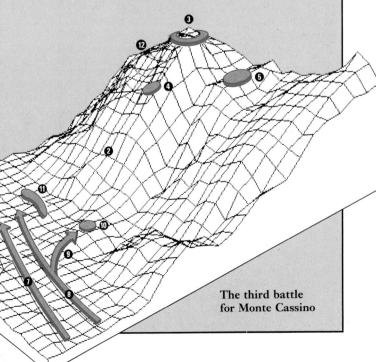

The third battle for Monte Cassino

117

Freyberg's second assault was called off on 23 March amid questions about the wisdom of expending such large quantities of troops on a frontal attack for no return.

Now General Alexander realized that the only way to overcome the obstacle of Cassino, penetrate the Gustav Line and open the way to Rome was to organize a major offensive. He began regrouping his forces for 'Operation Diadem' principally by bringing the Eighth Army, under Lieutenant-General Oliver Leese, over from the Adriatic, where the front was much quieter, to man the sector stretching from Cassino across the valley of the River Liri and by moving Mark Clark's Fifth Army to cover the line from the Liri down to the coast.

By 11 May all was ready. Alexander's preponderance of men and *matériel* far outweighed anything the Germans could muster in Italy at that stage of the war. Even so, Diadem's initial progress did not come up to expectations. The 2nd Polish Corps, on the Eighth Army's right flank, added its casualties to Cassino's stubborn slopes in a week of heavy fighting while the advance up the Liri Valley gathered momentum. But when the Eighth Army's efforts finally made the Gustav Line untenable for von Vietinghoff's Tenth Army, he ordered a withdrawal, which the gallant defenders of Cassino obeyed with the greatest reluctance. On 18 May, Polish troops made an unopposed entry into the ruins of the monastery.

As Diadem progressed, Alexander gave the go-ahead for the 6th Corps at Anzio, now reinforced to seven divisions, to break out of the beachhead it had held since 22 January, head northeast and cut off the German Tenth Army's line of retreat. Instead, Clark instructed it to advance north and clear a way to Rome, which it did. On 4 June, two days before the great Allied invasion of Normandy began, the Americans entered the Italian capital. The retreating German forces escaped northward to fight again.

From Cassino via Anzio, the bitter and bloody road to Rome—an open city of no strategic value—took five months to negotiate and cost the attackers 105,000 casualties, the defenders possibly 80,000. In military terms, the only benefit the Allied cause reaped from this sacrifice was the tying-down of German divisions which otherwise would have gone to reinforce the Eastern Front or those forces already stationed along the English Channel.

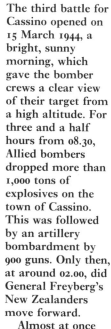

A missed opportunity

The Germans, hard pressed and without reserves, could easily have been driven out of Italy after the Allies took Rome. This in turn could have led to the occupation of Vienna and an advance into central Europe, with the result that many of those countries now behind the Iron Curtain might not have come under Russian control. The opportunity was squandered largely on the advice of General George Marshall, Chief of the US General Staff, who, with Eisenhower's agreement, opted instead for an invasion of southern France in support of the Normandy landings.

Kesselring was thus able to continue his brilliantly executed retreat northward, finally bringing the weakened Allied advance to a halt at the Gothic Line. There he held them from August 1944 until shortly before the German collapse in April 1945.

The Allied landing in southern France ranks among the great strategic blunders of the war, achieving little. The Germans withdrew before they could be encircled and the course of the campaign in Normandy was unaffected.

The third battle for Cassino opened on 15 March 1944, a bright, sunny morning, which gave the bomber crews a clear view of their target from a high altitude. For three and a half hours from 08.30, Allied bombers dropped more than 1,000 tons of explosives on the town of Cassino. This was followed by an artillery bombardment by 900 guns. Only then, at around 02.00, did General Freyberg's New Zealanders move forward.

Almost at once they encountered two unexpected obstacles. First, some 100 men from the first-rate German 1st Parachute Division had survived the awesome bombardment and now put up a vigorous defence. Second, the craters and mounds of rubble resulting from the bombing and shelling made tank movement impossible.

Allied bombing and shelling left not one building in Cassino intact (1). This deceived the Allies into thinking that the Germans had been annihilated.

Heaps of rubble (4) blocked the streets and huge craters (5), some as much as 18m/59ft across, made it impossible for the tanks (6) of the 4th New Zealand Armoured Brigade to advance into the town.

The New Zealand infantry (7) were, as a result, without tank support as they climbed over piles of concrete and twisted metal and scrambled through huge craters under heavy German small-arms fire. During the afternoon they penetrated about 230m/250yds into the ruins, with opposition from some 100 men—all that remained of the 2nd Battalion 3rd Parachute Regiment—who had sheltered in cellars and reinforced bunkers (3). When night fell, in heavy rain, the Germans filtered reserves into the town and began to use artillery against the attackers.

A ruined medieval fortress on the summit of Castle Hill (2) behind the town was fiercely defended by the Germans, who pinned the New Zealanders down with sniper fire. Finally they managed to work around to the rear of the fort and at 16.45, after a hard grenade battle, took it.

Kohima/Imphal/*March-July 1944*

Early in 1944 both British and Japanese forces were ready to go on the offensive in the difficult terrain of the Indian-Burmese border country. General William Slim was preparing his Fourteenth Army for a thrust across the River Chindwin as a prelude to the reconquest of Burma, which had been lost in the spring of 1942. While fighting continued at each end of the chain of mountains, 1,126km/700mls long, which formed the formidable boundary between India and Burma, he had been steadily building up strength in order to strike hard in the centre.

The jumping-off point for the main assault, to be headed by 4th Corps under Lieutenant-General Geoffrey Scoones, was Imphal plain in Manipur State, the only area suitable for airfields in thousands of square kilometres of rough country. Ground communication with what rapidly grew into a substantial forward supply base was limited to one narrow road winding 209km/130mls northward into Assam. It crossed a pass at Kohima, 1,524m/5,000ft high, before descending to Dimapur, a vast rear concentration of workshops, hospitals, storage depots and training facilities. There the vital road met the equally important Assam railway, which continued north and supplied General Joseph Stilwell's American/Chinese army.

General Renya Mutaguchi was, at the same time, planning to revive Japan's flagging fortunes by despatching his Fifteenth Army to secure the frontier passes before the monsoon broke. Their efforts began on 4 February with 'Operaton Ha-Go', a strong counter-attack in the southern sector, at Arakan, designed to divert and pin down Fourteenth Army's reserves. By the middle of the month, the main blow, 'Operation U-Go', was to be launched, but reinforcements were delayed and it was postponed until 6 March.

Slim and his staff had ample warning of the enemy's intention to attack the central sector and adjusted their plans accordingly. Once the Japanese were known to have crossed the River Chindwin in strength, 4th Corps' two forward divisions—the 17th Indian, under Major-General D.T. Cowan, to the south and the 20th Indian, under Major-General D.D. Gracey, to the east—were to pull back toward Imphal, where the battle would be fought on ground of their choosing against an enemy dangling at the end of almost impossibly long and difficult supply lines. Held in reserve on the large plain—64km/40mls long and 32km/20mls wide—was Major-General O.L. Roberts's 23rd Indian Division, the 254th

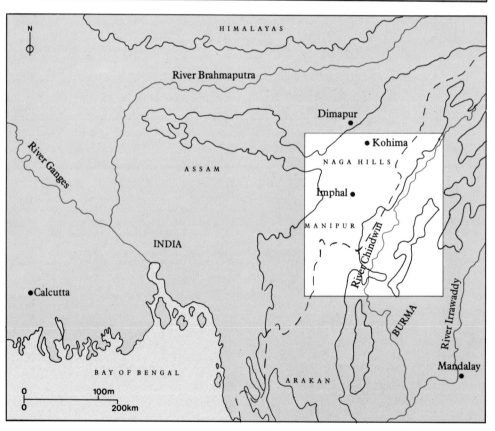

Japan, following her attack on US ships in Pearl Harbor on 7 December 1941, at first made spectacular conquests in three main areas: against the Dutch East Indies and the Philippines, against mainland Asia and into Oceania.

During the months of March and April 1942 she completely overran Burma, forcing the British and Indian contingents westward over the River Chindwin. There, however, the British established a defensive line, pinned on

Imphal, a base situated on a plain surrounded by jungle-clad mountains. This was the only site in the area where airfields could be constructed; moreover, the one serviceable road passed through Imphal to Kohima in

the north and then up to Dimapur, from which a railway line ran into India, enabling supplies to be brought forward.

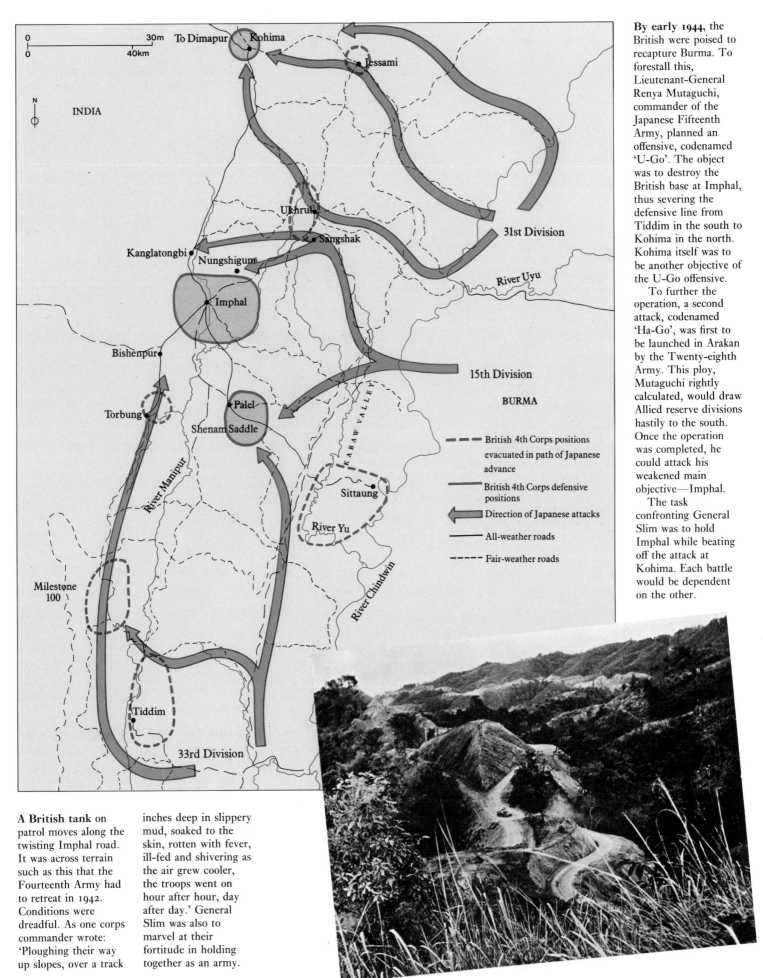

By early 1944, the British were poised to recapture Burma. To forestall this, Lieutenant-General Renya Mutaguchi, commander of the Japanese Fifteenth Army, planned an offensive, codenamed 'U-Go'. The object was to destroy the British base at Imphal, thus severing the defensive line from Tiddim in the south to Kohima in the north. Kohima itself was to be another objective of the U-Go offensive.

To further the operation, a second attack, codenamed 'Ha-Go', was first to be launched in Arakan by the Twenty-eighth Army. This ploy, Mutaguchi rightly calculated, would draw Allied reserve divisions hastily to the south. Once the operation was completed, he could attack his weakened main objective—Imphal.

The task confronting General Slim was to hold Imphal while beating off the attack at Kohima. Each battle would be dependent on the other.

Map labels: To Dimapur, Kohima, Jessami, INDIA, Ukhrul, Sangshak, 31st Division, River Uyu, Kanglatongbi, Nungshigum, Imphal, 15th Division, Bishenpur, BURMA, Palel, Torbung, Shenam Saddle, KABAW VALLEY, Sittaung, River Yu, River Manipur, River Chindwin, Milestone 100, Tiddim, 33rd Division

Map legend:
- - - British 4th Corps positions evacuated in path of Japanese advance
— British 4th Corps defensive positions
← Direction of Japanese attacks
—— All-weather roads
- - - - Fair-weather roads

Scale: 0 — 30m, 0 — 40km

A British tank on patrol moves along the twisting Imphal road. It was across terrain such as this that the Fourteenth Army had to retreat in 1942. Conditions were dreadful. As one corps commander wrote: 'Ploughing their way up slopes, over a track inches deep in slippery mud, soaked to the skin, rotten with fever, ill-fed and shivering as the air grew cooler, the troops went on hour after hour, day after day.' General Slim was also to marvel at their fortitude in holding together as an army.

Indian Tank Brigade and the 8th Medium Regiment, Royal Artillery. Last, but not least, there was a formidable source of firepower unmatched by the Japanese: 221 Group, Royal Air Force, commanded by Air Vice-Marshal Stanley Vincent.

Mutaguchi's opening move was to send two columns from his crack 33rd Division, led by Lieutenant-General G. Yanagida, against the 17th Indian in the Tiddim area 289km/180mls south of Imphal to attempt to cut it off. He almost succeeded. Cowan, whose troops had been doing well in the fierce clashes developing along their front, was a little slow to disengage. And when his huge column, which included 2,500 vehicles and 3,500 pack animals, finally moved back up the narrow road on 14 March, it often found its way blocked by enemy forces which had worked through the jungle to get behind it. Only by committing the bulk of his reserves could Scoones extricate the 17th Division from a potentially serious situation. The strength of the Indian tanks proved too much for Yanagida, who took an unusual step for a Japanese general in recommending that the attack should be called off; he was replaced immediately. Major-General N. Tanaka, who succeeded him, was made of sterner stuff, and conducted a vicious running fight up the Tiddim-Imphal road.

Meanwhile, Major-General T. Yamamoto was leading a third column from the 33rd Division, along with the bulk of Fifteenth Army's tanks and artillery, up the Kabaw Valley to join elements of Lieutenant-General M. Yamauchi's 15th Division in trying to overrun the 20th Indian Division. This force had withdrawn to prepare positions around the Shenam Saddle, protecting Palel, where one of Imphal's two all-weather airfields was situated. The area was the scene of much heavy fighting in the weeks following, including the only tank-to-tank engagement of the campaign, but Gracey's units consistently rebuffed the attempts of the Japanese to reach the plain.

As fierce and often confused fighting intensified south and east of Imphal during the first week of Operation U-Go,

Garrison Hill, *below,* as it looked after some of the fiercest fighting and bombardments of the battle. This was the 'last ditch' that withstood all Japanese attacks. Leafless trees, once so dense with foliage as to make the hillside almost impenetrable, and the pulverized ground, are grimly reminiscent of the Somme landscape during WWI. A lone parachute from a supply drop dangles forlornly from a denuded trunk.

During the night of 8–9 April, the Japanese launched a series of ferocious attacks on three sections of the Kohima garrison's defences, continuing their assaults the following day. Some of the most savage fighting took place around the Deputy Commissioner's bungalow, an area about 365m/400yds by 274m/300yds. The garrison held out, during incessant fighting at close range, for another 10 days before a relief column reached them.

Garrison Hill (1), where some of the fiercest fighting occurred, rose above the tennis court area. This was the site of Colonel Richards's command post.

Shellbursts around the Japanese positions (4) testified to the remarkable accuracy of two Indian Army mountain batteries, firing in support of their beleaguered comrades. Though shooting from 3.2km/ 2mls away to the north, they laid barrages of fire a mere 14 m/15yds in front of British forward positions.

When the British withdrew behind the bungalow, their forward positions (2) rested on the western edge of the tennis court (3). Soon the Japanese were a mere 20m/22yds away.

The Deputy Commissioner's bungalow (5) and another nearby (8) were overrun by the Japanese in darkness early on the morning of 9 April.

Once the Japanese had captured the bungalow area, they made skillful use of the dead ground (6) created by the terracing to regroup and reinforce their assault troops.

Most of the British battalion defending this fiercely contested sector took up positions at the top of the embankment behind the tennis court (11), around the tennis clubhouse (10) and on a low mound to its rear (9).

When the garrison was finally relieved on 18 April, all the trees in the area (7) had been stripped of foliage and the buildings reduced to rubble.

every man of the 4th Corps reserve was drawn into action. Slim realized that the enemy were approaching the plain much faster than he had expected and that it was essential to bring up reinforcements quickly. To achieve this, he instigated the biggest airlift operation in the Far East with the unstinting help of Admiral Lord Louis Mountbatten, Supreme Allied Commander South-East Asia. And from 17–30 March a stream of British and American transport planes ferried in the 5th Indian Division and all its equipment from the Arakan Front, some 482km/300mls to the south. On the flights out of Imphal the aircraft carried thousands of non-combatants so that only fighting men would be on the ration strength, a precaution that paid dividends later.

In the meantime, the 50th Indian Parachute Brigade, which had been moved forward to support Scoones's defence while the airlift got underway, was to play an important part in protecting Imphal at a critical period of the battle. The brigade was sent northeast up the track to Ukhrul to join a battalion of the 23rd Division guarding this approach to the plain. On 19 March their positions were attacked by strong columns from the Japanese 15th and 31st Divisions; after two days of bitter fighting they were forced to retire.

At Sangshak, about 16km/10mls south of Ukhrul, they made another brave stand, this time for six days. Outnumbered and desperately short of water, the remnants of this gallant blocking force received orders on 26 March to make a break for Imphal. Their delaying battles had bought enough time to allow major elements of the 5th Indian Division to arrive and deploy, somewhat reducing the tense situation around the edges of the plain.

Much fighting was still to be done at Imphal, the fluidity of which has been admirably summed up by Slim himself in his book about the Burma Campaign, *Defeat into Victory*: 'It swayed back and forth through great stretches of wild country; one day its focal point was a hill named on no map, the next a miserable, unpronounceable village a hundred miles away. Columns, brigades, divisions marched and counter-marched, met in bloody clashes and reeled apart, weaving a confused pattern hard to unravel.'

While the struggle was raging at Imphal in mid-March, a potentially much more dangerous situation was developing in the vicinity of Kohima, 97km/60mls north up the only road link with 4th Corps' main base at Dimapur. The road's long, exposed flank had not worried Slim overmuch. Even if Mutaguchi did send troops

Mountain guns

Artillery for pack transport had always posed a problem: a powerful gun was too heavy and bulky for a single mule to carry, while a gun small enough to be transported on a pack animal was too weak to be effective in mountain regions. It is thought that the solution originated in Russia, in 1876, when an artillery officer suggested making guns in two parts that could be screwed together. This and subsequent improvements allowed the 24th Mountain Regiment to deploy its weaponry at a site of their choosing in the defence of Kohima. Their guns were easy to manhandle, had good crest clearance and were, in addition, remarkably accurate.

The Mountain Regiment's position overlooking Kohima was ideal, for the height and range it afforded meant that the gunners could pour continuous, accurate fire on the Japanese while themselves remaining out of range of enemy guns. Moreover, the guns were manned and commanded by highly experienced artillerymen. At Kohima, they became so expert at determining the time and direction of Japanese attacks on the garrison that often an order from the beleagured West Kents was carried out before the message was received from the troops on the spot.

The Queen's Own Royal West Kent Regiment acknowledged their debt to the gunners in a book entitled *From Kent to Kohima*: 'The fire of these gunners was so careful and accurate that they were able to bring down fire at call on the other side of the tennis court with no danger whatsoever to our troops.'

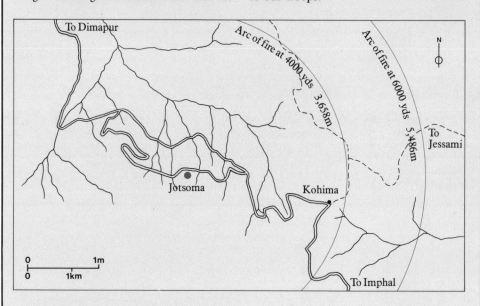

Guns of the 24th Mountain Regiment were sited in the jungle near Jotsoma and disguised as a native village. They were sufficiently close to the road for the guns to be manhandled into position and had an excellent site for their observation post on Punjab Ridge, about 1,097m/1,200yds ahead of them. They laid a deadly arc of fire to 3,200–3,658m/3,500–4,000yds. At unpredictable times they would extend their arc of fire to 5,486m/6,000yds, creating further havoc and injury among the Japanese lines.

A Japanese Model 92 70-mm Howitzer, *right*. Every infantry battalion had two of these guns.

Each Indian battery had four 3.7-in Pack Howitzers, *right*, and each weapon needed eight mules to transport it.

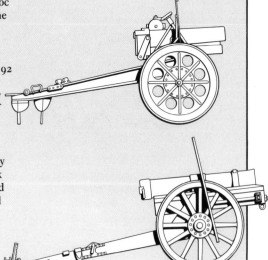

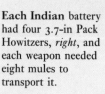

The defence of Kohima

The British had fully expected to have to fight to defend Imphal but had not anticipated having simultaneously to defend Kohima from heavy attack. They believed that the Japanese, if they undertook an attack, would be able to bring at most a regiment through 64km/40mls of thick jungle to cut the sole road running north from the Imphal plain into India. In the event, the Japanese brought up their entire 31st Division, together with its artillery.

The Battle of Kohima, which began on 5 April 1944, fell into three phases. The first, the siege, lasted 14 days, during which time Colonel Richards and a scratch force of

1,500 men stubbornly held out against General K. Sato's 31st Division, though their defensive perimeter shrank continuously in the process.

After the siege was lifted, the British brought up considerable reinforcements; nevertheless, Japanese resistance was fanatical. It took three and a half weeks for the British to clear Kohima Ridge, every bunker and strongpoint having to be dealt with separately.

Still the battle was not over. Large numbers of undernourished, diseased but battle-crazed Japanese troops continued to resist, and two British divisions had to be

called in to destroy them and reopen the vital road to Imphal.

General Sato, realizing that the situation was hopeless, ordered the withdrawal of his men from Kohima on 31 May without first seeking the army commander's permission. His superior, General Mutaguchi, faced with this *fait accompli*, agreed with Sato's decision for appearance's sake but ordered the retreating remnants of the 31st Division south to join the 15th Division fighting at Imphal, where he still continued to delude himself that victory was possible. Soon, however, the entire Japanese Fifteenth Army was obliged to withdraw.

General Sato's 31st Division, having reached the Kohima garrison's defences on 5 April, quickly took Transport Ridge, its southern outpost. The Japanese (1), pressing the greatly outnumbered defenders hard, captured Jail Hill (2) the next day and Detail Hill (3) on 10 April. Supply Hill (4) and Kuki Piquet (5) both fell on the night of 17 April, leaving only Garrison Hill and

the bungalow sector (6) on which the British could mount a stand. British casualties were tended on Hospital Ridge (7), the area within the garrison perimeter that was least exposed to Japanese fire.

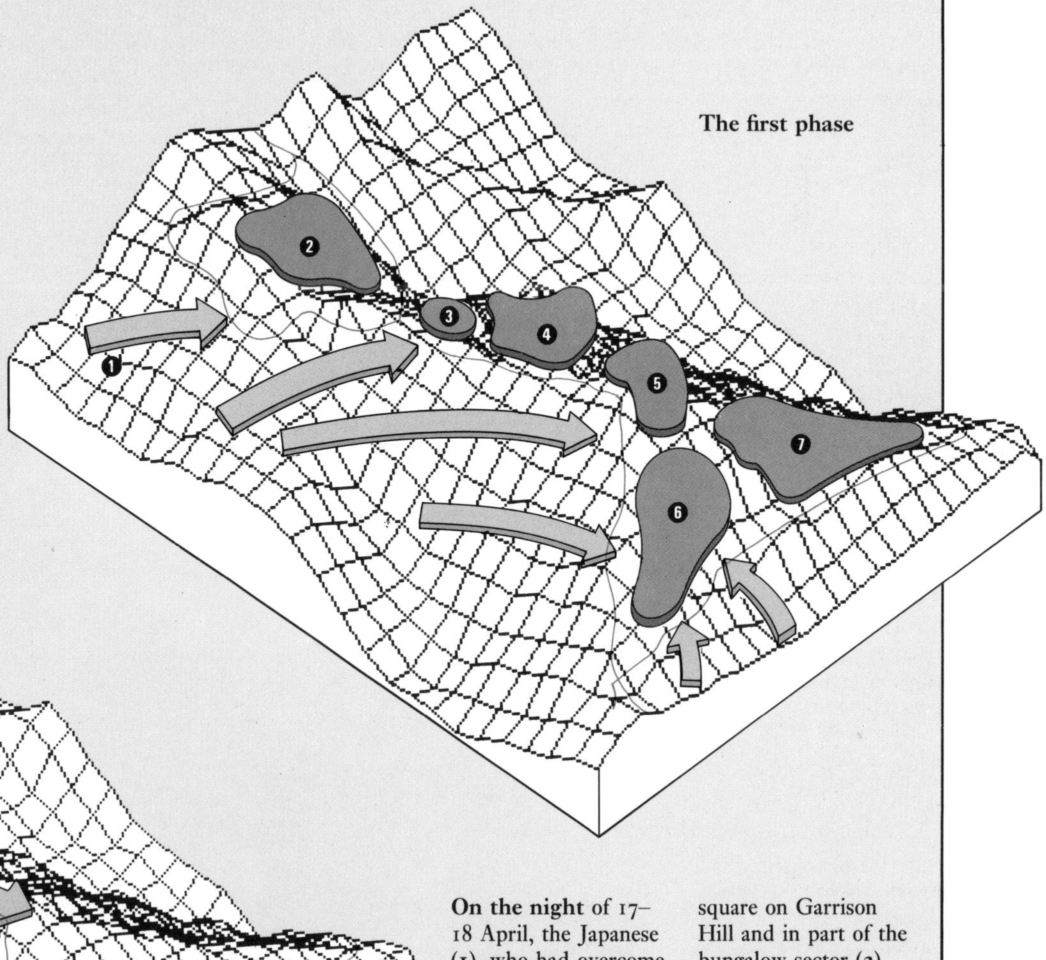

The first phase

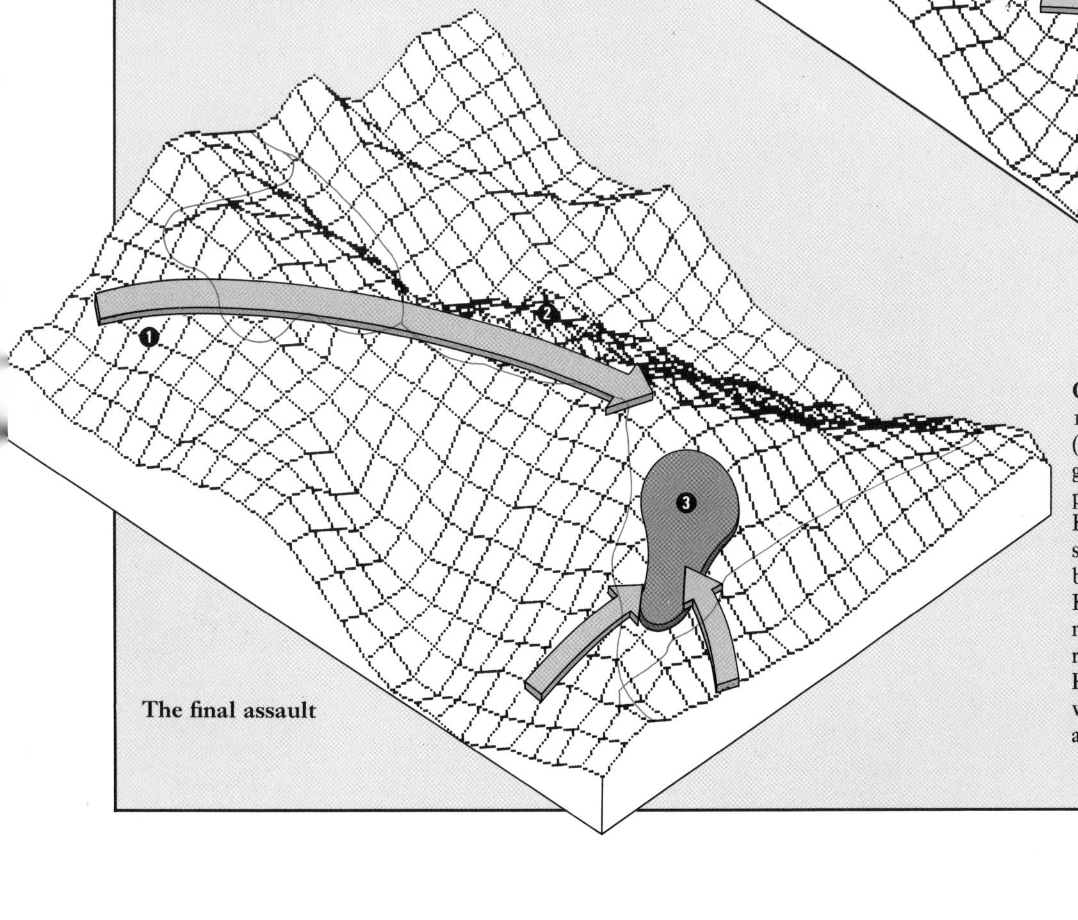

The final assault

On the night of 17–18 April, the Japanese (1), who had overcome garrison strongpoints piecemeal along Kohima Ridge (2) since 5 April, took both Supply Hill and Kuki Piquet. The mauled but defiant remnants of Colonel Richards's command were squeezed into an area 320m/350yds square on Garrison Hill and in part of the bungalow sector (3), where fighting had been intense for several days. On 18 April, the depleted garrison was finally relieved by units of the 2nd Division.

toward Kohima, the British reasoned that it was unlikely any force larger than a regiment, unsupported by artillery, would be able to get through the 64km/40mls of thick jungle between the Japanese positions on the River Chindwin and the road.

Because of this assessment of the situation, only one battalion of the Assam Regiment was assigned to cover the eastern approaches to Kohima, which in the early stages of the U-Go offensive continued to operate as the main staging point between Imphal and Dimapur. The village was a stores, administrative and medical centre, full of rear-echelon troops and civilian workers. Then came reports of enemy forces converging on Kohima. Even so, hurried preparations to defend the village were treated locally with less than the seriousness they demanded.

Slim, however, conscious of the danger

not only to 4th Corps' lines of supply and communication but also to the vast undefended Dimapur base, made arrangements to switch powerful forces to the area. This move could not be organized swiftly, so Colonel Hugh Richards, an imperturbable, 50-year-old infantry officer with much experience of jungle warfare, was despatched to Kohima as garrison commander to organize the defence properly. When he reached there on 23 March, he found that, apart from the battalion of men from the Assam Regiment picketed east of the base, a Native State battalion of questionable quality and a few platoons from the Assam Rifles, the garrison comprised odds and ends of a multitude of units, many of whom were unskilled in handling weapons. There were, however, plentiful supplies of food and small-arms ammunition.

Richards decided to base his defence on Kohima Ridge, a hilly spur about 1.6km/1ml long and 320m/350yds wide, around the base of which the road wound in a hairpin bend. Then, on 27 March, he learned to his astonishment that he would not be standing-off the anticipated enemy regiment: the whole of Sato's 31st Division was closing in on him. Three days later the Japanese succeeded in cutting the road between Imphal and Kohima, and the isolated command had to rely on its supplies being replenished by air.

As the crisis mounted at Kohima, a torrent of orders and counter-orders had troops moving into and out of the village

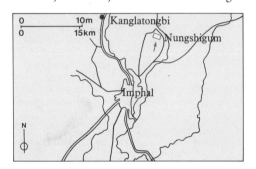

Hurribombers (1) strafed Japanese positions near the summit of Nungshigum. These Hawker Hurricane fighters, converted to carry a light bomb load, were used extensively in support of infantry campaigns in the Far East.

The Japanese positions (2), ringing the top of the hill, were not held in strength when the Dogras attacked. Nevertheless, their fearless resistance cost the Japanese 100 casualties.

In the second week of April 1944, units of the Japanese 51st Regiment of the 15th Division took up positions on Nungshigum, a hill 1,158m/3,800ft high overlooking Imphal and the main airstrip 10km/6mls to the southwest. The British at once realized that if the Japanese were allowed to assemble there in strength, Imphal would be in dire peril.

On the morning of 13 April, a hot and humid day of brilliant sunshine, two companies of the 1/17 Dogra Regiment, one of the crack Indian infantry units, supported by six tanks from B Squadron, 3rd Carabiniers— 5th Division's artillery—together

with two squadrons of Vengeance dive-bombers and a Hurribomber squadron, combined to dislodge the Japanese from their dominating position.

The Japanese were astonished when six Grants (3) climbed the steep approaches to Nungshigum. The tanks moved up to the summit at such a sharp angle that their drivers could not see the ground ahead. The

vehicle commanders, spurning personal safety, stood up in the open turret hatches to direct the drivers, simultaneously harassing the Japanese with hand grenades (4)

and handguns (6). Five of the six commanders were killed.

At the summit, A and B companies of the 1st Dogras (5) met fierce resistance from those Japanese who had survived the

aerial and artillery bombardments, but the Dogras finally cleared the ridge with a bayonet charge.

with bewildering frequency, making Richards's unenviable task even more difficult. He never knew from one day to the next how many soldiers would be available to man the weapon pits which had been dug. His worries seemed over, however, when Slim sent the 161st Indian Infantry Brigade from Dimapur, where it had been flown in from the Arakan Front. But the day it arrived at Kohima it was sent back to guard the big rear base, a manoeuvre that led the 161st's brigadier to nickname his command 'The Duke of York's Own'—it had been marched right up to the top of the hill, then marched right down again.

On 5 April, the day the Japanese infantry first clashed with the Kohima garrison and after most of the Native State battalion had deserted, Colonel Richards was delighted to have his scratch force strengthened by a good British unit, the 4th Battalion of the Queen's Own Royal West Kent Regiment, which had been detached from 161st Brigade and sent to help defend the pass. With the West Kents came a battery from the 20th Mountain Regiment, Indian Artillery; Richards's command was now swelled to 1,500 first-class fighting men and 1,000 non-combatants.

Although the Colonel expected to have to hold out for a few days at most because he knew that Slim was airlifting massive reinforcements into Dimapur, he showed amazing prescience in issuing 14 days' rations and ammunition to all positions. They would be needed.

As well as moving 15,000 soldiers through the Assam jungle—a major feat in itself—Sato had also brought up 75-mm infantry guns to shell the ridge. Assault after assault by waves of fresh troops was launched against the hard-pressed defenders, the Japanese attacks being prefaced by short-range artillery bombardments and flurries of mortar bombs and grenades. Such overwhelming force began to have its effect and Richards's perimeter started to shrink as outlying positions became untenable. In one sector, only the width of a tennis court behind the Deputy Commissioner's bungalow separated the two forces.

Some remarkably accurate gunnery was demonstrated in the bungalow area also. The battery of the 20th Mountain Regiment had been unable to deploy under the close-range bombardment of the Japanese, but its officers now directed fire from the remaining guns of 24th Regiment on a hill at Jotsoma, 3km/2mls northwest of Kohima. There the whole brigade had been blocked by Sato's forces while on its

Supplies by air

In the Imphal-Kohima area, such roads as existed were mostly unsuitable for heavy traffic, except, of course, the main highway to India, which had been cut by the Japanese. The two main forms of transportation in this remote area were, therefore, mules and aircraft. Mules could withstand the heat and carry great amounts of food and ammunition through thick jungle and across narrow mountain passes. But with the simultaneous sieges of Kohima and Imphal, aircraft became of crucial importance, dropping supplies to the former and landing reinforcements, rations, munitions and equipment at the latter.

The ideal aircraft for the task was the Douglas Dakota, which could carry up to 3,400kg/7,500lb and was capacious enough to accommodate jeeps and mules. Secured on a platform, the pack animals were sometimes dropped by parachute to troops operating in inaccessible areas. They were usually loaded up and ready to move off within 20 minutes of landing.

The Dakotas, once they had completed their drops, landed on the nearest British or American jungle airstrip to pick up casualties and ferry them to hospitals in India. The Dakotas were made available largely as a result of a request from General Wavell, Commander-in-Chief India, to Winston Churchill in 1943. Hitherto, priority for all aircraft and supplies had been given to the Middle East theatre and to Europe.

A Dakota of 194 Squadron being loaded on 24 March 1944 with a jeep crammed with supplies. Airlifts were the quickest and surest means of supplying forward troops in the jungle.

After the Japanese had been repulsed in the Arakan, Lord Louis Mountbatten, Supreme Allied Commander South-East Asia, ordered 24 Dakotas to be transferred from China to airlift an entire division northward to the relief of Kohima and Imphal—the first time such an exercise had been undertaken on so great a scale in the Burma campaign.

194 Squadron earned the nickname of the 'Flying Elephants' from the emblem painted on the fuselage of their Hudsons and Dakotas. During March to July 1944, this squadron averaged more than 2,000 flying hours a month, principally in dropping supplies to the garrisons at Kohima and Imphal and to Chindit groups operating behind Japanese lines. It was part of 177 Wing, which in eight months had transported 31,217 troops and evacuated 28,898 casualties.

The defence of Imphal

When General Mutaguchi initiated the 'U-Go' attack by launching his Fifteenth Army at the British base on the Imphal plain early in March 1944, he expected to achieve his objectives within three weeks. This misplaced confidence led him to operate in difficult terrain with extended lines of communication and virtually no air cover. He calculated that infantry weapons, artillery and a few light tanks would be adequate to bring him victory. Moreover, he considered it unnecessary to provide his army with rations to last the campaign: when his troops had consumed the limited amount of food issued to them, he told them that they could capture and eat their enemy's supplies.

Mutaguchi ordered the 33rd Division up roads to the south and east of the plain, advanced the 15th Division around to the north and despatched the 31st Division to Kohima to sever Imphal's only road link. He was confident his plan was tactically sound and would lead to certain victory.

His assault columns at first came up against Lieutenant-General Scoones's 4th Corps. Scoones was expecting an attack and had prepared a defence plan. Advance units were to fall back on strong positions, from which they could defend the plain from encircling Japanese forces. There they would have to stand and fight but could ignore the need to keep open lines of communication with other units, for rations and ammunition were to be provided by air drops. Reinforcements were also to be flown in to the self-contained defensive box by the workhorse Dakotas.

The garrison of British, Indian and Ghurka troops, supported by the fire power of artillery, tanks and fighter and bomber aircraft, kept the Japanese at bay and finally forced them to retreat after inflicting enormous casualties on Mutaguchi's men, by then starving and ridden with disease.

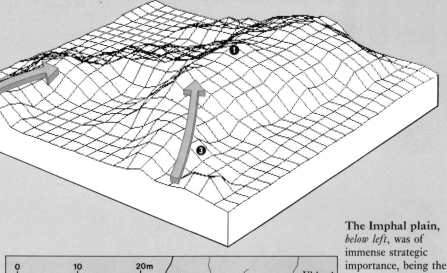

Troops of the Japanese 15th Division, *left*, first appeared on Nungshigum Hill (1) on 6 April 1944. Although driven off the following day, they returned in greater strength on 11 April and occupied the summit, threatening Imphal and its main airfield a few miles away on the plain below. On 13 April, after heavy air and artillery bombardment, the two steep spurs (2, 3) leading up to the Japanese positions were scaled by companies of infantry from the 1/17th Dogra Regiment; they were accompanied by six tanks. After heavy fighting, the Japanese were forced to withdraw.

The Imphal plain, *below left*, was of immense strategic importance, being the only place flat enough for airstrips. The British, since stemming the Japanese advance in May 1942, had developed it as a base from which to reconquer Burma.

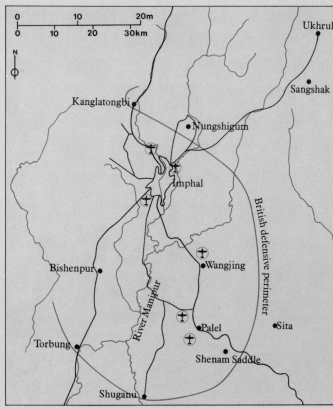

Troops and tanks, *above*, approaching Nungshigum in April 1944. The Japanese occupied the summit of the hill, which rose 305m/1,000ft above the surrounding plain and gave them an uninterrupted view of the British headquarters and main airfield at Imphal. To the British, it was imperative to drive them from such a commanding position. The earth, just prior to the monsoon period, was at its most parched, causing the tanks to throw up thick clouds of dust.

way yet again to assist Richards. The accuracy of the shooting was so great that they were laying a barrage of defensive fire just ahead of the garrison's positions.

For eight tough days the determined defenders amazingly succeeded in stopping Sato's onslaughts; then came the 'black 13th'. Japanese artillery found the range of the hospital trenches filled with wounded, and most of a parachute supply drop of much-needed water and mortar ammunition fell behind enemy lines, while the attacks by Sato's infantry reached a new peak of intensity.

The dwindling garrison had been sustained by repeated promises of relief from the nearby 161st Brigade and from elements of the British 2nd Division which were following it down the road from Dimapur; but their situation was now desperate. Even so, they had to find the power to resist for another four dreadful days before reinforcements finally broke through the Japanese roadblocks north of Kohima. When the relief forces arrived on 18 April, they found Richards and his men crowded into a stinking, shell-pocked box 320m/350yds square, battered but uncowed. They had suffered more than 600 casualties.

The battle of Kohima was, however, far from over. The Japanese had diverted part of their force to build a strong, fortified line in the pass which they now manned. Slim ordered Lieutenant-General M. Stopford of 33rd Corps, now commanding operations on the Kohima Front, to put relentless pressure on Sato and by mid-May the enemy, much depleted and without adequate supplies, was on the defensive and suffering, but not prepared to capitulate. The same situation applied all around the Imphal plain, though it was evident that the U-Go offensive was doomed.

Having built up a three-to-one superiority, Slim went over to the attack on all fronts; even when the monsoon broke at the end of May he insisted on momentum being maintained. Little by little, the Japanese were forced to give ground, and on 22 June the line of land communications was opened once more when tanks of the 2nd Division advancing from Kohima met an infantry patrol from the 5th Division coming up the road 16km/10mls north of Imphal.

Mutaguchi's Fifteenth Army was now in full retreat across the River Chindwin. In the prolonged battles around Kohima and Imphal the Japanese sustained 53,000 casualties, 30,000 of whom were dead. Slim, who had lost 16,000 men, could now commence the reconquest of Burma.

The monsoon, which regularly began in late May, was preceded by intermittent rain showers and long periods of intense heat. By June, however, downpours had turned the baked, dusty tracks into muddy swamps, *left*, while the rivers that irrigated the area swelled into torrents, *below*, making progress, which was always difficult, at times impossible.

The Burma Star

Servicing and repairing Hurricanes, *left*, was easier than with most other aircraft. Unlike more sophisticated machines, the Hurricane was constructed of wood and fabric with a metal-tube framework. This enabled mechanics familiar with the aircraft to service it in the field, rather than having to send it to repair factories in India.

The Burma Star, *left centre*, with its striking ribbon, was the campaign medal issued to all men and women who served in the South-East Asia Command during the years 1942–5.

The Commanders

General Sir William Slim (1891–1970), a man of outstandingly clear mind, imbued all those who served under him in the Fourteenth Army with confidence. Slim had always maintained that his best chance of re-entering Burma was by decisively defeating the Japanese before he crossed the River Chindwin, since if he did not, he feared they could concentrate overwhelming forces against him on the east bank. Thus the Japanese, by crossing the river to attack Imphal, gave him just the opportunity he had been seeking.

Lieutenant-General G.A.P. Scoones (1893–1975), an intellectual with an analytical mind, was considered by Slim to be the most intelligent senior officer on his front. Scoones's orders were 'to hold the Imphal Plain and destroy any enemy who entered it'; to do this, he formed defensive 'boxes' around strategic points. Scoones and Slim, in an otherwise superlative tactical action, made one miscalculation: they thought Mutaguchi could launch only one regiment against Kohima; in fact he succeeded in deploying a whole division.

Lieutenant-General Renya Mutaguchi (1888–1966), was a fearless, ruthlessly ambitious man who revelled in war. Following the Japanese occupation of Burma, he argued strongly that the mountainous, roadless jungle between Burma and India, the diseases indigenous to the area, and Japan's extended supply lines combined to make further advance perilous. Later, following Wingate's overcoming the problems of operating in the jungle, Mutaguchi changed his mind and decided to attack the British bases at Imphal and Kohima.

The Kohima Cross
Because of the extreme heat at Kohima, corpses had to be buried immediately. Makeshift crosses were erected by surviving soldiers and later a larger, more durable cross was made, *above*. This wooden cross is now preserved at Maidstone, Kent. The practice of units erecting monuments in memory of their comrades was rare in WWII although common in WWI. After the war, 1,287 British and Indian graves were gathered in a single cemetery and marked by an altar and a Cross of Sacrifice made from local stone. The inscription reads:

> **When you go home**
> **Tell them of us and say,**
> **For their tomorrow**
> **We gave our today.**

Kohima—Imphal: turning point in the East
After the decisive battles of Kohima and Imphal, the initiative in Burma passed irrevocably into Allied hands. The Japanese Army had suffered around 92,000 casualties—dead, wounded and missing—since the 1944 campaign began; the survivors, now inadequately supplied, were on the verge of starvation.

The Japanese, far from being reinforced, were actually shorn of units, Burma having become a low priority theatre for their High Command because US Pacific offensives were converging on mainland Japan. Moreover, Japanese losses at the Battles of the Coral Sea, Midway and Leyte Gulf had eliminated their navy as a competent fighting force.

In the air, too, the Allies had overwhelming superiority. By October 1944 they had 392 fighters and more than 150 bombers in the Burma theatre; the Japanese could muster only about 50 aircraft in operational condition. After Kohima and Imphal, Japan's Burma Area Army became outnumbered, ill-equipped, unsupplied and virtually cut off. Ultimate defeat was inevitable but most Japanese soldiers fought on with stubborn bravery, some isolated pockets of men holding out for years.

General Slim paid them tribute: 'We all talk about fighting to the last man and the last bullet. The Japanese soldier was the only one who did it.' He was also most generous in praise of his own troops. 'Burma was a *soldiers'* war', he wrote; 'It was they who turned Defeat into Victory.'

The Normandy Campaign/*June-August 1944*

On 6 June 1944—D-Day—the Allies stormed Hitler's 'Fortress Europe' with the most powerful invasion force ever assembled, so opening the Second Front, which Stalin had been demanding since 1941. But even before the Soviets began insisting on action to relieve German pressure on the Eastern Front—in fact, since shortly after the Dunkirk evacuation in 1940—the British had planned to carry the war back to Europe, 'if necessary, alone' in Prime Minister Winston Churchill's defiant words. It was a question of gathering sufficient men and *matériel* for the task, while resisting both the Axis and Japanese forces in other theatres; it took four years to do so.

The invasion of Europe was discussed when Churchill and Roosevelt met at Casablanca in January 1943, but it was not feasible that year: the resources were not available. It was agreed, however, to appoint the British Lieutenant-General Frederick Morgan as Chief of General Staff to the Supreme Allied Commander designate (COSSAC) to make a detailed plan for a full-scale assault on Occupied France. Morgan's scheme for an attack through Normandy beginning on 1 May 1944, codenamed 'Overlord', was approved at the planning conference held in August 1943 in Quebec and attended by Churchill and Roosevelt.

But it was not until December that the leader of the Allied Expeditionary Force was named: General Dwight D. Eisenhower, who had led the successful Allied landings in North Africa and Italy. The rest of the 'top brass' for Overlord were British—Deputy Supreme Commander, Air Chief Marshal Sir Arthur Tedder; Allied Naval Commander, Admiral Sir Bertram Ramsay; Allied Air Commander, Air Chief Marshal Sir Trafford Leigh-Mallory; Allied Ground Forces Commander, General Sir Bernard Law Montgomery.

The tempo of preparations for the invasion now increased dramatically. Both Eisenhower and Montgomery thought that the COSSAC assault plan was too weak on too narrow a front. A further two seaborne divisions and an airborne division were, therefore, added to the original five divisions for the initial assault, on a front extended from 56km/35mls to 80km/50mls in the Baie de Seine, east of the Cherbourg Peninsula. But this enlargement of the plan created a new problem: there were not enough landing craft. Eisenhower supplemented his fleet at the expense of General Sir Harold Alexander's campaign in Italy, and he put back the invasion date from May to June

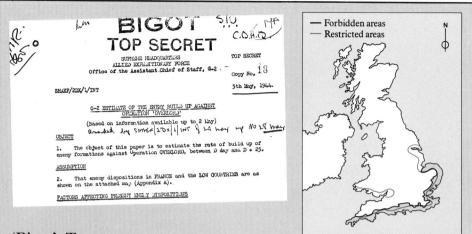

— Forbidden areas
— Restricted areas

'Bigot': Top secret

In the months leading up to the Normandy landings, the Western Allies had to ensure the Germans received no information about their plans. Elaborate precautions were taken to maintain secrecy, and access to large areas of Britain was severely restricted (*see map*). The highest security classification was codenamed 'Bigot', formed by the reverse spelling of 'To Gib', the stamp used on documents of personnel sent to Gibraltar. These papers could be seen by 'Bigots' only, a few people who had been positively vetted and cleared. All Bigots were kept under continual scrutiny and forbidden to take any action that might expose them to capture and interrogation.

There were many scares concerning documents classified as Bigot, the first occurring in March 1944 when the FBI found a parcel containing Bigot papers had accidentally broken open in a Chicago postal sorting office. In the event no damage was done, and despite such lapses, Bigot security was so tight that German Intelligence never discovered the landing points chosen by the Allies.

Snares and stratagems

Secrecy on its own was not enough. With hundreds of thousands of troops, their weapons and supplies, being assembled in southern England, it was impossible to disguise the fact that an invasion of Europe, almost certainly of northern France, was imminent. It might be possible, however, to deceive the Germans as to the exact location of the landings. A deception scheme was therefore devised.

While the invading force was assembling in southwest England, bogus camps, tanks and landing barges (*above*) were established in the southeast, to give the impression of an army in readiness. On D-Day, Allied aircraft dropped tons of metallic strips over the Calais area, and ships set others adrift; on German radar screens they appeared as aircraft and warships. In consequence, 19 German divisions were kept inactive around Calais, while nearly 322km/200mls to the southwest Allied forces were securing a bridgehead. So effective was this scheme that, for six weeks after the landings, Hitler still believed that the main attack was to come in the Pas de Calais.

The United Kingdom became an armed camp in the months immediately preceding the Normandy landings. All along the south coast, ports and harbours were crammed with shipping, *left*, weapons and supplies, and vast depots of additional supplies were sited inland. In the south of England, areas of flat ground everywhere had been turned into airfields; woods concealed military vehicles. And, for the time being, sealed camps became home for hundreds of thousands of Allied servicemen.

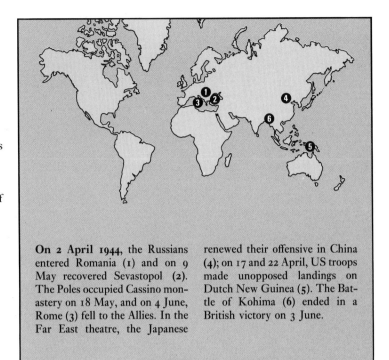

On 2 April 1944, the Russians entered Romania (1) and on 9 May recovered Sevastopol (2). The Poles occupied Cassino monastery on 18 May, and on 4 June, Rome (3) fell to the Allies. In the Far East theatre, the Japanese renewed their offensive in China (4); on 17 and 22 April, US troops made unopposed landings on Dutch New Guinea (5). The Battle of Kohima (6) ended in a British victory on 3 June.

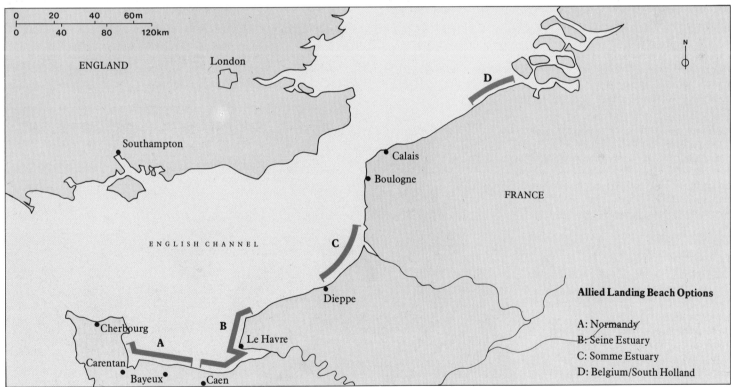

Allied Landing Beach Options

A: Normandy
B: Seine Estuary
C: Somme Estuary
D: Belgium/South Holland

The British started planning an invasion of Europe only days after France had capitulated to Germany. On the night of 23 June 1940, a flotilla of RAF high-speed launches carried about 100 British soldiers across the Channel to Boulogne and Le Touquet, where they attacked buildings occupied by Germans, killing two. The military effect of the raid was minimal, but as a gesture of defiance it was unsurpassed.

Then, in July 1941, when Great Britain was still on the defensive, the Inter-Services Training and Development Centre produced the first detailed plan for an amphibious assault on France. On 19 August the following year, Canadian and British assault troops sailed from the south of England to raid the harbour of Dieppe. They were repulsed with heavy losses, but the lessons learned proved to be invaluable in 1944.

The problems facing the Allies were similar to those that had deterred Hitler from invading England in 1940. Not least was the difficulty of finding the ideal spot at which to land. The Pas de Calais was rejected because the area was the most heavily fortified along the French coast.

Brittany was rejected as being too far from Germany, so entailing long lines of communication. To the east, Holland and Belgium could be quickly reinforced by the enemy.

This left only one possibility: the Cotentin Peninsula and the area around Caen, a lodgement bounded by the Seine, Eure and Loire rivers. Caen became the main objective, with a subsidiary attack on the east coast of the peninsula to facilitate the early capture of the port of Cherbourg.

133

so as to benefit from another month's production of landing craft.

In the months preceding the invasion, detailed reconnaissance was made of the Normandy coast. Information provided by daring aerial photographic runs was augmented by occasional clandestine visits to the shore to inspect the lie of the land and the defences that had been installed by the Germans. These were growing increasingly formidable as the weeks passed, thanks to the efforts of Field Marshal Erwin Rommel, who, in November 1943, had been appointed by Hitler to command Army Group B in France. He was given special responsibility for improving the inadequate fortifications all along the Atlantic Wall.

Rommel reinforced concrete bunkers and gun positions; strengthened and extended existing fieldworks and increased the number of machine-gun nests and mortar batteries. On the beaches, various devices—some explosive, some simply obstacles—were liberally distributed to deter landing craft. From the outset, Rommel was convinced that the war would be won or lost on the beaches, a

view not held by his immediate superior, Field Marshal Gerd von Rundstedt, Commander-in-Chief West, who planned to cut off and destroy the invaders as they moved inland. To attempt this, Rundstedt had Army Groups B and G, commanded respectively by Rommel and Colonel-General Johannes Blaskowitz, and Panzer Group West under General Geyr von Schweppenburg.

He had 38 infantry divisions on coast defence duty, stretching from Holland to the Franco-Spanish border and along the south of France; seven reserve divisions were concentrated in the Pas de Calais sector and three in Normandy. Four of his ten panzer divisions formed the mobile strategic reserve to deal with an invasion. Hitler gave Rommel control of one panzer

division, the 21st; the other three were to remain uncommitted until Hitler ordered them to move. The Luftwaffe in France mustered only 160 serviceable aircraft, 70 fighters and 90 bombers; and the Kriegsmarine had only a few destroyers, E-boats and U-boats in the Channel.

Against this motley assortment of German forces was arrayed the accumulated strength of the Western Allies—39 divisions (20 US, 14 British, 3 Canadian, 1 Free French and 1 Polish); nearly 11,000 combat aircraft (of which 5,000 were fighters); 2,300 transport planes and 2,600 gliders; and more than 6,000 warships, transports and landing craft.

The assault was to be led by specially developed 'swimming tanks' and other ingenious armoured vehicles. Supplies

In the early hours of the invasion, it was essential for the Allies to safeguard the flanks of the beachhead by preventing the Germans from bringing in reinforcements. Eisenhower had total air superiority, but his aircraft could not take out small targets at night or in bad weather, so he decided to use airborne troops to seize strongpoints, blow up or secure bridges and keep the Germans off balance and confused. The task of seizing and holding the Caen Canal bridge at Bénouville and the River Orne bridge at Ranville on the left flank was given to the British 6th Airborne Division. These crucial targets were about 0.4km/¼ml apart on the coast road.

The three Horsa gliders assigned to the capture of the bridge at Bénouville (1), later renamed Pegasus Bridge after the airborne troops' insignia, followed each other a minute apart. The Germans had begun digging holes (10) for 'Rommel's Asparagus'—poles designed to rip open the bellies of landing gliders; it seemed they expected an attack.

The first glider (7) came in at 00.16 and had to use its chute to reduce speed; this lifted the tail, and it ploughed into a barbed wire fence and smashed the nose. The pilot and co-pilot, still strapped into their seats, were thrown out of the cockpit unconscious—the first

Allied troops to land on French soil. Inside the Horsa, everyone was momentarily knocked senseless. Major John Howard, the commander, hit the roof, and his helmet smashed down over his eyes; when he came to, he at first thought he had been wounded and blinded.

The pilot had, nevertheless, brought the glider down in exactly the right place by the canal (3). Within seconds the men regained consciousness, leaped out and went for their target. Luckily a German anti-tank gun (6) beside the bridge was unmanned.

The first landing achieved complete surprise. Two teenage sentries pacing the bridge in opposite directions, mistook the crash of the glider's landing for a piece of a damaged Allied bomber hitting the ground.

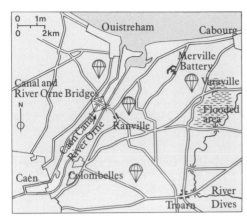

One minute later, the second glider (8) landed, and its contingent joined the first group at the east end of the bridge. Their primary task was to clear the trenches on the far side of the road of German troops and take out a pillbox (4).

As they ran across the road, the third glider (9) crash-landed and the unit's doctor, sitting behind the pilot, was thrown through the windscreen.

As Howard and his men cleared the trenches and pillbox, more troops from the first and second gliders stormed the bridge from the eastern end. One of the German sentries fled to the western end, shouting 'Paratroopers! Paratroopers!' His comrade fired his Very pistol (2) and was immediately cut down.

Some men (5) ran over the bridge to seize the Gondrée café (11) and other buildings, while the sappers removed demolition fuses from the bridge but found no explosives. Within 10 minutes of landing, the small force had captured the bridge; they held it for two hours until relieved by men from the main drop farther east of Ranville.

would be landed at two huge artificial harbours and fuel would be pumped direct to Normandy from England via Pluto (Pipeline Under the Ocean).

The Germans realized that an invasion was likely in the summer of 1944, but the exact date and location remained the best-kept secret of the war. Indeed, the Allies mounted a complex and successful deception operation to convince the enemy that the Pas de Calais coast was the target.

Following the postponement of Overlord in May, the first period offering the desired combination of a moonlit night and a low tide just after dawn was 5, 6 and 7 June; Eisenhower settled for 5 June. When June arrived, however, the weather deteriorated to such an extent that the worried General delayed the operation for 24 hours. At a meeting of his senior commanders at 04.00 on 5 June, meteorologists cautiously forecasted a limited break in the bad weather next day. Balancing this option against a prolonged delay, Eisenhower opted for 6 June with the laconic words, 'OK, we'll go.'

The Germans were confused. On the evening of 5 June, they had heard the BBC broadcast two lines from Paul Verlaine's poem 'Chanson d' Automne' and correctly identified them as the signal to the French Resistance that an invasion was imminent; yet the weather was so bad that such an attack seemed inconceivable. Rommel certainly thought so, for he decided to take leave to visit his wife. Then, on the night of 5–6 June, the Germans picked up signs on their radar of surface and air activity in the Boulogne and Dieppe areas. There were also reports of parachute drops. It was all part of a clever Allied plan to rivet enemy attention on the wrong localities.

Meanwhile, as an immense fleet of warships and troop carriers steamed toward Normandy under cover of darkness, British and American glider and parachute forces landed behind enemy coastal defences to secure the flanks of the beachhead, which was divided into five zones: Utah, Omaha, Gold, Juno and Sword.

The British 6th Airborne Division went in to cover Sword Beach on the Allied left flank and achieved all its objectives, including the daring capture of the two bridges over the Caen Canal and the River Orne. Two US airborne divisions, the 82nd and the 101st, protected the area inland from Utah Beach on the right flank, but their drop was much more scattered and they suffered more casualties than the British. Some German troops were aware of the airborne assaults and did their best to repel them, but the coastal defences were, inexplicably, not put on full alert.

The Mulberry harbours

Transporting a huge invasion force to Normandy, and successfully landing it in the face of determined opposition, posed difficult and diverse problems; no less difficult was the task of keeping the troops supplied once they were established ashore. Since it was perilous, if not actually impossible, to mount a head-on attack against one of the heavily defended ports, such as Cherbourg, the Allies built artificial harbours that could be towed in sections to the landing points and assembled there.

This top-secret project, codenamed 'Mulberry', was approved at the Quebec conference in August 1943, and completion was called for by 1 May 1944. In just seven months, 20,000 workers in construction firms throughout Britain succeeded in producing two enormous prefabricated ports, each as big as Dover Harbour, which could be towed to the French coast. In charge of assembling and placing the Mulberry harbours was Rear-Admiral W.G. Tennant, who, in 1940, had masterminded the evacuation at Dunkirk.

On D-Day + 1, the first 45 of 70 old ships were sunk at Arromanches off the British beaches, and at St Laurent off the American beaches, to form breakwaters; then the sections of the harbours were floated into position. The British harbour made an enormous contribution to the success of the campaign, but the American harbour at St Laurent was so badly damaged on 19 June by the worst storm in the Channel for 80 years that it was never completed.

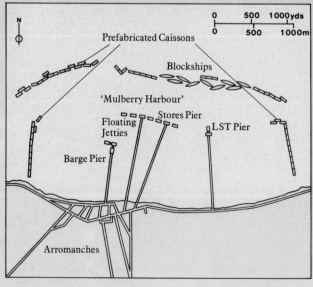

More than two million tons of steel and concrete were towed to the French coast to build the Mulberry harbours. Concrete caissons—some 18m/6oft high and weighing 6,000 tons—formed the outer walls of the harbours. Inside, hydraulically operated piers, which rose and fell with the tide, were connected to land by floating roadways. The British Mulberry, *left*, handled 12,000 tons of cargo and 2,500 vehicles a day.

The capture of Pointe-du-Hoc

The slaughter and confusion on 'Easy Red' was more than matched by the scene 8km/5mls to the west at Pointe-du-Hoc, a commanding promontory, on top of which the Americans believed there was a powerful German battery of six 155-mm guns. These had a range of more than 19km/12mls, and dominated the coast from Port-en-Bessin in the British sector to a point northwest of Utah Beach. It was fear of the power and range of these guns that led to the US landing craft being lowered some 18km/11mls offshore, subjecting the troops to an exhausting three-hour ride through rough seas.

The US Rangers, who had been training for weeks in similar conditions, were given the dangerous task of scaling the cliffs under concentrated fire to silence the guns. Some 200 Rangers, equipped with rocket guns firing grapnels, ropes and ladders, were to be put ashore at H-Hour. Their landing craft, however, moved east of the landing site; when the error was discovered, they had to approach it by a course parallel to the shore, exposing them to fire from the cliff top. A number of vessels were sunk; others were so badly damaged their cargo had to be jettisoned.

The pre-invasion naval bombardment had stopped when the Rangers reached their correct landing point, and the Germans had remanned the fortifications. Soaked, suffering from seasickness, and under heavy small-arms and grenade attack from above, the Rangers battled to scale the cliff. To assist them, the US destroyer *Satterlee* opened fire on German positions on Pointe-du-Hoc, enabling the first men to reach the top within five minutes of landing on the beach.

When they reached the summit, the Rangers found that the guns, the destruction of which had been the object of their desperate endeavour, were no longer there. To save them from earlier aerial and naval bombardment, the Germans had moved them to a more secure site, an orchard 1.6km/1ml inland, where the Rangers later discovered them; they had never been fired. Having taken Pointe-du-Hoc, the Rangers moved on to cut the coastal highway between Vierville and Grandcamp and establish a defensive position there.

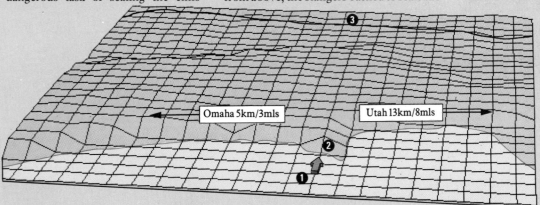

Omaha 5km/3mls

Utah 13km/8mls

Coastal artillery, such as the German 155-mm gun battery at Pointe-du-Hoc, needed the correct type of fire control equipment to perform its principal task —the destruction of enemy warships. Coastal artillery always outgunned ships because its firing platform was more stable and its range was greater than that of all but the biggest naval guns.

Before the main American landings began on Omaha and Utah Beaches at 06.30 on 6 June, a raiding force of 225 US Rangers (1) went ashore to knock out a German gun position on top of Pointe-du-Hoc (2), which dominated both landing areas. After scaling the 30-m/100-ft cliff under strong attack, the Rangers found that the heavy artillery had been removed. Later they came across—and destroyed—the missing guns near the main road (3) a short distance inland from their original position.

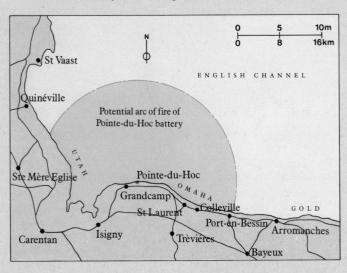

Rangers scaling the cliffs at Pointe-du-Hoc

waves of landing craft were unloading men and vehicles wherever possible. Timetables and plans were forgotten as confused, displaced units sought whatever cover they could.

This was the scene on the Easy Red sector in the centre of Omaha Beach as Bradley weighed his options. In the event, he

decided not to withdraw and gradually, with the arrival of tanks, artillery and supporting gunfire from destroyers operating close inshore, the battered infantry managed to break out, storm the hills above the beach and establish a firm foothold.

The landing area stretched for 6km/4mls between Vierville in the west and Colleville in the east. The entire length of the beach was backed by grassy slopes, 46km/150ft high (**1**), which provided ideal defensive positions for the Germans.

On the ridge, which commanded an unbroken field of fire over the shore, the

Germans had eight heavy guns, 35 anti-tank guns and 85 machine-guns in well-fortified positions (**2**). They had taken care to bracket the four exits leading up from the beach (**3**). In addition to this formidable fire power, there were infantry with small-arms, grenades and mortars.

The area between the slopes and the concrete sea wall was wired and mined (**4**). Without the benefit of armoured vehicles designed to clear such obstacles quickly, men of the 16th Infantry Regiment (**5**) were exposed to enemy fire for long periods as they tried to force their way through.

Obstacles of many types were placed at random on the beach below the high-water mark to impede landing craft; some had mines attached to them (**6**). This type (**7**) was called a hedgehog by the Allies. As they waded ashore under heavy fire, US soldiers turned the presence of the obstacles to advantage by taking cover behind them.

Omaha Beach

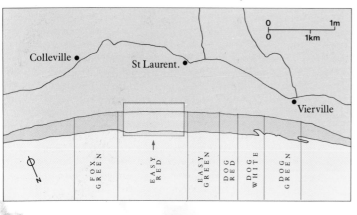

Between 08.00 and 09.00 on 6 June, the American forces on Omaha Beach seemed in so perilous a position that the US commander, General Omar Bradley, considered withdrawing them.

The bombardment of enemy positions by warships and aircraft before H-Hour—06.30—had been ineffective. Rough seas, whipped up by the deteriorating weather, swamped almost all the amphibious tanks; the shore was littered with corpses and vehicles, caught by heavy, accurate German fire, which also pinned down those troops who had gained the shelter of the narrow shelf of shingle.

The opposition was much fiercer than the veteran US 1st Infantry Division had been led to expect because the Germans' crack 352nd Division had moved into the area.

To add to the chaos and confusion on this stretch of the Normandy coastline, following

D-Day

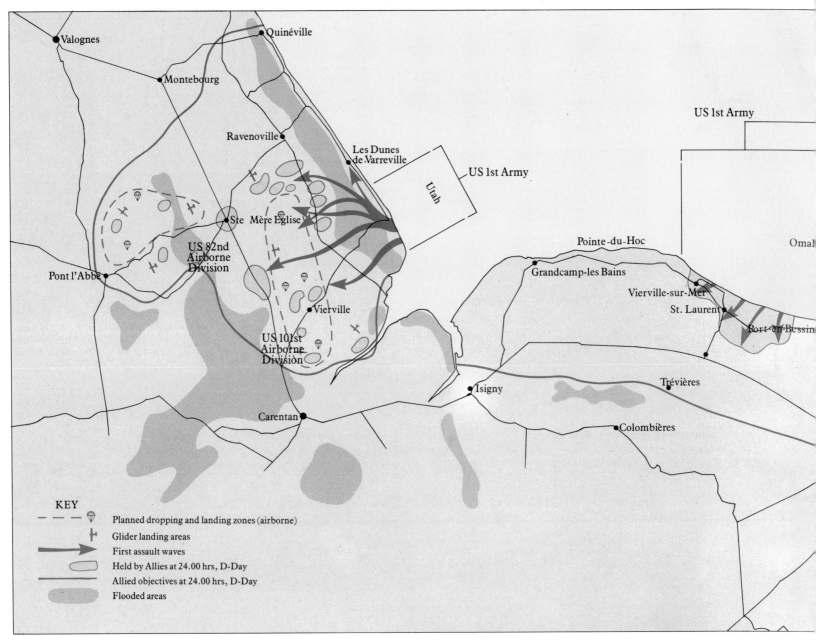

KEY

- ⛑ Planned dropping and landing zones (airborne)
- ⊬ Glider landing areas
- ➤ First assault waves
- ◯ Held by Allies at 24.00 hrs, D-Day
- —— Allied objectives at 24.00 hrs, D-Day
- ▨ Flooded areas

The logistical and tactical problems of invading France were dauntingly numerous and complex, but the strategy was simple.

The US First Army was to land on two beaches, Utah and Omaha, while their 82nd and 101st Airborne Divisions dropped to the west to protect the Army's right flank and, with the Utah forces, to cut off the Cotentin Peninsula. The British were to land on Gold and Sword Beaches, and the Canadians on

Juno, with the object of rapidly overrunning the communications centres of Bayeux and Caen. Their exposed eastern flank was guarded by the 6th Airborne Division.

Follow-up forces were to be brought in speedily, both to resist counter-attacks and to build up numbers for a breakout into northern France. The plan was to land eight divisions on D-Day, a further five by D-Day + 1 and 21 more by D-Day + 12.

Many of the US

airborne troops were captured; others dropped into meadows flooded by the Germans to defeat such a landing. The paratroopers were so dispersed that they spent most of the first day regrouping. On Omaha Beach, disaster was only narrowly averted, and 2,500 US soldiers became casualties. Progress by the British forces was encouraging: by the end of the first day they were 10km/6mls inland and were poised to take Caen.

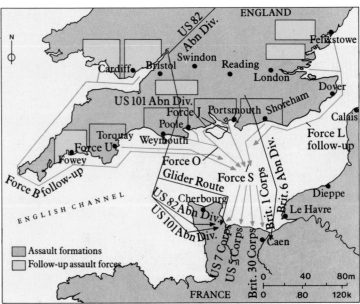

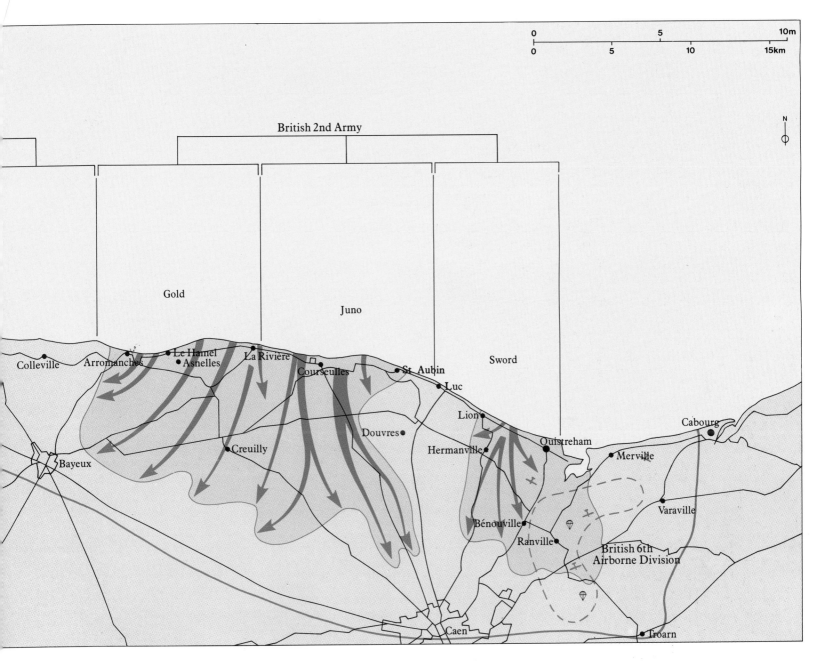

British 2nd Army

Gold

Juno

Sword

Colleville
Arromanches
Le Hamel
Asnelles
La Rivière
Courseulles
St Aubin
Luc
Lion
Douvres
Hermanville
Ouistreham
Cabourg
Merville
Bayeux
Creuilly
Bénouville
Ranville
Varaville
British 6th
Airborne Division
Caen
Troarn

0   5   10m
0   5   10   15km

N

German engineers,
above, running for
cover as an Allied
aircraft flies low to
photograph beach
obstacles.

The commissioning
of a massive German
15-in gun, *below*, one
of many along the
Atlantic Wall.

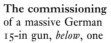

Omaha Beach stretched for 6km/4mls between the towns of Colleville (1) and Vierville (2). The whole landing zone was overlooked by fortified high ground. This part of the Normandy coast, the target of two US infantry regiments, was divided by the Americans into six sectors. The 116th Regiment landed on Dog Green (8) Dog White (7) Dog Red (6) and Easy Green (5), while the 16th Regiment went in on Easy Red (4) and Fox Green (3). Ernest Hemingway, the author, was on Fox Green and wrote an account of the carnage. The arrows show the direction US troops took up the heights, after being pinned down on the shore.

Only a handful of Sherman DD (duplex drive) amphibious tanks (8) reached the shore with the first wave on this part of Omaha Beach; they were insufficient to make a significant impact on the German defences. As the morning wore on, however, more tanks (9) and artillery landed and began to take out gun positions and pillboxes.

Once ashore, the shingle shelf (10) that ran almost the whole length of the beach was the only protection US soldiers had from ferocious enemy fire. If they were to move inland at all, gaps had to be made in the bank of loose stones to allow tanks and other vehicles to pass through. It was not until 10.00, when the rising tide was approaching the shingle, that engineers managed to make the necessary openings.

Some landing craft were blown up by direct hits, others had their bottoms ripped out by obstacles hidden under the water as the tide rose. Only a few marked channels through these obstacles had been made by demolition teams, so a huge jam of landing craft built up offshore.

American casualties were heavy on Omaha Beach and particularly so on Easy Red sector. Dead and wounded lay sprawled over the entire beach, and bodies bobbed in the water as the tide came in. Discarded equipment and the wreckage of landing craft were also strewn along the shore.

v

Reinforcements for the US Army, *top left*, crammed aboard a landing craft on their way to Normandy on 12 June 1944. Their cheerfulness and confidence stem from the knowledge that the Allied foothold in France, though limited, was by then secure.

LSTs discharging their cargo at Omaha Beach, *left centre*, on the afternoon of D-Day + 1. Massed ships at sea await their turn to unload. By midnight on 6 June, more than a quarter of a million men were ashore in Normandy.

Frenchmen greeting a soldier of the 1st Battalion, The Hampshire Regiment in Arromanches on D-Day, *left below*. Not all the French were overjoyed at being liberated, since warfare disrupted their lives, destroyed their homes and farms and exposed them to danger.

Paratroopers of the British 6th Airborne Division, *below*, dropped in advance of the glider landings, guard crossroads near Pegasus Bridge on D-Day. Many gliders broke up on landing, but the action was totally successful.

Hobart's 'Funnies'

Winston Churchill, haunted by the high casualties sustained by the invading infantry in the Gallipoli campaign of WWI, was determined to keep Allied losses to the minimum when Europe was invaded. His fears of a bloodbath were heightened in August 1942, when a raid in strength on Dieppe was repulsed on the shoreline with heavy loss. It was clear that some sort of specialized armour would be needed to go in ahead of the infantry to clear paths through the Germans' coastal defences.

In March 1943, Major-General Percy Hobart was given command of the 79th Armoured Division and ordered to devise means of breaching the Atlantic Wall. Working at speed, he and his team produced an imaginative selection of bizarre but effective tanks in time for the D-Day landings. These machines undoubtedly saved many lives, particularly on the British beaches where they were widely used. The Americans were offered 'Hobart's Funnies', but they showed interest only in the amphibious Shermans. The heavy casualties suffered by the US Army on Omaha Beach might have been avoided had specialist British armour been deployed.

Major-General Percy Hobart was serving with the Home Guard when he was given command of the 79th Armoured Division. An expert on armoured warfare, Hobart was appointed by the Chief of the Imperial General Staff, Sir Alan Brooke, who recognized in this eccentric officer the innovative talent needed to design special tanks with which to break through the defences of Atlantic Wall.

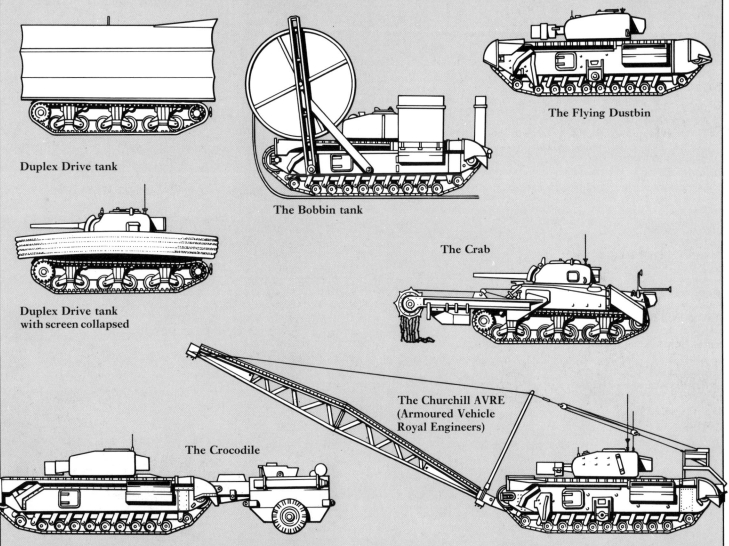

Duplex Drive tank

The Bobbin tank

The Flying Dustbin

Duplex Drive tank with screen collapsed

The Crab

The Crocodile

The Churchill AVRE (Armoured Vehicle Royal Engineers)

Duplex Drive tank
This 33-ton Sherman MkIV—the 'swimming tank'—amphibious once waterproofed, was fitted with twin propellers and given an inflatable canvas screen for buoyancy.

The Bobbin tank
Churchill tanks were adapted to lay a roadway over sand or soft ground. They carried 34m/110yds of tough fibre matting on a spool 3m/10ft wide, hanging over the front.

The Crab
A Sherman tank with revolving chain flails fitted on the front became an effective minesweeper. In an hour it could clear a path 3m/10ft wide and 2.5km/1½mls long.

The Churchill AVRE
This version of the tank carried a small box-girder bridge, capable of supporting a load of 40 tons. A gap 9m/30ft wide could be bridged in 30 seconds.

The Flying Dustbin
This Churchill tank, fitted with a 290-mm mortar, could fire an 18-kg/40-lb shell, shaped like a dustbin, three times a minute. It was used to smash concrete strongpoints.

The Crocodile
This version of the Churchill MkVII carried a flame-thrower, with a range of 110m/120yds, mounted on its hull; it towed a 1,018-l/400-gal fuel tank.

Each seaborne landing was timed for one hour after low water, but because the tide in the Channel rises earlier at the Cherbourg Peninsula end of the beaches, the Americans had to hit Utah and Omaha at 06.30, while the British and Canadians had to wait until 07.25 before conditions were right on Gold, Juno and Sword.

Not one of the Allied landings was driven back into the sea as Rommel wanted. On Utah, the thrust of the 4th US Infantry Division, led by amphibious Sherman tanks, had little difficulty in cracking the Atlantic Wall, held as it was by second-rate troops. They advanced 10km/6mls on 6 June and made contact with the 101st Airborne Division.

At Omaha Beach, regimental combat teams from the 1st US Infantry Division, supported by only five swimming tanks, were met by well-directed fire from the sole veteran German infantry unit then in Normandy, the newly arrived 352nd Divi-sion. Having declined the use of British armoured vehicles designed to clear a path through minefields, those American in-fantrymen who survived the dangerous sprint up the beach found themselves pinned down in the dubious shelter of a 6m/20ft wide shelf of shingle running the length of their front. In the face of heavy casualties, General Omar Bradley, com-manding the US forces from a warship offshore, seriously considered abandoning the Omaha landings. By 11.00, however, his infantry was making headway against the German positions, and eventually pushed through their defences as far as the coast road.

The British forces that assaulted Gold Beach between Asnelles and La Rivière at 07.25 comprised the 50th Infantry Divi-sion and the 8th Armoured Brigade, whose tanks stormed the German defences. The heaviest fighting took place at the village of Le Hamel, which was garrisoned by a detachment of the crack German 352nd Division. But soon the Gold beachhead was 13km/8mls deep.

On Juno Beach, stretching either side of the fishing village of Courseulles, the 3rd Canadian Infantry Division encountered strong opposition as they waded ashore. Although initially unsupported by tanks because of the difficulty of landing them in rough seas, the Canadian troops smashed aside enemy resistance and pushed 11km/7mls inland. The last Allied landing area, Sword Beach, extended from Lion sur Mer to the mouth of the River Orne at Ouistreham. There the 3rd British Infan-try Division and the 27th Armoured Brigade overcame all coastal strongpoints, repulsed a counter-attack and carved out a perimeter 10km/6mls wide and deep.

By the close of 6 June, the Allies had more than 150,000 troops and their equip-ment ashore and had seized some 207sq km/80sq mls of Occupied France. Their

British landings on Gold Beach began at 07.25 on 6 June. On the right flank, at Le Hamel, A and B Companies of the 1st Battalion, The Hampshire Regiment, led the way ashore, followed 20 minutes later by C and D Companies—seen here under heavy artillery and small-arms fire as they closed with the powerful beach defences. The landing might well have been repulsed by units of the German 352nd Division had it not been for the tanks, notably Hobart's 'Funnies', which enabled the Hampshires to force a gap through the barbed wire and minefields east of the strongly defended town of Le Hamel.

Le Hamel presented a formidable target for the Hampshires. The terrain was typical of that part of the coast—a flat, sandy beach, bounded by a belt of low sand dunes. A gentle slope led up to a sea wall and the inland plateau.

The German gun positions had interlocking fields of fire over the beach. At the eastern end, in Le Hamel, there was a concealed battery of 75-mm guns (8), capable of enfilading the entire beach. Machine-gunners and riflemen were stationed in every building overlooking the shore. Le Hamel itself was protected on three sides by an anti-tank ditch.

The Germans had transformed the area into a fortress. The beach had been littered with some 2,500 obstacles, mostly of the tetrahedral type (2)—triangular steel cones, 0.8m/2½ft or 1.2m/4ft high. These were embedded in the sand, and were invisible at high tide; they could rip open the bottom of a landing craft. At the top of the sandy slope, a continuous barrier of barbed wire had been laid in front of a concrete wall (7), which was interrupted by strongpoints, guarded by more barbed wire and minefields.

Four of the five flail tanks (3) landed were destroyed as they made their way toward Le Hamel. Rough seas prevented DD tanks being 'swum' ashore, delaying their arrival until the LCTs could run them on to the beach. The men of the Hampshires were thus temporarily without the support of heavy weapons, and a breakdown in radio communications stopped their calling on the Navy's guns for assistance.

Tanks—both Shermans (4) and 'Funnies' (1)—went ashore on LCTs (5). While flail tanks whipped the sand to detonate mines, the bobbins laid matting over patches of soft, treacherous blue clay. Bridging tanks laboured over the beach, straddling craters and anti-tank barriers with narrow box girders.

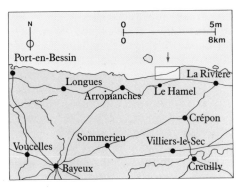

C and D Companies (6) made for the shelter of the sea wall. They grouped east of Le Hamel and at 09.00 exploited a gap forced in the coastal wire and minefield belt to capture the village of Asnelles.

Le Hamel had been so heavily fortified that earlier aerial and naval bombardments had failed to destroy it. The Hampshires, having forced a flanking movement from Asnelles, managed to storm it from the rear in mid-afternoon—eight hours after landing—in heavy house-to-house fighting.

casualties were low, considering the size of the operation—about 6,000 Americans and 3,500 British and Canadians had been killed or wounded.

There was much against the Germans: Rommel and other senior commanders were away from the front when the blow fell; lack of transport prevented rapid deployment of their infantry; and contradictory orders kept the only panzer division near the coast moving ineffectually to and fro. Meanwhile, three other panzer divisions remained idle because nobody was willing to wake the sleeping Führer to tell him of the invasion and seek his permission to commit the tank reinforcements to battle.

Despite overwhelming evidence to the contrary, Hitler, Rommel and the rest of the German High Command decided that the Normandy landings were subsidiary to a main assault on the Pas de Calais coast. Their first-rate Fifteenth Army was kept on alert around Boulogne, and only the panzers were finally released to bear the brunt of the invasion. Soon the German military realized their error as the Allied hold on Normandy strengthened.

Hitler alone remained unconvinced, and to counteract the big attack he was still sure would come across the short Channel route, he ordered the use of the first *Vergeltungswaffen* (reprisal weapons), the V1 flying bomb. On 13 June, the first of 2,000 V1s fell on London's civilian population, beginning a terror campaign which had no influence on Allied military operations. Had the flying bombs been aimed at harbours such as Portsmouth or Southampton, through which supplies were being shipped to Normandy, they might have affected the progress and conduct of the battle.

Even though Allied advances after D-Day were slowed to a crawl, particularly by ambushes among the hedgerows of the *bocage* country, both Rundstedt and Rommel realized that their only hope lay in retreating to form a new defence line. But Hitler would have none of it. On 18 June, the Americans cut off the huge fortified port of Cherbourg when they gained control of the Cotentin Peninsula. The next day it became imperative that the docks were captured, for the worst summer storm in the Channel for 80 years blew up, destroying the US Mulberry harbour and damaging the British one.

At the end of June, while the Anglo-American forces were still making only limited progress, Rundstedt and Rommel again pleaded with Hitler to permit them to carry out a strategic withdrawal to the River Seine. This the Führer refused.

The French Resistance

Members of the French Resistance were of value to the Allies in two respects. First, they were numerous—it is thought that there were about 50,000 along the Atlantic Wall alone. Although, individually, they provided only snippets of information, when collected and passed through MI6 to the Intelligence cell in London, these helped to build up a reliable picture of German troop dispositions and fortifications. Photographs, surreptitiously taken, conversations overheard, troop movements observed—all were reported to London.

The French Resistance was not, however, a single body under an overall command but comprised disparate groups, most concerned not only, or principally, with aiding the Allied war effort but in securing a vantage point from which to take power in liberated France. There was, also, a second, more ambitious aim in the French Resistance: to build their units into a strategic, fighting weapon. Throughout the country, but particularly in the north in the months before the invasion, groups of Resistance fighters blew up bridges, derailed trains and assassinated German servicemen. Often these efforts were coordinated by British and Free French agents who had been parachuted in or landed by aircraft, together with weapons and supplies.

In all occupied countries, patriots defied the Germans, risking interrogation under torture and almost certain execution if they were captured, and sometimes exposing whole communities to reprisals by their clandestine activities.

Shortly before D-Day, Allied bombers intensified their attacks on the French railway system and took out major road and rail bridges over the Seine, Eure and Loire rivers, which formed the boundary to the proposed lodgement area, *left*. German troop and tank movements were further hindered by the French Resistance, who also destroyed bridges, ambushed troops and derailed trains, *above*.

The Commanders

Von Kluge   Von Rundstedt   Model   Eisenhower   Leigh-Mallory   Tedder

Field Marshal Guenther von Kluge (1882–1944) had been Commander-in-Chief of the Central Front in Russia and in 1944 briefly commanded the German Army in the west. Though he was servile to Hitler, hypnotized by his personality and overawed by his earlier military triumphs, von Kluge was implicated in the attempt on Hitler's life in July 1944 and replaced; he committed suicide on 18 August.

Field Marshal Gerd von Rundstedt (1875–1953) was transferred, after service in Russia, to overall command in the west in 1942. With the exception of an interlude between July and September 1944, he remained in that post until the end of the war. There was friction between von Rundstedt and his subordinate, Field Marshal Rommel, commander of Army Group B in northern France. Rommel believed that the Allied invasion must be stopped on the beaches; Rundstedt, on the other hand, held that the invaders should be halted and destroyed in the interior.

Unlike von Rundstedt, who was an aristocrat, contemptuous of the Nazis and not involved in politics, **Field Marshal Walther Model** (1891–1945) was a dedicated Nazi and one of Hitler's favourite commanders. He held a number of commands on the Eastern Front, halted the Soviet offensive near Warsaw in 1944 and succeeded von Kluge in France as Commander-in-Chief West. After the disaster at Falaise, Model supervised the German withdrawal; later he oversaw the defence of Arnhem. He shot himself in 1945, when defeat was inevitable.

A new, younger type of Allied commander was appointed after the disasters of Dunkirk and Pearl Harbor. The outstanding example was **General Dwight D. Eisenhower** (1890–1969), the Supreme Allied Commander of the Allied landings in Normandy. Prior to 1942 he had been a staff officer and had never commanded troops in battle, but despite this he was given charge of the 'Torch' landings in

North Africa and the subsequent campaigns in Tunisia and Italy. He was surprised at his appointment to command 'Operation Overlord', a responsibility given to him because of his bold, original thinking, his strength of character and coolness under stress, and his ability to ensure cooperation between his senior subordinates.

Sir Trafford Leigh-Mallory (1892–1944) commanded the Allied Expeditionary Air Force for the Normandy invasion. Unlike Eisenhower, he aroused considerable personal animosity, caused friction with the Americans and often seemed hesitant or pessimistic. He was killed in 1944 when his aircraft crashed.

An air commander of completely different character was **Sir Arthur Tedder** (1890–1967), a man of cool mind, wit and the ability to work unceasingly for the Allied cause. He had commanded the RAF in the Middle East (1941–3) and became General Eisenhower's deputy.

A20 Boston medium bombers of the US Ninth Air Force attacked the six-gun battery at Pointe-du-Hoc, west of Omaha Beach, before the Allied landings.

The chief burden of maintaining pressure on Germany had long been laid on the air forces; indeed, both invaders and defenders believed that a landing in France would be impossible without overwhelming air superiority. John Ehrmann in his book *Grand Strategy*, wrote: 'Without the reduction of the Luftwaffe's capacity and the widespread delay of movement by land, the assault might well have failed'; and after

the war, Gerd von Rundstedt succinctly remarked, 'It was all a question of air force, air force and again air force.'

By June 1944, the Luftwaffe had been almost swept from the skies, and very much greater numbers of better-armed Allied aircraft played the part that German aircraft had taken in the blitzkrieg against the Low Countries and France in 1940. They dropped paratroops and supplies, searched out and destroyed enemy fortifications, and so crippled roads and railways that the Germans had immense difficulty in bringing up reinforcements.

Rundstedt was furious and, on 2 July, after remarking that the only thing the Germans could sensibly do in Normandy was to sue for peace, he was replaced by Field Marshal Guenther Hans von Kluge.

In spite of spirited resistance by the panzers, the Allies were starting to push out their perimeter. On 9 July, British and Canadian forces finally captured Caen, which had, in fact, been one of the objectives on the first day of the invasion. A week later, to the south, the Americans took the key town of St Lô. Everything was now poised for a break-out.

Montgomery planned to make a major attack southward from Caen toward Falaise on 18 July. Apart from inflicting considerable damage on the enemy, Montgomery's aim was to draw off German forces from Bradley's front at St Lô, allowing him to smash through their consequently weakened defences. Then to the Germans' great dismay, Rommel was seriously wounded on 17 July when his staff car was strafed.

'Operation Goodwood', Montgomery's attack, was not entirely successful. An immense aerial and naval bombardment failed to neutralize the panzers and artillery, which knocked out over 400 British tanks. And before heavy rain put a stop to armoured operations, the Germans had started to move up reinforcements.

Less than a week later, in good weather, Bradley opened a blitzkrieg offensive around St Lô and achieved the desired breakthrough. Into the gap poured Major-General George S. Patton's newly formed US Third Army, with one column on the left swinging north behind the Germans and another driving west into Brittany.

Shortly afterward, to the horror of Kluge and his generals, Hitler ordered all his available panzers—about 250 tanks—supported by infantry, to counter-attack inside the area, which was being sealed off from the north by the British and Canadians and from the west and south by the Americans. The US forces made for Falaise to join the Canadians, advancing from the north to close the battered and almost surrounded enemy's last line of retreat. The Canadians did not, however, arrive before the German withdrawal began and, though the slaughter and destruction were terrible, perhaps as many as 30,000 enemy troops managed to escape before the remaining 50,000 finally surrendered on 22 August.

In the middle of August 1944, remnants of the German Seventh Army and the Fifth Panzer Army were in danger of being enveloped by Allied forces pressing from the north, west and south. The only escape route lay through a gap, 19km/12mls wide, south of Falaise, which was being rapidly closed.

By 19 August, the only way out for the retreating Germans was a corridor 3km/2mls wide between the villages of St Lambert to the north and Chambois to the south, across which ran the River Dives. So severe were their losses that the Germans called the area *Das Korridor des Todes*, the 'Corridor of Death'.

There were only three crossing points over the River Dives (5) in the St Lambert–Chambois area: two small bridges (4), both on the outskirts of St Lambert (1), and a ford in the middle at Moissey. Although the Dives was a narrow river, it had extremely precipitous banks up to 2.5m/8ft high, which vehicles could not negotiate.

All types of vehicle (2), from horse-drawn wagons to Tiger tanks, clogged the narrow roads. Bottlenecks built up, providing sitting targets for Allied gunners and pilots.

The RAF's rocket-firing Typhoon fighter-bombers (3) pounded the fleeing Germans. They bombed the front and rear ends of columns, then strafed the vehicles stranded in between.

As the German columns moved slowly through the gap, they also came under artillery fire (6) from Polish batteries to the south and Canadian batteries to the north. Allied patrols made contact on 19 August, but it was not until the 21st that the remaining Germans were finally trapped.

After the gap was sealed, the corridor was found to be littered with 252 abandoned guns, 1,778 trucks, 669 cars, 157 light armoured vehicles and 187 tanks and assault guns. The Germans lost 10,000 dead and 50,000 prisoners. It is estimated that some 30,000 managed to escape through the narrowing gap.

143

Arnhem/*September 1944*

In September 1944, when the Allied advance on western Germany was halted by a combination of inadequate supplies and stiffening resistance, Field Marshal Sir Bernard Montgomery devised a spectacular plan to defeat the enemy by Christmas. The scheme entailed massive use of airborne troops, with a crucial role for the British 1st Airborne Division.

At that time Montgomery's Twenty-first Army Group, comprising the British Second and Canadian First Armies, was within 160km/100mls of the Ruhr, one of the Third Reich's two most vital industrial regions; General George Patton and his US Third Army were within the same distance of the other, the Saar. However, both of these controversial commanders had had the momentum of their armoured thrusts checked by shortages of fuel and stores. Each knew that whoever managed to get priority for supplies would win the kudos of being first into Germany.

Forsaking his customary caution, Montgomery went to the Supreme Allied Commander, General Dwight D. Eisenhower, on 10 September with a daring scheme to rush Germany by a back-door route through the Netherlands—to be undertaken by the end of the week.

In essence, he wanted airborne forces to land in the east of occupied Holland, capture five bridges on the main road linking Eindhoven and Arnhem and hold open a 'corridor', 103km/64mls long, until ground troops of the British Second Army could drive up from their current positions on the Belgian-Dutch border. From Arnhem, Montgomery believed it would not be difficult to turn the flank of the Germans' western frontier defences and storm into the Ruhr.

Eisenhower was not totally convinced, but he agreed. While Patton fumed at Metz in eastern France, Montgomery began intense and intricate planning for the attack, which was to commence on Sunday 17 September. 'Market' was the codename for the airborne side of the attack, 'Garden' applied to the role of the infantry and armour—hence 'Operation Market Garden'.

Even before units had been assembled for the operation, doubts were voiced by the senior commanders. Major-General Robert Urquhart, the commander entrusted with capturing the road bridge over the Lower Rhine at Arnhem, Montgomery's principal objective, was later to record in his account of the battle remarks that passed between Lieutenant-General Frederick Browning, Deputy Commander, The First Allied Airborne Army, and Field Marshal Montgomery at

British troops, *top*, of the First Allied Airborne Army, were photographed at their allotted stations in a C-47 just before they took off from an English airfield on 17 September for their flight to dropping zones at Arnhem.

US paratroopers, *above*, already airborne, show the same confidence and cheerfulness as the British. Newspaper correspondents accompanying the paratroopers all remarked upon their high morale. In Army uniform, with the American Red Cross insignia on his helmet, is a field director (third from left) of that organization. These men accompanied US troops on their missions to act as their advisors and confidants.

On 21 July 1944, US Marines landed on Guam (1). Eleven days later (1 August) the Warsaw uprising (2) by patriots against the Germans began. Bucharest (3) fell to the Russians on 31 August, two weeks after the Allies' 'Operation Anvil' landings on the coast of southern France (4) began on 15 August.

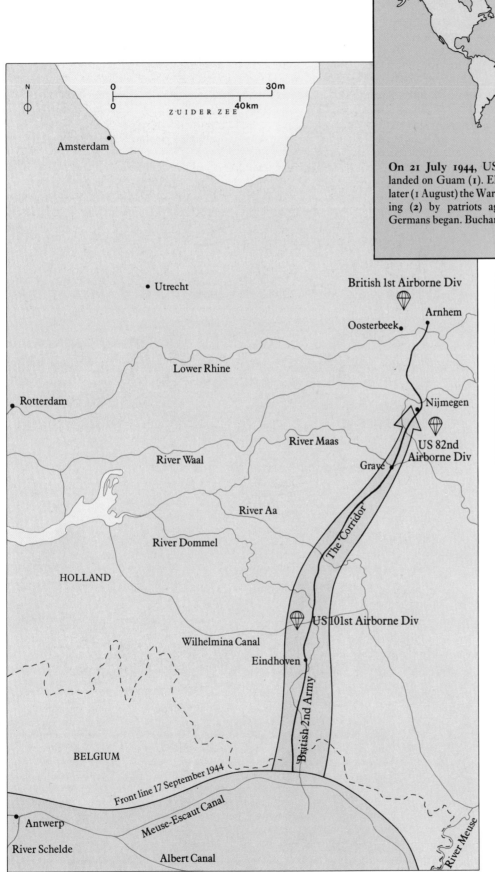

By early September 1944, Allied troops were approaching the Rhine on a wide front. Then a logistical problem arose: supplies became scarce because they had to be brought from ports in distant Normandy. There were thus inadequate resources both for Montgomery to thrust forward through Holland and into Germany's industrial Ruhr and for General Patton's US Third Army to strike through the Saar toward Frankfurt am Main. Unable to accommodate both commanders' needs, General Eisenhower compromised by giving neither of the Allied spearheads priority. German resistance stiffened and soon both wings came to a halt.

Montgomery devised an audacious plan to speed up his advance on the Ruhr by dropping three airborne divisions behind enemy lines to seize the bridges on the Eindhoven to Arnhem road. This, Montgomery calculated, would create an Allied corridor along which his Second Army could make a dash for the German frontier. But a series of mishaps and miscalculations turned this imaginative plan into an Allied disaster.

the final conference before the airborne assault was launched. Browning asked how many days it would take for the British Second Army to reach and relieve the paratroopers dropped behind enemy lines. Montgomery replied with confidence, 'Two days.' Browning, studying a map of the area, said, 'But, sir, I think we might be going a bridge too far'—words that proved prophetic within a week.

In England frantic efforts were made to assemble and get ready 5,000 assorted aircraft for what would be the biggest-ever airborne operation. Three divisions—the British 1st and the US 101st and 82nd—plus the 1st Polish Parachute Brigade were to be landed and supplied over a period of three days because senior air force officers estimated that there were not enough aircraft for them to drop all the men in a single day.

The 101st's drop zone was near Eindhoven at the southern end of the corridor; the 82nd was to secure the central section around Nijmegen. The task of capturing Montgomery's main objective, the big road bridge over the Lower Rhine at Arnhem in the north, was given to the 1st Airborne and the Poles, under the command of Major-General Urquhart. His 'Red Devils' would have to hold out longest until the Second Army arrived, and if things went wrong they would be on their own.

In spite of reports coming in from the Dutch Resistance indicating German armoured units near Arnhem—a fact corroborated by RAF reconnaissance photographs—the men of the 1st Airborne were told at their briefing to expect weak opposition from second-rate troops.

Next, the first rule of every airborne operation—drop close to the target to ensure surprise—had to be broken because the airmen refused to risk their planes close to the bridge in the belief that the area was heavily protected by anti-aircraft batteries. Urquhart's only alternative was to land on patches of open ground west of his objective.

Even though the vital element of surprise had been removed, there was no stopping or revising the operation. The first half of the division climbed aboard transports and gliders on the morning of Sunday 17 September and, once airborne, joined a mighty fleet of British and American aircraft heading east toward Holland.

The landings, in the early afternoon, went well and to begin with met little opposition. But the old men and boys that Allied Intelligence had believed to be defending Arnhem turned out to be two

The British airborne assault on Arnhem began just after 13.00 on 17 September 1944. Parachutist 'pathfinders' arrived first to mark the landing zones, some 10km/6mls west of the town. Then gliders of the 1st Airlanding Brigade, loaded with infantry, guns and jeeps, descended; they were followed by paratroopers of the 1st Parachute Brigade. Here units of the first wave land on the flat, open fields between Wolfheze and Heelsum.

The glider landings worked well in general, and crews and passengers on both Horsas (3) and the bigger Hamilcars (6) swiftly unloaded their machines. However, not all gliders landed without mishap (5).

Douglas C-47 aircraft (1), known to the British as Dakotas, were used to ferry the paratroopers to their drop zones. These aircraft also served as 'tugs' for the gliders.

Small groups of paratroopers dropped west of Arnhem before the main assault to mark landing zones with coloured smoke flares (2).

Drifting among the paratroopers as they descended were scores of red, brown and yellow parachutes (4), coloured to designate the type of supplies they carried.

As the parachute drop began, infantry from the gliders moved off (7) to take up defensive positions on the perimeter of the landing zones.

147

combat-hardened divisions of SS Panzers and a Panzer Grenadier battalion, which was equipped with experimental multi-barrelled, rocket-propelled mortars.

The German attack was fought off by the 1st Airlanding Brigade, which was tasked to secure the landing and drop zones for the second wave coming in next morning. Meanwhile, the 1st Parachute Brigade's three battalions set out for the bridge, each following a different road. Their progress was slowed by crowds of excited Dutch people, who pressed fruit and drinks on the British soldiers, welcoming them as their liberators. As the troops moved on through wooded and built-up areas, it was discovered that their radio sets were malfunctioning, a serious situation which would have a considerable effect on the conduct, and eventual outcome, of the battle. Units of the 1st Airborne were not only out of touch with each other in what was developing into a very confused fight, they also had no outside contact.

The 1st and 3rd Battalions of the Parachute Regiment, moving along main roads into Arnhem, were soon obstructed by heavy enemy fire. But Lieutenant-Colonel John Frost and his 2nd Battalion, using a secondary road alongside the river, advanced quickly. The Germans blew up a railway bridge before Frost could capture it, and a small pontoon bridge farther upstream was found to be unusable but their main objective—the road bridge—was intact. Darkness was falling when Frost and his men began to take up positions in houses overlooking both sides of its long, concrete northern approach ramp.

Although brave efforts to storm the strongly held southern end of the bridge were repulsed by Panzer grenadiers, the mere fact that British paratroopers were on the north side was enough to cause major difficulties for the commander of the 2nd SS Panzer Corps, Lieutenant-General Wilhelm Bittrich. He wanted to transfer one of his divisions rapidly away from the town to assist in beating off Allied attacks on Nijmegen, and while he attempted to move some tanks on to the south bank using a tiny ferry some way to the east—a painfully slow process—he ordered his troops to clear the bridge, whatever the cost.

Soon Frost's battalion was engaged in a fierce gun battle, as tough SS troopers tried time after time to dislodge it. In one flurry of well-directed fire the paratroopers wrecked a column of 22 scout cars and halftracks, which tried to bulldoze through from the south. Around the north end of the bridge houses were burning or

The paratroopers' equipment
A sergeant of the Parachute Regiment, fully equipped for the drop on Arnhem. As well as his parachute, reserve parachute, his weapon—either a 9-mm Sten sub-machinegun or a .303-in Lee Enfield No 4 rifle—ammunition and kit, each para-trooper was expected to carry additional battlefield equipment or supplies. This NCO has a large valise containing a light machine-gun. It could be released by pull-ing the handle, using his right hand, after he jumped from the aircraft, so that the container dangled 6m/20ft beneath him and hit the ground first. Many British paratroopers carried bulky loads in excess of 45kg/100lb and complained of hardly being able to climb aboard their aircraft.

A British paratrooper preparing to break open a supply container on an Arnhem drop zone. Hundreds of these strong metal containers, usually about 1.5m/5ft long by 0.6m/2ft in diameter, were dropped from aircraft at the same time that the men of the Parachute Regiment jumped. They contained weapons, equipment or stores.

The heaviest field guns used by the 1st Airborne Division at Arnhem were 75-mm howitzers of the 1st Light Regiment, Royal Artillery. Here one is seen in action shortly after it and its operators had landed.

Gliders into action

Gliders had played no part in British or American military thinking until they were used with spectacular success by the Germans in 1940 in their attack on the Belgian fortress of Eben Emael. It was, nevertheless, not until 1942 that Great Britain began to use unpowered air transport operationally; American gliders did not enter combat until 1943.

The outstanding British gliders were the Horsa, which carried a platoon of infantry or three tons of equipment, and the larger Hamilcar, able to transport twice as much.

The Americans favoured Wacos, smaller craft mass produced by the Ford Motor Company. There were two models, one which carried nine men and a larger type capable of carrying fifteen.

Gliders, which were used extensively during the Allied invasions of Europe in 1944, were mostly made of wood and carried the minimum number of instruments. They were towed at fairly low speed behind a 'tug' aircraft for most of their journey, during which time they were notoriously unstable. As soon as the gliders were released, however, they became more manageable and their pilots could often land accurately and smoothly without great difficulty. There were nevertheless accidents, many of them fatal, because the craft were so flimsy. The gliders were designed so that, by removing eight pins, the fuselage could be split just behind the wings to allow equipment to be unloaded swiftly. In practice, a jeep and trailer could be removed in two minutes, but at Arnhem many gliders were damaged on landing, and unloading became a prolonged and difficult operation.

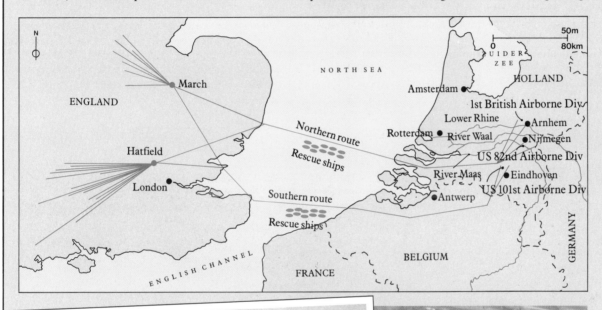

The first waves of transport aircraft and gliders, some 2,000 in all, carrying 19,000 troops and their equipment, took one of two routes from bases in England. The British 1st Airborne Division, bound for Arnhem, and the US 82nd Airborne Division, going to Nijmegen, took the northern route. Units meeting over Cambridgeshire crossed into Holland south of Rotterdam; 129km/80mls of the journey was over enemy territory. The US 101st Airborne Division took the southern route; units met over Hertfordshire and crossed into Belgium before turning north to Eindhoven. Only about 97km/60 mls of this route was over German-held territory.

A Douglas C-47, pulling a Waco glider, takes off to begin its journey to the American landing zones around Eindhoven. The glider is carrying its full complement of 15 men.

Men of the 1st Airlanding Brigade loading a jeep into a Horsa glider. Horsas could carry not only jeeps but trailers or light artillery; alternatively, they could transport up to 29 men.

149

disintegrating under artillery fire, while the cellars beneath them were filling with dead and wounded.

Shortly after the first landings, Major-General Urquhart, balked by the failure of his radio link, left divisional headquarters in the drop zone and drove in a jeep to assess what was happening among his scattered command. In time he caught up with his deputy, Brigadier-General Gerald Lathbury, commander of the 1st Parachute Brigade, who was advancing with the 3rd Battalion. Just then, however, prolonged street fighting broke out on all sides, stopping the two senior officers of the division from exercising any sort of overall control at a critical stage of the operation. Lathbury, wounded in the leg, was taken prisoner; Urquhart had to hide in an attic for several hours before he managed to regain British positions.

When he learned that divisional headquarters was now at the Hartenstein Hotel in Oosterbeek, 4.8km/3mls west of the town, Urquhart took over a jeep and sped there under fire. When he arrived, after an enforced absence of almost 40 hours, he discovered that he had been reported captured.

Much had happened during that time, nearly all of it for the worse. The second wave, bringing the rest of the 1st Airborne Division, had been delayed by bad weather on the morning of Monday 18 September. When it finally arrived over Arnhem at 16.00, the Germans, who had found a copy of the Market-Garden plan in a crashed glider at Nijmegen, knew what to expect and had prepared a rough reception. Moreover, there was little co-ordination between hard-pressed airborne units, scattered over a wide area, some of

which were trying to hold off Panther and Tiger tanks and self-propelled assault guns with rifles, Sten guns and grenades. But perhaps most disappointing of all, nothing had been heard of the Second Army, whose spearhead—the Guards Armoured Division—should have been nearing Arnhem if the Garden part of the operation were proceeding according to plan. The only encouraging piece of news was that the 2nd Battalion still dominated the north end of the bridge, though its losses were severe.

On Tuesday the situation deteriorated still further. Every effort made by other battalions to fight their way through to relieve Colonel Frost's diminishing command was blocked 1.6km/1m from the bridge by fresh German infantry and armour brought in to reinforce Bittrich. Casualties were heavy on both sides.

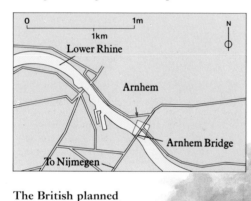

The British planned to capture intact the road bridge over the Lower Rhine at Arnhem, the key to Operation Market Garden, and hold it until the early arrival of ground forces from the British Second Army.

Only Lt-Col John Frost's 2nd Battalion, The Parachute Regiment, managed to reach the bridge and, though for a time they dominated the northern approach, they were quickly cut off by the Germans, who made frequent and ferocious attacks to dislodge them. One of the fiercest attacks against the paratroopers took place at about 09.30 on 18 September, when an armoured column of the 9th Panzer Reconnaissance Battalion tried to dash across from the southern end of the bridge.

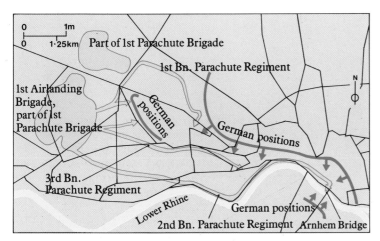

The British 1st Airborne Division approached the bridge at Arnhem in three battalions: the 1st Battalion in the north, the 3rd in the centre and the 2nd to the south. Only Frost's 2nd Battalion reached the objective, but it was quickly cut off. The others were halted by SS units.

The German attack was led by Captain Paul Grabner, who was killed during the action. Most of his vehicles were destroyed or set on fire. Two halftracks, swerving through the smoke and explosions, smashed through the parapet (4) and fell on to the road below.

To reach the northern ramp of the bridge, the vanguard of the German column (1) had to surmount the hazards of wrecked vehicles left from earlier fighting and Teller mines laid by British paratroopers. The Germans were allowed to get some way along the northern ramp before the paratroopers, positioned in houses on the west side (3) and in weapon pits on the embankment (5), raked the attacking enemy force with concentrated fire from anti-tank weapons, machine-guns and small-arms. This massive wall of fire was laid across the width of the road and 12 of the 22 German vehicles on the bridge were destroyed.

British fire was also directed against the Germans from buildings on the east side of the bridge (2), occupied by Captain Eric Mackay of the Royal Engineers and a few other Corps troops. Though they had only rifles, sub-machineguns and grenades, they caused heavy casualties.

Through the clamour of battle could be heard the triumphant British paratroopers shouting 'Whoa Mohammed', a war cry they had first adopted in North Africa in 1942. The cry enabled the British to distinguish friend from foe when fighting house to house and among the mounds of rubble. The battle cry also seemed to hearten the paratroopers even in the toughest and most difficult situations.

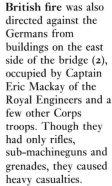

Though Urquhart was unaware of it, most of his much-needed 1st Polish Parachute Brigade was delayed by bad weather in England and could not be flown out that day. Glider-borne elements of the Polish force did get away late from airfields in the south, but when they descended on their landing ground they found themselves in the middle of a battle and were shot at by friend and foe alike.

That same Tuesday, the division was expecting a consignment of vital supplies. Because the drop zones had been captured, Urquhart repeatedly transmitted a request for the incoming aircraft to offload their containers near his HQ at the Hartenstein Hotel. His radio, however, was still malfunctioning and the messages did not get through. With great courage, RAF pilots flew through a barrage of flak to deliver their precious cargo, most of which floated down into German hands. Out of 390 tons of ammunition, food and medical supplies, only 31 tons were received by the 1st Airborne Division.

Acutely aware that his command was fragmented and sustaining heavy losses, Urquhart came to a hard but unavoidable decision on the night of 19 September: Frost's isolated battalion would have to fend for itself while what remained of the rest of 1st Airborne was pulled back to form a defensive box around the Hartenstein Hotel. There the survivors would try to stand off attacks until the overdue Second Army broke through. In fact, British tanks were only 16km/10mls to the south, after battling up the road they had named 'Hell's Highway'.

When signallers at last managed to get a radio set working properly, Urquhart sent an urgent request: he wanted the Polish paratroopers, now expected on 20 September, not to go in as planned at the southern end of the bridge, which remained in enemy hands, but to switch to Driel, 8km/5mls to the west. A small ferry was still running there which could carry the Poles over to 1st Airborne's positions, since part of their perimeter ran along the north bank of the Lower Rhine. Continuing bad weather, however, still kept the bulk of the Polish brigade in England.

At Oosterbeek crossroads, in the centre of Urquhart's defensive box, enemy fire of all calibres was so intense that his men called it the 'Cauldron'. All around, the Germans were pressing on the thinly held lines. Down by the bridge in Arnhem, Colonel Frost, now wounded, and what was left of his brave 2nd Battalion, realized that the end of their magnificent three-day stand was close. By late evening, those still able to fight were down to their last rounds

A patrol of British paratroopers, *above*, clearing enemy snipers from houses in Oosterbeek. The British Sten sub-machinegun proved highly effective in house-to-house fighting. It had a magazine capacity of 32 rounds and could fire either single shots or bursts.

Men of the 1st Paratroop Division, *right*, took cover in shell holes.

Reporting the battle
Men of the Army Film and Photographic Unit, who took graphic still and ciné pictures of the 1st Airborne Division's epic fight at Arnhem, were themselves photographed on their safe return to Britain after the battle. Such servicemen provided extensive press coverage of the operation, with some of the most vivid film of the war.

Many, exposed to dangers as great as those experienced by fighting men, were wounded or killed during World War II. Sergeant D.M. Smith, *left*, was wounded in the shoulder during the battle. Sergeant C.M. Lewis, *right*, had enlisted in 1940 and was twice wounded during the Tunisian Campaign. These servicemen/photographers were not only skilled cameramen but also trained fighting soldiers and experienced paratroopers: Smith made 18 descents before the end of the war.

Allied cameramen and radio reporters operated in all theatres during World War II, making it the most swiftly and extensively reported conflict in history. Of the few vital messages that reached England detailing the confused battle situation at Arnhem, most were sent not by the army but by a BBC set, specially supplied for British war correspondents.

The Commanders

Sosabowski

Frost

Urquhart

Bittrich

The Allied landings and subsequent troop deployments at Arnhem were dogged by ill luck. The commander of the Polish Parachute Brigade, **Major-General Stanislaw Sosabowski (1892–1967)**, was first delayed in taking off by bad weather; then, when his brigade finally landed, most of the men were dropped into enemy positions and were badly mauled.

Lieutenant-Colonel John Frost's (1912–) 2nd Battalion was the only unit to reach the bridge at Arnhem but was then cut off and, although the paratroopers fought with the utmost courage, their positions were overrun three days later.

Major-General Robert Urquhart (1900–), in overall command of the 1st Airborne Division and the Polish contingent, had not before led paratroopers or glider operations. He was, however, a highly experienced infantry officer, which is why he was chosen to command this daring assault. Though victory eluded him, his resourcefulness and courage in a desperate situation were exemplary.

SS Lieutenant-General Wilhelm Bittrich (1894–1979), commander of the 2nd SS Panzer Corps, strongly recommended to his superior, Field Marshal Walther Model, that the bridges, which in his view were the Allied target, should be destroyed. Model disagreed: 'No matter what the English plan,' he insisted, 'these bridges can be defended.' Later the mere presence of paratroopers on the north side of the Arnhem bridge was enough to prevent Bittrich's moving one of his divisions over to help defend the bridge at Nijmegen, which was captured.

German troops, *left*, of the Hohenstaufen Division, approach the Museum, which is situated at the top of the hill overlooking Arnhem town. Their rifles, nonchalantly slung over their shoulders, indicate that the battle is virtually over. The Museum is cordoned off with German tanks and the last British paratroopers surrounded.

German StuG III self-propelled assault guns, *right*, were used with infantry support to clear streets of snipers during the battle. The ripple effect was caused by Zimmerit anti-magnetic mine paste, which had been applied to the machine's skin to prevent enemy infantry from fixing limpet mines to it. This was a major hazard with this type of vehicle, which lacked machine-gun protection.

and their positions were overrun. As dawn broke on 21 September, Bittrich's panzers were able to cross the Lower Rhine bridge and confront the oncoming Second Army.

Later that Thursday, the 1,500-strong 1st Polish Parachute Brigade at last dropped on Driel, only to find the Germans waiting for them and the ferry inoperable. About 200 men swam over to join Urquhart; the remainder dug in on the south bank. Early the following morning, four days and 18 hours after the first drop, a detachment of armoured cars from the Second Army arrived in Driel and made the first direct contact with the battered 1st Airborne Division, holding on 366m/400yds away across the river.

Over Saturday and Sunday, British infantry came up in force on the south bank. In the meantime, the plight of Urquhart's men steadily worsened. Their supplies were almost exhausted, and all attempts to replenish them failed. Then, when a brave effort by the 4th Battalion of the Dorsetshire Regiment to cross the river came to nothing on the Sunday night, plans were made to evacuate the remnants of 1st Airborne. Shortly after 06.00 on Monday 25 September, General Urquhart was given the order to withdraw. That night, while keeping up a pretence of manning the perimeter as usual, men with boots and equipment muffled made their way silently down to the Rhine, where a few boats waited to ferry them over.

As their ordeal ended, there was a final irony: no one had expected so many men to get out and there was not enough transport to cope with them. Exhausted soldiers, who had endured eight days of fierce fighting, had to march 18km/11mls to the Second Army's main positions at Nijmegen. Of the 10,005 men of the 1st Airborne Division, 2,163 reached Driel, together with 160 Poles and 75 men of the Dorsetshire Regiment from the abortive relief attempts. They left behind 1,200 dead and 6,642 wounded, captured or missing. The Germans reported 3,300 casualties, a third of whom were dead.

In his *Memoirs* Montgomery was insistent on the reasons for the failure of the operation. Supreme Headquarters had never regarded the landings as a spearhead attack into the Ruhr; troops were not landed on their targets; the depleted 2nd SS Panzer Corps proved unexpectedly formidable and, lastly, the weather was unfavourable. He was, however, deeply aware of the exertions and sacrifices made by his men and later wrote of the action: '. . . there can be few episodes more glorious than the epic of Arnhem.'

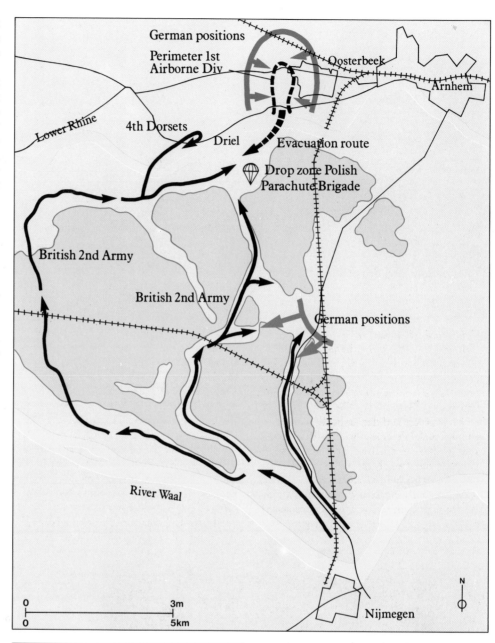

Germany's revenge on Arnhem

As gliders and paratroopers began to land in force to the west of Arnhem, the Dutch were overjoyed for, it seemed, they were to be liberated from German occupation. Orange, the Dutch national colour, was worn openly on the streets by crowds gathering to welcome the British. Unintentionally, the local residents slowed the advance as they crowded around and pressed refreshments on the soldiers.

When the battle was over and the British survivors had been evacuated, the Germans took their revenge: they drove the entire population out of the town, declaring it a military area. It was not until spring 1945 that the people of Arnhem were able to return to the ruins of their homes.

The rescue attempts were to culminate in a successful withdrawal of Allied troops. Shortly before 22.00 on the night of 25–26 September, the evacuation of 2,500 paratroopers from their positions on the north side of the Lower Rhine began. The night was dark and wet with occasional light from burning buildings and German flares. All around was devastation as detachments, making their way with the aid of white guide tapes, moved to the embarkation stations. By 24.00, despite heavy and continuous German bombardment, British and Canadian sappers were in position on the south bank with 14 assault boats and some smaller craft, ready to evacuate the beleaguered paratroopers.

Over 2,000 men were evacuated before the Germans sent tanks into the perimeter, taking about 300 wounded troops prisoner. Many were returned to freedom by the Dutch Resistance.

Five heroes of Arnhem

Five Victoria Crosses were awarded at Arnhem, four of them posthumously. The painting, *above*, by Terence Cuneo depicts **Lance-Sergeant John Baskeyfield** who operated, single-handed, a 6-pounder anti-tank gun at Oosterbeek. The citation dwelt on his coolness and daring in allowing each enemy tank to come well within 91m/100yds before opening fire. Baskeyfield knocked out two Tiger tanks and a self-propelled gun before being killed.

Major Robert Cain was cut off with his company but survived six days of repeated attacks by tanks, self-propelled guns and infantry. His courage and fine leadership prevented a vital sector being taken by the Germans. After the war, Major Cain returned to civilian life.

Lieutenant John Grayburn, a platoon commander of the 2nd Parachute Battalion, was entrusted with seizing the bridge at Arnhem. He was wounded in the shoulder while trying to capture the southern end of the bridge but pressed on until ordered to retreat. Later he was wounded in the back while defending a critical house; when it became untenable, he directed his men's safe retreat but was himself killed.

Flight Lieutenant David Lord was the pilot of a Douglas Dakota supply aircraft which was twice hit and the starboard engine set ablaze. Nevertheless, he made two runs over the dropping zone before ordering his crew to bale out; a few seconds later, the aircraft crashed in flames.

Captain Lionel Queripel and his company, while advancing on Arnhem, came under heavy fire. Despite being hit in the face when carrying a wounded sergeant to safety under fire, and later receiving wounds in both arms, he pushed on until enemy fire became so intense that he ordered his men to retire. He covered their retreat, with an automatic pistol and a few hand grenades, but was never seen again.

Captured British paratroopers, *above*, many of them wounded, were disarmed by German soldiers. Hundreds of Allied prisoners were held until the war ended eight months later, though some escaped and were given sanctuary by the Dutch. Survivors of the battle, *right*, their morale still high, were sent home on leave.

The Battle of The Bulge/*December 1944-January 1945*

By the late summer of 1944, the hard-pressed forces of Nazi Germany were being squeezed in a vice. British and American armies were approaching the Third Reich from the west; the Russians were closing on its eastern frontier. But those in the Allied camp who believed that the war would be over by Christmas—and there were many—had underestimated Adolf Hitler.

The Führer was not prepared to remain on the defensive and eventually be overwhelmed by the Allies' superior power. The drain on his resources caused by having to fight on two fronts may have robbed him of any chance of complete victory by force of arms, but by winning one more major battle he conjectured that a situation might be created which could be turned to Germany's advantage.

There was no point in trying to take on the Red Army; it was far too strong. His only hope lay on the Western Front, where Anglo-American forces were experiencing supply and reinforcement difficulties—caused by over-extended lines of communication. If he could inflict a major defeat in this theatre, he believed that a negotiated peace with Britain and the United States of America was possible. He could then turn his full attention—perhaps even helped by his former enemies—to destroying Communist Russia.

On 16 September, while listening to a situation report about the Western Front, Hitler had an inspiration. Tapping the battle map, he announced: 'I shall go over to the offensive ... out of the Ardennes, with the objective, Antwerp.' A surprise attack from this hilly, forested region in eastern Belgium had worked for the Germans in 1940, and it might work again.

This sector, which separated the axis of advance of the main British and American armies, was lightly held, and a blitzkrieg-style drive across Belgium to recapture the port of Antwerp (which was still unusable by the Allies) would sever General Dwight D. Eisenhower's already shaky supply lines and cut off Field Marshal Sir Bernard Montgomery's Twenty-first Army Group in Belgium and southern Holland. More than 20 enemy divisions stood to be destroyed if this bold plan, deceptively called 'Wacht am Rhein' (Watch on the Rhine), were properly executed.

But Hitler, who spent more than a month secretly working on this scheme with a handful of trusted aides, was living in a dream world, the product of his megalomania. As soon as Field Marshal Gerd von Rundstedt, the recently reinstated Commander-in-Chief of German forces in the west, and other senior

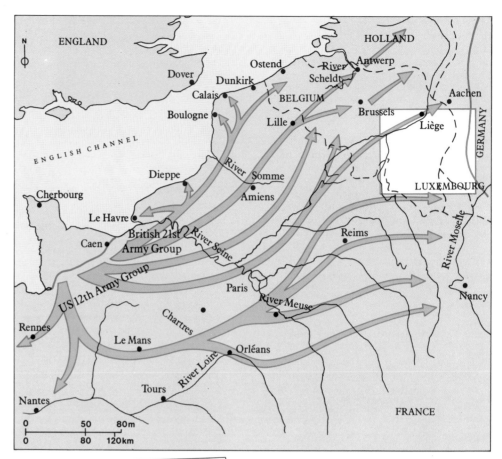

After the Allied armies broke out of the Normandy beachhead in August 1944, General Eisenhower decided to pursue the retreating Germans on a broad front. General Montgomery's Twenty-first Army Group made rapid progress through northern France and then Belgium, but after the failure to seize Arnhem, their thrust lost momentum.

At the same time, General Bradley's US Twelfth Army Group had pushed east and north through France. Paris was freed on 25 August, and by mid-September American forces were near the German border. After heavy fighting, US troops broke through the West Wall defences in November and took Aachen, the first big town to fall. It seemed as if the war might soon be over.

The Americans were caught off balance by the magnitude and ferocity of the German attack and lost much equipment. These propaganda pictures show a Nazi soldier directing follow-up troops past a knocked-out US halftrack, *above left*, and German soldiers advancing rapidly on the first day of the offensive, *left*. Speed was an essential element in Hitler's plan.

Three German armies launched a surprise counter-offensive against US positions in the Ardennes region on 16 December 1944. Forging westward on a front 145km/90mls wide, the Germans drove a salient into the Allied front line. This might have been larger and their advance more extensive had they managed to oust the US 101st Airborne Division from Bastogne and taken St Vith to the north more quickly, for these two American 'breakwaters' were to cripple German operations.

On Christmas Day, units of the Fifth Panzer Army reached the farthest point of penetration—almost to the River Meuse—before being turned back by mounting Allied pressure. While the British 30th Corps, borrowed from Montgomery's Twenty-first Army Group, pushed at the tip of the salient, the US First Army in the north and the US Third Army in the south began to squeeze the Germans. Within a month, the opposing front lines were back in almost the same positions they had held on the eve of the German offensive.

Following the D-Day landings (1) on 6 June 1944, Caen fell on 9 July and Paris was liberated on 25 August. Brussels was taken on 3 September; the following day Antwerp was captured. The unsuccessful Arnhem operation (2) began on 17 September. On the Eastern Front, the Russians captured Minsk (3) on 3 July.

The Japanese were defeated at Imphal (4) on 4 July; on 21 July US troops landed on Guam and on 20 October in the Philippines (5).

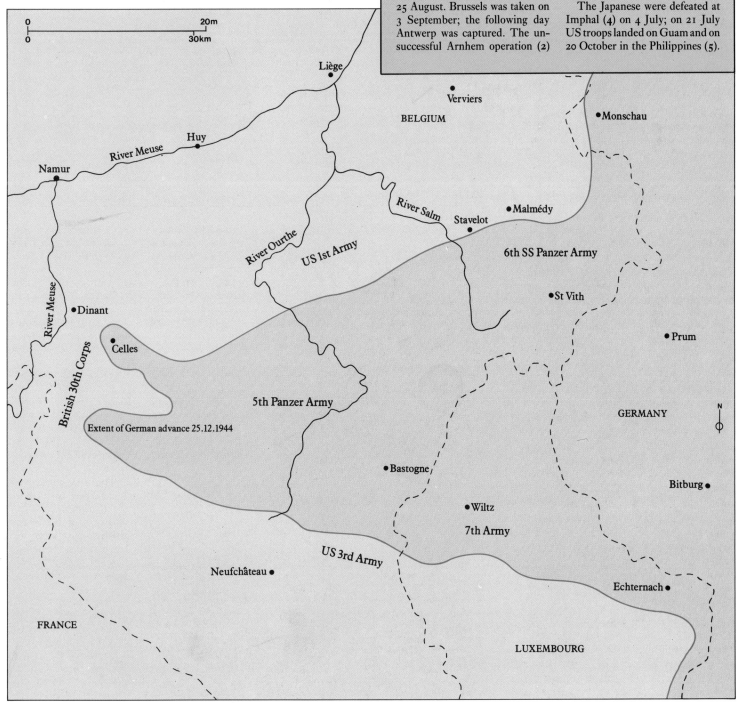

combat officers learned the details of 'Wacht am Rhein', they were appalled. The Wehrmacht simply did not possess the resources for a task of such magnitude.

Though German industry produced a record quantity of weapons and ammunition in 1944, it did not match Allied output. The tanks available for the offensive—970 for the opening wave, 450 for follow-up support—fell short of the 2,500 deployed in the blitzkrieg into France in 1940. Moreover, Germany no longer enjoyed air superiority: only about 1,000 fighter-bombers were available in comparision with 2,000 in 1940. In addition, the Allies, now fielding a more numerous fighting force, could call on considerable reserves: by the fourth day of the offensive, American strength in the Ardennes had doubled to 180,000.

The plan, though strategically sound,

was doomed from the start, as von Rundstedt acknowledged after the war when he said, 'It was obvious to me that the available forces were far too small for such an extremely ambitious plan. It was a nonsensical operation, and the most stupid part of it was the setting of Antwerp as the target. If we had reached the Meuse we should have got down on our knees and thanked God, let alone try to reach Antwerp.' But Hitler, running true to form, would not listen to the advice of the professional soldiers.

Though von Rundstedt and other generals tried to interest the Führer in a more modest counter-attack, he insisted that his decision was irrevocable. It was up to them to make it work. All he would agree

to were changes in the launch date from 25 November to 10 December, then to 16 December, to give his troops more time to redeploy and prepare for the offensive. He also changed the name of the operation from 'Wacht am Rhein' to 'Herbstnebel' (Autumn Fog). Thus, the scene was set for one of the biggest battles to be fought in the West in World War II.

Designated to make the breakout in the Ardennes were the newly formed Sixth SS Panzer Army, commanded by Colonel-General Joseph 'Sepp' Dietrich, and the Fifth Panzer Army under General Hasso von Manteuffel, supported by General

On 20 December 1944, four days after the offensive began, some units of Kampfgruppe Peiper, a strong column of tanks, artillery, self-propelled guns and mechanized infantry, had established a bridgehead on the south bank of the River Amblève at Cheneux. Their idea was to hold this forward position as a springboard for the resumption of the main body's westward push as soon as fuel had been brought up.

However, the Americans were closing in. The task of taking Cheneux

was given to Colonel Reuben Tucker's 504th Parachute Infantry Regiment of the 82nd Airborne Division. The fighting lasted throughout the night of the 20th and most of the next day. In a series of encircling attacks, of which the action at Cheneux was just one, US forces smashed Colonel Peiper's Kampfgruppe, and the survivors had to struggle back to the German lines on foot.

The village of Cheneux (1) was occupied by most of Peiper's light flak battalion and a company of the 2nd SS Panzer Grenadier Regiment (2).

The approach to the German positions in Cheneux (366m/400yds across open fields) was punctuated by barbed wire fences (3), which slowed the US infantry and so caused many casualties

On the afternoon of 20 December, in heavy mist, Colonel Tucker

sent B and C companies of his 1st Battalion (4) forward to attack the village. Several times during the night they tried to storm German positions, but they came under concentrated fire from machine-guns, mortars and 20-mm flak wagons.

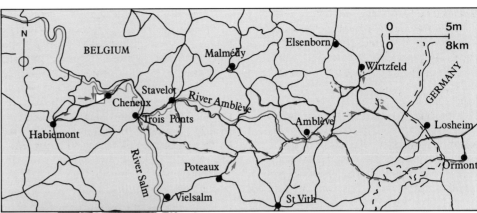

The main advance of Peiper's column, *map above*, is shown with a solid line; diversions with dots, and the route of the group in the south with dashes.

The paratroopers battled against strong opposition without artillery support until the arrival of two tank destroyers (5). Had they had the benefit of covering fire, these two companies would probably not have lost so many men—23 killed and 202 wounded.

Before dawn, US troops secured a foothold in buildings on the western edge of the village (6). While they hung on there, Tucker sent his 3rd Battalion on a six-hour flanking march to bring them in on Cheneux from a northerly direction.

The Germans in Cheneux were cut off by late afternoon. A few escaped to rejoin the Kampfgruppe's main body on the north bank of the Amblève, but they left behind 'heaps of dead', according to one eyewitness, and a large quantity of equipment, including 14 flak wagons and a battery of 105-mm long-range guns.

Erich Brandenberger's Seventh Army. The plan was for the Panzers to attack on a 145-km/90-ml front, from Monschau in the north to Echternach in the south, with the Sixth SS Panzer Army on the right, the Fifth Panzer Army on the left, and the infantry of the Seventh Army screening the armour's southern flank. Anticipating poor visibility, which would keep Allied aircraft grounded, Hitler expected the Panzers to reach the River Meuse within two days. From there, Dietrich was to make a dash for Antwerp, while von Manteuffel was to move on the port by way of Brussels.

To help spread confusion among the Allies in the opening stages of 'Herbstnebel', Hitler had decided to send a picked force of English-speaking, American-uniformed troops, carrying US arms, behind enemy lines to disrupt the Allied forces by switching signposts, misdirecting armoured columns and soldiers, and the like. They were to be led by the daring SS Colonel Otto Skorzeny, who sprang to fame after rescuing Mussolini from his mountain prison.

On 10 December, six days before his counter-offensive was due to begin, the Führer, although tired and ill, insisted on moving his headquarters from the 'Wolfschanze' (Wolf's Lair) in East Prussia to the 'Adlerhorst' (Eagle's Eyrie) in the Taunus Hills near Bad Neuheim in the Rhineland. From this base, he intended to take personal control of the coming battle, just as he had when the successful assault on the French had been unleashed through the Ardennes in 1940.

During November, while preparations for the onslaught were proceeding, the Americans launched attacks on Hitler's 'West Wall' frontier defences, breaking in north of the Ardennes and capturing Aachen, the first sizeable German town to fall to the Allies. These operations were carried out by the understrength and largely inexperienced First, Ninth and Third Armies of General Omar Bradley's Twelfth US Army Group on either side of the Ardennes front. This 129km/80ml long stretch was manned by only four divisions of the US 8th Corps, under Major-General Troy Middleton. It was looked on as something of an easy sector because Allied Intelligence discounted the Germans' ability to launch a major armoured offensive through the area. So, of the four divisions spread thinly along this line, the 28th and the 4th were nursing their wounds after taking part in earlier heavy fighting, and the 9th Armoured and the 106th had never been in action.

Though information was coming in

The price of duplicity

On 21 October 1944, Hitler received at his headquarters in East Prussia a man he held in high regard: Colonel Otto Skorzeny, the soldier who had masterminded the rescue of Mussolini from imprisonment following his overthrow. The Führer outlined his plan for the Ardennes offensive to Skorzeny and entrusted him and his 150th Panzer Brigade with a major role in the forthcoming operation.

Skorzeny's orders were twofold: first, small motorized columns under his command were to be sent in advance to capture and hold the Meuse bridges before the arrival of German armour; secondly, English-speaking units, wearing captured US uniforms, were to infiltrate enemy lines, then cut telephone wires and spread rumours of the German advance among Allied soldiers and the civilian population.

The Americans over-reacted to the danger posed by Skorzeny's force by imposing stringent security checks. Jeeps, even staff cars, were repeatedly stopped and their occupants questioned minutely on such aspects of American culture as the private lives of film stars and the league positions of baseball teams. Many senior officers, ignorant of the correct answers, were briefly incarcerated and interrogated.

This German soldier, dressed in American uniform, is guarded by military police of the US 30th Division near Malmédy. Few of Skorzeny's men captured while trying to come through American lines escaped execution.

Hundreds of empty 23-1/5-gal fuel cans, *left*, lie piled in heaps at a US supply depot near Stavelot in Belgium. The Americans destroyed such dumps to ensure that the advancing Germans, who were short of fuel, could not use it against them.

A German soldier stops to examine a captured US anti-aircraft gun mounted on a truck, *left*. The Luftwaffe mustered 1,035 Focke-Wulf 190s and Messerschmitt 109s for the battle and inflicted heavy damage on Allied aircraft surprised on the ground. But, having lost more than 300 aircraft and most of their experienced pilots, the Luftwaffe was a spent force.

Hitler's super weapons

Despite intensive bombing of industrial targets, vital German tank and aircraft factories still produced technically advanced weapons. During the Battle of the Bulge, formidable weapons were available, but their deployment in limited numbers was inadequate in the face of the massive numerical superiority of Allied weapons. Germany possessed two closely related armoured vehicles. The PzKwVI Tiger II tank, known as the King Tiger, was the biggest tank of the time with the most powerful gun. Its relative, the Jagdtiger, a self-propelled gun or tank destroyer, was built on the Tiger II chassis. It was the largest and heaviest armoured fighting vehicle of World War II and carried the biggest gun, the 128-mm Pak 44. But its bulk and slow speed made it an easy target.

Some German aircraft also were farther advanced technically than those of the Allies. The single-seat Messerschmitt Me 262, for instance, powered by two Junkers Jumo 004B turbo jet engines, was the first jet aircraft to fly in combat. It came in a fighter version, the 'Schwalbe' (Swallow), and also a fighter-bomber version, the 'Stürmvogel' (Stormbird), and was the precursor of a new age in military aviation.

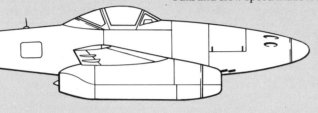

Messerschmitt Me 262 Maximum speed: 869kmh/540mph; range: 966km/600mls; armament: fighter—four 30-mm cannon mounted in the nose; bomber—various weapons, including rockets, with a total weight of 1,020kg/2,250lb.

PzKwVI Tiger II Weight: 68 tons; road speed: 38kmh/25mph; range: 110km/68mls; maximum armour thickness: 185mm/7¼in; armament: one 88-mm gun, two 7.92-mm machine-guns.

JgPz VI Jagdtiger Weight: 76 tons; road speed: 38kmh/25mph; range: 110km/68mls; maximum armour thickness: 250mm/9¾in; armament: one 128-mm Pak 44 gun, one 7.92-mm machine-gun.

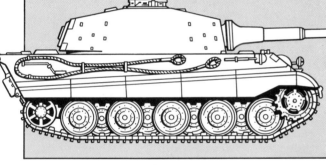

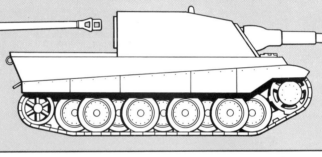

Infantrymen of the 83rd US Division, crouching beside a 57-mm anti-tank gun on a road near Bovigny in Belgium in readiness to repel any sudden German attack. They are covering their comrades, advancing through the snow-covered fir trees on either side of the forest road. Hitler had timed the offensive to coincide with a period of bad weather, predicted by his meteorologists. It was dark and frosty as German troops moved up to their assault positions on 15 December, the landscape covered with a cold, thick mist—precisely the conditions that would ground Allied aircraft and prevent their attacking German supply lines, as they had to such terrible effect in Normandy. For the next five days Hitler's luck held and the weather remained unchanged.

from many quarters concerning an enemy build-up close to the borders of Belgium and Luxembourg, General Eisenhower's Intelligence staff miscalculated Hitler's intention. Based on their appreciation of German resources, they concluded that a limited counter-attack was being prepared against US positons around Aachen.

Measured against this false assumption, it is no wonder that the Americans were taken completely by surprise at 05.35 on 16 December, when the dark and foggy Ardennes countryside was lit by a massive German artillery barrage from 2,000 guns, as a forerunner to heavy assaults by infantry and panzers.

The initial dash of the Army and SS units may have been inspired by von Rundstedt's eve-of-battle message: 'Soldiers of the West Front! Your great hour has arrived. Large attacking armies have started against the Anglo-Americans. I do not have to tell you anything more than that. You feel it yourselves. We gamble everything! You carry with you the sacred obligation to give everything to achieve things beyond human possibilities for our Fatherland and our Führer!' The old Field Marshal, whose heart had never been in 'Herbstnebel', was doing his duty in exhorting his troops, but at the same time he was telling them no less than the truth about their situation, for they were involved in a high-risk, last-ditch action which would require a super-human effort to succeed.

Contrary to Hitler's expectations, Colonel Skorzeny's advance units, masquerading as GIs, failed to cause much confusion behind the Allied lines, and many of these misguided soldiers faced a firing squad for their deceit. In fact, the assaulting German armies received much greater assistance from the long spell of bad weather, on which the operation had been predicated, and which protected them from concentrated air attacks. This, together with a slow response by US ground forces, gave them an initial advantage. Startling inroads were made into the American positions, eventually creating a salient up to 80km/50mls deep and giving the action its name—the Battle of the Bulge.

Von Manteuffel's Fifth Panzer Army, which crashed through the US 28th and 106th Divisions, enjoyed the greatest successes. His

At 07.30 on Christmas Day 1944, Kampfgruppe Maucke—a mixed armoured and infantry force, led by Colonel Wolfgang Maucke—attempted to break through the US 101st Airborne Division's defences around Bastogne. The formation, though newly arrived in the area, was sent against the supposedly weak northwest sector of the American perimeter without benefit of reconnaissance.

Nineteen MkIV tanks and StuG III assault guns, painted white to camouflage them in the snow and accompanied by Panzer grenadiers wearing white snow suits, began their advance in the early morning darkness. On nearing the American lines, the Kampfgruppe split up: seven vehicles and a company of infantry turned north toward the village of Champs, while the remainder thrust south to Hemroulle.

When Colonel Steve Chappuis of the 502nd Airborne Infantry Regiment learned that German forces were approaching, he sent his B and C companies to reinforce A Company in Champs. During their march, the paratroopers, sighting the enemy, took cover along the edge of a wood (**2**), separated from the road to Champs by an open field, and opened fire with small-arms, machine-guns and bazookas.

The German armoured vehicles, with some grenadiers riding on top of them and others following on foot, rushed the American positions in line abreast, but broke off when brisk fire cut the infantry to pieces.

As the tanks and guns turned to regroup, they exposed their right flank to two self-propelled guns (**1**) from the US 705th Tank Destroyer Regiment which, unknown to the paratroopers, were concealed in the same wood where they had taken cover.

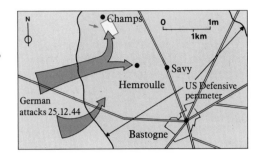

A StuG (**4**) and two MkIV tanks (**3**) were destroyed at a range of 366m/400yds; a bazooka claimed another tank, and farther down the road a StuG was set ablaze by a small force protecting Rolle Château, 502nd Regiment's HQ. One tank reached Champs but was disabled; the last tank turned for Hemroulle, where it was captured.

Of a company of Panzer grenadiers, 67 were killed and 35 taken prisoner. All the German armour in the second column heading south toward Hemroulle was also destroyed.

forward units ultimately penetrated as far as Celles, just 10km/6mls from the Meuse, but could make no further progress, justifying von Rundstedt's appreciation of German military capability. But there was one obstacle deep inside the Bulge that blocked the Fifth Panzer Army's main supply route and put a brake on the speed of its advance—the important crossroads town of Bastogne. This was bravely defended by the 101st US Airborne Division until it was relieved by General George Patton's Third Army. When invited to surrender what the American troops graphically described as 'the hole in the doughnut', Brigadier-General Anthony McAuliffe of the 101st's blunt refusal astonished the Germans. The 101st carried on fighting, obtaining essential supplies by air drop.

On 'Herbstnebel's' southern flank, Brandenberger's Seventh Army had been checked before it got far; while in the north, Dietrich's Sixth SS Panzer Army failed to carry the Elsenborn Ridge not far from its starting point, though some units struck deep through the Losheim gap. The latter were, however, unable to exploit their gains, mainly through lack of fuel and stiffening opposition.

Hitler had expected much more from his SS Panzers, who on 19 December were still a long way from their objective of 17 December, the River Meuse. Nevertheless, he obstinately refused to sanction von Rundstedt's request to move part of Dietrich's command south to lend added power to von Manteuffel's more successful thrust.

On the same day, 19 December, the Supreme Allied Commander, General Eisenhower, was meeting his senior generals at Verdun to plan the repulse of 'Herbstnebel'. Though there was an undeniably large salient in the Allied line, 'Ike' opened proceedings with these words: 'The present situation is to be regarded as one of opportunity for us and not disaster. There will be only cheerful faces at this conference table.' Probably the most significant decision taken that day was to switch Patton's Third Army from its east-facing position on the Saar front and move it 241km/150mls north to attack the left flank of the Bulge, a massive logistical feat which the Americans carried out superbly.

On the following day, 20 December, having steadily gathered up all the reserves he could find to pit against the 17 enemy divisions deployed against him, Eisenhower announced a temporary change in command to enable the Allies to operate effectively on the two distinct

The turning point: Bastogne relieved

Bastogne, the headquarters of the US 8th Corps, was situated at the centre of the road network on the German line of advance. If the Americans could hold the town, German chances of reaching the River Meuse would be greatly reduced.

By 20 December, the Germans had encircled Bastogne. All American troops in the area were placed under the command of Brigadier-General McAuliffe of the 101st Airborne Division, the senior officer present. Despite intense German artillery and bomber attacks, the Americans, supplied from the air, held grimly on. Meanwhile, General Patton committed the 4th Armoured Division to the relief of the important local centre of Bastogne.

Three converging columns struck at the German 5th Parachute Division south of the town. The final breakthrough was made by Combat Command R, supported by 94th Armoured Field Artillery and the 37th Tank Battalion, thrusting through the village of Assenois, 4.8km/3mls from the town. Assenois was subjected to artillery fire from 04.45 on 26 December; American tanks burst into the village while US shells were still falling. Hand-to-hand fighting ensued, but the American advance could not be halted: Bastogne was relieved later that day. Nearly 12,000 Germans died and around 3,900 Americans. Tank losses were also huge: 150 American and 450 German tanks were destroyed.

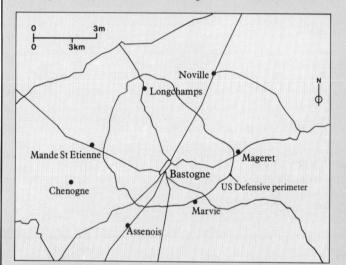

The morning of 23 December was cold but clear: Allied aircraft could again operate after a period of impenetrable mist and cloud. At once aircraft of US Troop Carrier Command began dropping supplies to the besieged garrison at Bastogne. In the space of four hours, 241 aircraft, each carrying 544kg/1,200lb of cargo, dropped parapacks over the area.

On 26 December, 289 aircraft again delivered supplies, mainly of ammunition, but doctors and medical necessities were also parachuted in. There was a bonus for the defenders: the cargo craft were protected by fighters and these, their mission over, strafed enemy positions before turning for home.

Massacre at Malmédy

On the morning of 16 December, Colonel Jochen Peiper took command of a unit consisting of about 100 MkIV and MkV Panther tanks and a battalion of 40 King Tigers, supported by a battalion of motorized infantry. Their task was to act as a spearhead in the Ardennes offensive.

Peiper's drive across Belgium left a trail of death. At Honsfeld, a rest area for the 349th Regiment of the 99th US Infantry Division, paratroopers riding on the sides of Peiper's tanks jumped off to round up American troops; 19 who did not surrender were shot and their bodies looted. Near Bullingen, Peiper overran a small airfield and forced captured GIs to refuel his tanks; the task completed, they were shot. At

Ligneuville, eight further prisoners died.

The advance continued toward the town of Malmédy, where a column of Americans, equipped with small-arms only, were obliged to surrender to Peiper's tanks and machine-guns. The Germans, having searched their prisoners, herded them into a field, where they were ordered to line up in eight rows, each of 15 men. Then two tanks were brought forward and the men shot down with machine-gun fire. Of the 120 men, 20 miraculously survived, and although most were wounded, they made a dash for the relative safety of a nearby wood. About 12 Americans reached the sanctuary of a café, but the Germans set fire to the building and shot all the men as they

stumbled out, choked by the acrid smoke. When a report of the massacre reached First Army HQ later that day, it was at once made public. This proved the turning point of the campaign, for instead of panicking the American soldiers as Hitler had envisaged, it strengthened their resolve to beat back the Germans in revenge for the slaughter of their comrades.

After the war, Peiper and his accomplices were arrested and tried for the murder of 308 soldiers and 111 civilians, although the total was probably nearer double those figures. Peiper was sentenced to death, but this was commuted to imprisonment in September 1948; and on 22 December 1956, he was released.

Three units of Battery B of the 285th US Field Artillery Battalion, comprising 140 men and 30 vehicles, moved south from Malmédy on 17 December. The column continued down the N32 road toward Baugnez, where five roads met. A military policeman on duty waved the column on, then turned to enter a café (1). A moment later,

he heard the sound of tank cannon (2) and saw the column under fire. A unit from Kampfgruppe Peiper (3), advancing north on a secondary road, had opened up on the Americans. Germans jumped from their tanks and stormed across the open field (4), firing small-arms. The execution of prisoners that followed became known as the Malmédy massacre.

Men of the 291st Engineers, *left,* numbering the frozen bodies of victims. German brutality at Malmédy gave rise to American retaliation on prisoners.

Leading elements of Kampfgruppe Peiper, *above,* at a crossroads on their westward advance, riding in a versatile amphibious Volkswagen 166 *Schwimmwagen.*

fronts formed by the V-shaped salient. The southern front was to be controlled by General Bradley, who was upset at having to give up some of his troops to Field Marshal Montgomery, who was called in to direct the fighting on the northern front. Between them they were to put pressure on the Germans and squeeze them out of the Bulge.

Despite Dietrich ousting Brigadier-General Robert Hasbrouck's 7th US Armoured Division from the bitterly contested town of St Vith on 21 December, it was clear to von Rundstedt, at least, that the tide was beginning to run against the Germans. The next day he asked Hitler's permission to start a withdrawal. He was refused and told to commit his reserves so that the offensive could be reinvigorated. Thus more days of fierce fighting were assured in this scattered, confusing action, carried out in the depths of winter and ultimately involving a million men.

Now that the weather had cleared and the Allies could at last make full use of their overwhelming air superiority to blast German armoured columns, enemy casualties increased greatly. There was not much that the depleted Luftwaffe could do to stop the rain of bombs on both forward positions and areas in the rear, even with the help of its new, jet-propelled Messerschmitt fighters.

On Christmas Eve 1944, the Allies had 32 divisions in that sector and were at last bringing their superior weight to bear on the hard-pressed Germans in a string of sharp counter-attacks. The Bulge was beginning to shrink, and von Rundstedt was once more appealing to Hitler to allow him to disengage. Perhaps the crushing defeat of a large part of von Manteuffel's Fifth Panzer Army on Christmas Day, followed by the relief of Bastogne on Boxing Day, served to convince the reluctant Hitler that his grandiose scheme to blitzkrieg his way to Antwerp had been little more than wishful thinking. Clearly there was no way through the ever-stronger Allied lines, so he consented to a withdrawal on 27 December, while still maintaining that 'Herbstnebel' had been worth the effort. But had it?

By early January 1945, the front line in the Ardennes was almost back to where it had been when the offensive began. And in some of the worst fighting of the war, the Germans had suffered 100,000 casualties, the Americans 81,000 and the British, who did not play a large part in the battle, 1,400. Losses in guns, tanks and equipment had been enormous on both sides, but the Allies could quickly replace their's, the Germans could not.

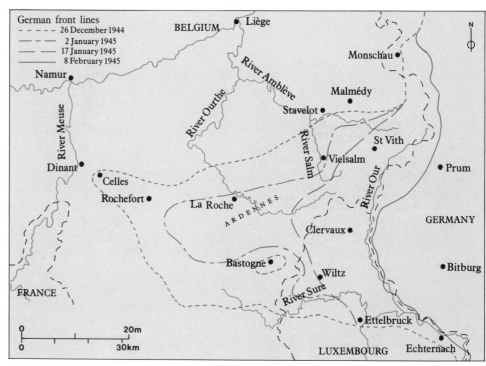

German front lines
- - - - - 26 December 1944
— - — - 2 January 1945
— — — 17 January 1945
———— 8 February 1945

Troops of Patton's Third Army fought their way up the Assenois road to relieve Bastogne. Von Manteuffel was thus obliged to divert some formations from their advance on the River Meuse to counter these attacks. The Germans were soon severely handicapped by lack of fuel, and, on 23 December, the skies cleared and the full weight of Allied air power fell on them. While Patton attacked from the south, the US First Army, units from the US Ninth and from Montgomery's Twenty-first Army Group, pressed from the north and west. By 26 December, the German attack was faltering.

The offensive ended in total failure for the Germans. They gained nothing and suffered heavy casualties and loss of vital *matériel*, which might have been deployed along the formidable natural defence of the Rhine. The Allies should have been able to cut through the base of the Bulge to prevent any German formations escaping eastward. As it was, although the Germans abandoned their tanks for lack of fuel, they fought a dogged retreat and thousands got away.

A still, *left*, from a German propaganda film, showing German troops with captured US equipment, including a Colt .45 pistol, a belt of machine-gun bullets and an ammunition box. An integral part of the German plan was to use captured Allied supplies, especially fuel.

The Commanders

Von Rundstedt

Von Manteuffel

McAuliffe

Field Marshal Gerd von Rundstedt (1875–1953) was an aloof, apolitical officer of the old Prussian school, whose age and prestige placed him at the head of the officer caste system. Hitler disliked him but needed an elderly, experienced commander for his offensive in the Ardennes. So in September 1944, Rundstedt was summoned from semi-retirement to the 'Wolf's Lair', where Hitler treated him with marked diffidence and respect. Rundstedt agreed to serve as Commander-in-Chief West, but was not told of Hitler's intentions until much later. After the war, he stated

that, while he recognized the merit of Hitler's operational plan, he realized that '... all conditions for the possible success of such an offensive were lacking.' Rundstedt was captured in 1945, tried and imprisoned, but was released four years later.

General Hasso Freiherr von Manteuffel (1897–1978) was an extremely small man—around 1.6m/5ft 2in tall and weighing only 54kg/120lb—and, like Rundstedt, shunned politics. After infantry service in WWI, he transferred to the cavalry and soon recognized the possibilities of armour, as advocated by the young

Guderian. In 1941, he was posted to the Russian Front and served there with great distinction.

Brigadier-General Anthony C. McAuliffe (1898–1975), US commander in Bastogne, was given an ultimatum by the Germans who had encircled the town: surrender or be annihilated. McAuliffe's reply—'To the German commander: Nuts! From the American commander'— gained wide currency as the most succinct rebuff of the war. McAuliffe later served as US Army Commander in Germany.

By 31 December, the German offensive had been halted, but it took a month of heavy fighting for the Allies to eliminate the Bulge. The weather had become much colder since the start of the campaign, the fog thicker and the snow deeper. The narrow, twisting roads in the Ardennes were icy, and vehicles, such as these 90-mm tank destroyers, stalled on inclines. Others slithered to the verge and had to be pushed aside to allow those coming behind at a crawl to pass. Bridges had been destroyed by the Germans and the sites defended. In such conditions, an advance of 3km/2mls in a day was an achievement. Freezing fog and poor visibility prevented the Allies from flying sorties on most days.

Berlin/*April-May 1945*

Early in 1945, when the Third Reich was on the verge of collapse, a prize remained that Josef Stalin wanted above all others—Berlin, the German capital and last refuge of Adolf Hitler. For a time it had looked as if Field Marshal Bernard Montgomery's Twenty-first Army Group, curving into north Germany from Holland, might get there first; then the Supreme Allied Commander, General Dwight D. Eisenhower, moved the main axis of advance away from the direction of Berlin.

He now focussed his attention on central Germany, where he felt that General Omar Bradley's Twelfth Army Group was in a good position to make a rapid junction with Soviet troops around Dresden, thereby cutting the stricken country in half and making the subjugation of its remaining forces much easier. Eisenhower took the view that any last stand by the Germans would take place in the south and that, as a consequence, Berlin had become no more than a name on a map. He therefore sent a personal message to Stalin on 28 March 1945, informing him of his intention and inquiring about the Red Army's plans.

While Eisenhower waited for the Soviet leader's reply, the British protested vigorously at his change of plan. Prime Minister Winston Churchill spelled out his disquiet in a letter to the ailing US President, Franklin D. Roosevelt, telling him that to Germans everywhere the fall of Berlin would be 'the supreme signal of defeat'. Then he tackled the point that really worried him: 'If the Russians take Berlin, will not their impression that they have been the overwhelming contributor to the common victory be unduly imprinted in their minds, and may this not lead them into a mood which will raise grave and formidable difficulties in the future?' Churchill believed that, from a political standpoint, Berlin should be taken by Anglo-American forces if they had the opportunity. Zones of occupation, which had been discussed at the Yalta Conference in February, could be sorted out later by the Allies.

The Americans, whose main goal at that time was a military victory, closed ranks behind Eisenhower, who was encouraged when he received Stalin's response on 2 April. The Russian leader welcomed his proposal, concurring that the main thrust of their converging armies should be Dresden, and adding that, as a result, he would send secondary forces toward Berlin, which he agreed had 'lost its former strategic importance'. He estimated that his offensive would begin toward the middle of May.

Nothing could have been further from

Stalin's devious plan
Stalin distrusted the Western leaders and believed that they were preparing to seize Berlin before the Russians could. This was, indeed, the plan advocated by Field Marshal Montgomery—a single thrust in overwhelming strength from north of the Ruhr—but Eisenhower had vetoed it in favour of a drive in the direction of Dresden in order to cut Germany in half.

While ostensibly cooperating with Eisenhower, Stalin had a plan of his own: to enhance Russian prestige and to establish Communist control in central as well as eastern Europe by entering Berlin first. To this end, he personally masterminded the outline plan for his last offensive without informing Eisenhower.

It was this duplicity in Stalin's nature that led him to mistrust his allies, mistakenly thinking they must be as devious and secretive as he was himself.

A **member** of the Volkssturm (Home Guard) and his grandson, a boy of the Hitler Youth, *below*, armed with a *panzerfaust*, a recoilless anti-tank gun. Toward the end, the defence of Berlin was left largely to the old and the very young, or to bicycle troops, using small-arms and *panzerfausten* against Russian tanks and artillery.

A **German** government newspaper of 27 April, *above*, for the 'Defenders of Greater Berlin', claiming that the capital had become a deathtrap for Soviet tanks. The Germans were fighting not only in defence of Berlin, the editorial claimed, but of European civilization.

After the decisive Battle of Kursk in July 1943, the Germans never regained the strategic initiative in the east. The Russians advanced remorselessly westward, expelling the enemy first from the Soviet Union and then, step by step, from eastern Europe. By August 1944, they had reached Warsaw and captured Bucharest. In the last week of October they entered East Prussia and by April 1945 were poised for an attack on Berlin. Stalin, determined to capture the capital before his Western allies, took command of the final operations. He summoned to the Kremlin Zhukov, commander of the First Belorussian Front directly east of Berlin, and Koniev, commander of the First Ukrainian Front to the south, to determine the opening date of the offensive, troop compositions and objectives. Zhukov was ordered to capture Berlin while Koniev struck west to the Elbe south of the city. With a pencil, Stalin then began to draw on a map the demarcation line between the two commands. When his pencil reached Lübben, southeast of Berlin, he suddenly, and without explanation, stopped. No one spoke, but Koniev took this to mean that, if his forces achieved a rapid breakthrough, he was authorized to take Berlin himself from the south. In this way, Stalin implicitly invited the two rival commanders to compete for the capture of the city.

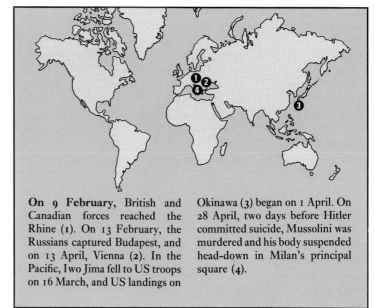

On 9 February, British and Canadian forces reached the Rhine (1). On 13 February, the Russians captured Budapest, and on 13 April, Vienna (2). In the Pacific, Iwo Jima fell to US troops on 16 March, and US landings on Okinawa (3) began on 1 April. On 28 April, two days before Hitler committed suicide, Mussolini was murdered and his body suspended head-down in Milan's principal square (4).

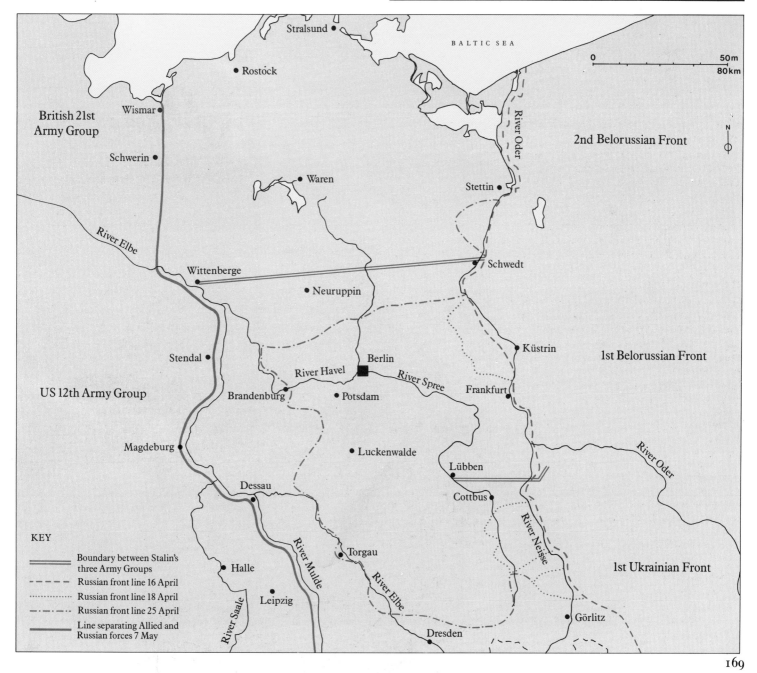

British 21st Army Group

US 12th Army Group

2nd Belorussian Front

1st Belorussian Front

1st Ukrainian Front

BALTIC SEA

Stralsund

Rostock

Wismar

Schwerin

Waren

Stettin

River Oder

River Elbe

Wittenberge

Schwedt

Neuruppin

Küstrin

Stendal

Berlin

River Havel

River Spree

Frankfurt

Brandenburg

Potsdam

Magdeburg

Luckenwalde

Lübben

River Oder

Dessau

Cottbus

River Neisse

Torgau

River Mulde

River Elbe

Halle

Leipzig

River Saale

Dresden

Görlitz

0   50m
0   80km

KEY

	Boundary between Stalin's three Army Groups
	Russian front line 16 April
	Russian front line 18 April
	Russian front line 25 April
	Line separating Allied and Russian forces 7 May

the truth. When Stalin read Eisenhower's telegram, he immediately suspected an Anglo-American plot to race the Red Army to Berlin. Before replying, he had called in his two senior Field Marshals, Georgi Zhukov and Ivan Koniev, briefed them on what he perceived to be Eisenhower's real intention, and asked pointedly, 'Who will take Berlin? We or the Allies?' Both Zhukov and Koniev, who were rivals, offered to storm the German capital, so Stalin gave each marshal just 48 hours to prepare a plan of attack. After weeks of heavy fighting, they had been hoping to rest, re-equip and reinforce their commands before the start of the next big offensive expected in May, but now it was obvious that their leader meant them to move much sooner than that.

Zhukov, whose First Belorussian Front (or Army Group) was on the River Oder, 80km/50mls east of Berlin, with a bridgehead on the west bank at Küstrin, based his scheme on an opening bombardment by some 10,000 guns followed by an unusual pre-dawn attack: 140 anti-aircraft searchlights, beamed at the German lines, would be switched on to blind the defenders as his infantry rushed them. The main thrust would be delivered out of the Küstrin bridgehead by four field and two tank armies, and two more armies would support each flank. With over 750,000 men at his disposal and complete air superiority, he expected quickly to overwhelm the opposing German forces.

Koniev, whose First Ukrainian Front rested on the east bank of the River Neisse and was 121km/75mls southeast of Berlin at its nearest point, had to rely on mobility rather than weight if he were to succeed. After a two-and-a-half hour bombardment by around 7,500 guns, he would force a crossing at dawn under a smoke screen, using five field and two tank armies (more than 500,000 men). The tank armies, concentrated on his right flank, would smash through the German defences then swing northwest toward Berlin. He was promised two more armies in support, but he could not count on their arriving on time—and time, as it turned out, was short. Stalin approved both of their plans but, to Koniev's great disappointment, he gave Zhukov priority to go for Berlin because his forces were nearer to the capital. However, fanning the competition between the two field marshals,

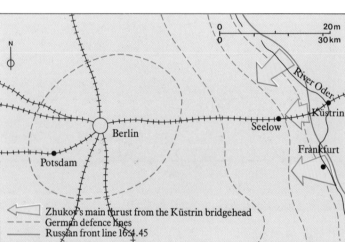

Zhukov's main thrust from the Küstrin bridgehead
German defence lines
Russian front line 16.4.45

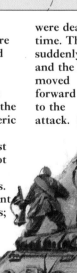

At 04.00 on 16 April 1945, three red flares, fired by the Russians in their Küstrin bridgehead, illuminated the sky and the River Oder. A moment later, 140 searchlights, beamed at the Germans, were switched on. Then three green flares were fired, the signal for the opening of the greatest artillery bombardment ever mounted on the Eastern Front. Some 10,000 guns of all calibres—mortars, tanks, self-propelled guns, light and heavy artillery and 400 Katyushas—pounded the German lines. The eruption was so terrible that entire villages collapsed and blocks of concrete, steel girders and trees were tossed into the air. An atmospheric disturbance was created and forest fires blazed as hot winds roared between the trees. The bombardment lasted 35 minutes; it was so intense that men shook and were deafened for a time. Then it suddenly stopped, and the Russians moved forward to the attack.

The searchlights (3), some probably stripped from Moscow's defences, were operated by women soldiers of the Red Army. Adding to their intense glare, all tank headlights (4) were also switched on to blind the Germans, while the Russians could see every movement.

Russian T34 tanks (5) had been produced since 1940 and were continually improved by strengthening armour and increasing fire power. By 1945, the T34's turret had been redesigned, and it carried an 85-mm gun. Tank tactics had to be adapted to every technical innovation. As early as 1943, close support from soldiers on foot and in carriers was needed to destroy infantry-manned anti-tank weapons, which were becoming more and more deadly.

Russian infantry (6) attacked with pitiless ferocity, fired by a longing for revenge. Many had fought at Leningrad, Moscow or Stalingrad and had seen their homes destroyed and their land laid waste. Prisoners recently released from captivity by the advancing Red Army were regarded as traitors and were used to clear mines.

Total air superiority was enjoyed by the Russians, enabling the 6,500 bombers stationed along Zhukov's and Koniev's fronts to pound the enemy ahead of the advancing tanks (7) without harassment.

The Russians were, however, deluded in thinking that their massive artillery bombardments had destroyed the Germans' ability to resist. For few Germans were in the area: General Heinrici, forseeing such an attack, had ordered most of his troops back to the second line of defence during the previous night. So the shells fell on unmanned positions (2) and the searchlights merely served to spotlight the Russian tanks and infantry for waiting German gunners.

It was impossible to prevent a Russian breakthrough because of their vast numbers, but the Germans bought time by holding up their advance. Heinrici's men had fortified and now manned the Seelow Heights (1), a sandy ridge west of Küstrin, ranging from 30-61m/100-200ft in height, which barred the main road to Berlin. From there they raked the advancing Russians with gunfire and managed to hold out until the evening of 17 April—upsetting Zhukov's timetable for the capture of Berlin and allowing Koniev to close on the city from the southeast.

Stalin tactitly indicated to Koniev that if he had a chance to make a dash for Berlin before Zhukov, he was free to do so.

The date for these simultaneous offensives was set for only 13 days ahead, 16 April. But five days before the Russian attacks began (and a day before President Roosevelt died), the leading elements of Lieutenant-General William Simpson's US Ninth Army reached the banks of the River Elbe, 80km/50mls west of Berlin. By 15 April, American troops were across the river at Barby and there was little that General Walther Wenck's motley Twelfth Army could do to prevent a determined push for the capital.

Wenck could not stop the Ninth, but Eisenhower did. He ordered Simpson to stand fast on the Elbe while the first priority—a link-up with the Russians around Dresden—was pursued. Next morning, at 04.00, massed fire from thousands of guns announced the start of the Red Army's push for Berlin.

How was the German capital to be defended? There were those, professional soldiers mostly, who regarded it as indefensible with the limited resources at hand. Principal among them was Colonel-General Heinz Guderian, Chief of the General Staff, who was dismissed on 28 March for suggesting that the time had come to negotiate with the enemy. And there was a school of thought prevalent in the unreal atmosphere of the Führer's bunker under the Chancellery that the Russians would suffer their biggest defeat at the gates of the city. Hitler, in failing health and more irrational than ever, based his optimism on the coloured flags on his war map symbolizing a mass of intact Army and SS units, though many of them, in fact, had ceased to exist and others were vastly under-strength.

The one sensible move that the Führer made at the end of March was to relieve Reichsführer SS Heinrich Himmler, the chicken farmer turned secret police chief, from his unlikely post as Commander-in-Chief of Army Group Vistula and give it to Colonel-General Gotthard Heinrici, a veteran of the Russian Front who knew how to direct large formations in combat.

Short of armour, ammunition, equipment, supplies and adequate reserves, Heinrici's new command (which had not seen the River Vistula for some time) comprised three armies. The Third Panzer Army was led by General Hasso von Manteuffel and occupied a 153-km/95-ml front north of Berlin to Stettin. General Theodor Busse's Ninth Army defended 129km/80mls along the Oder, east of the

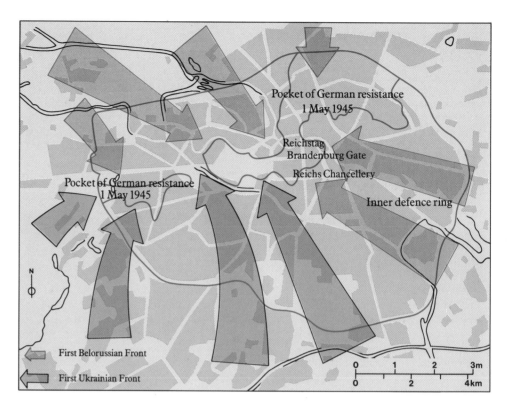

Pocket of German resistance
1 May 1945

Pocket of German resistance
1 May 1945

Reichstag
Brandenburg Gate
Reichs Chancellery

Inner defence ring

N

First Belorussian Front

First Ukrainian Front

0 1 2 3m
0 2 4km

Berlin was defended house by house, often room by room, by every able-bodied male. The Germans were inadequately armed, the Russians numerically superior and the outcome never in doubt. The Soviets launched powerful attacks from all sides, preceded by saturation bombardments. German resistance was at its most intense among rubble, which provided excellent cover.

Throughout the war, both Allied and Axis forces made great use of propaganda leaflets, usually dropped by aircraft. During the Battle of Berlin, many copies of a leaflet advising surrender, *left*, were showered on the city by the Red Air Force. 'Further fighting', it read, 'means the destruction of German industry, disruption to family life and useless personal sacrifice.' Few Germans responded to this call while Hitler lived.

WEITERMACHEN
bedeutet:

FÜR DEUTSCHLAND-

Ständig wachsende Verheerung durch Material-schlachten auf deutschem Boden im Osten und Westen. Vernichtung der letzten Voraussetzungen für den Wiederaufbau nach dem Kriege.

FÜR DEINE FAMILIE-

Ständig wachsende Gefahren durch den ein-rollenden Krieg. Selbstmörderische Volkssturm-Einsätze, Bombardierungen, immer mehr Nahrungsknappheit, Parteiterror und schliesslich Chaos.

FÜR DICH-

Ständig wachsende Material-Unterle-genheit, in der Deine Opferbereitschaft allein nichts ausrichten kann. Ein Selbst-opfer in letzter Stunde, das seinen Zweck verloren hat.

ZG 119

Hitler's last days

The Führerbunker was sited in the lower of two storeys in the Chancellery air-raid shelter, built 15m/50ft beneath the ground and covered with a heavy layer of reinforced concrete. The upper storey contained the kitchens, staff living quarters and rooms for Goebbels's family. The Führerbunker below comprised 18 small rooms, leading off a central passageway. The passage was divided in the middle by a partition, the first half being used as a daily conference room. To one side, apartments were set aside for Hitler and Eva Braun: she had a bed-sittingroom, bathroom and dressing-room, Hitler a bedroom, sitting-room and study.

Across the corridor there was accommodation for Goebbels and for Hitler's personal physician and a surgery, as well as the telephone exchange, guards' room and generators and air-purification machinery. Other senior Nazis still in Berlin—notably Martin Bormann—were housed in other nearby air-raid shelters.

Access to the Führerbunker was by a heavy steel door; inside, security was stringent, even generals being subjected to the indignity of a search. Particular attention was given to briefcases, since one had been used to introduce a bomb into the 'Wolf's Lair' in the attempt on Hitler's life on 20 July 1944.

The interior of the bunker was brilliantly lit and comfortably furnished. The atmosphere, however, was oppressive. Mental and physical exhaustion, incessant air raids, fear, despair, and the certain knowledge that, with the Russians already on the outskirts of the city, defeat and death could not be averted for long, created in almost all the occupants a tension not far removed from hysteria. Hitler alone, once he had made his decision to commit suicide, was at times serene.

Much of the day and night was taken up with conferences, during which symbols for non-existent or grossly depleted armies were moved from spot to spot on a map. Meals were the only bearable interlude. After them, Hitler would play with a gift from Bormann, his Alsatian, Blondi, and her puppies; one of these, Wolf, whom he had brought up on his own, had Hitler's special affection. He would fondle him on his lap, endlessly repeating his name.

Generals and high-ranking Nazis summoned to the bunker all remarked on the eerie atmosphere, wholly divorced from reality, that prevailed among its occupants. Colonel-General Heinrici summed it up when he whispered to his operations chief, Colonel Eismann, on one of the last days of Hitler's life: 'Just think: three years ago Hitler had Europe under his command, from the Volga to the Atlantic. Now he's sitting in a hole under the earth.'

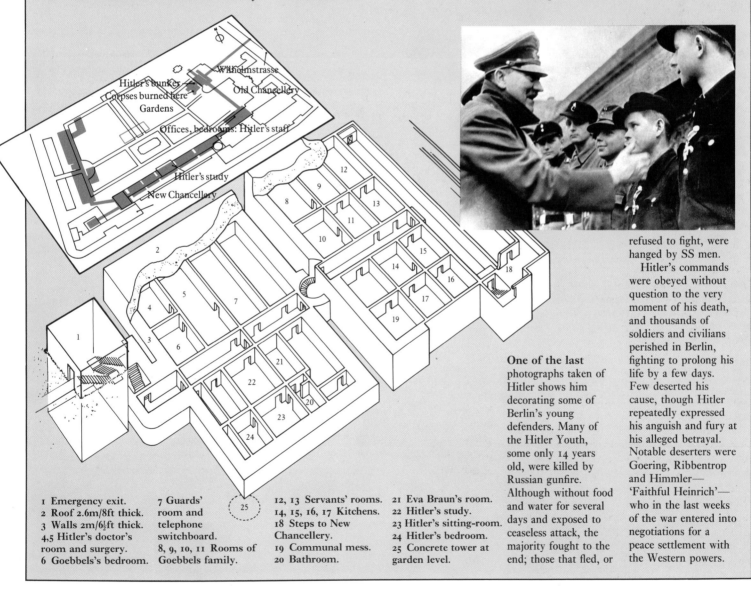

1 Emergency exit.
2 Roof 2.6m/8ft thick.
3 Walls 2m/6½ft thick.
4,5 Hitler's doctor's room and surgery.
6 Goebbels's bedroom.
7 Guards' room and telephone switchboard.
8, 9, 10, 11 Rooms of Goebbels family.
12, 13 Servants' rooms.
14, 15, 16, 17 Kitchens.
18 Steps to New Chancellery.
19 Communal mess.
20 Bathroom.
21 Eva Braun's room.
22 Hitler's study.
23 Hitler's sitting-room.
24 Hitler's bedroom.
25 Concrete tower at garden level.

One of the last photographs taken of Hitler shows him decorating some of Berlin's young defenders. Many of the Hitler Youth, some only 14 years old, were killed by Russian gunfire. Although without food and water for several days and exposed to ceaseless attack, the majority fought to the end; those that fled, or refused to fight, were hanged by SS men.

Hitler's commands were obeyed without question to the very moment of his death, and thousands of soldiers and civilians perished in Berlin, fighting to prolong his life by a few days. Few deserted his cause, though Hitler repeatedly expressed his anguish and fury at his alleged betrayal. Notable deserters were Goering, Ribbentrop and Himmler—'Faithful Heinrich'—who in the last weeks of the war entered into negotiations for a peace settlement with the Western powers.

Berlin/4

city, down to the river's confluence with the Neisse, where it flanked Field Marshal Ferdinand Schörner's depleted army group which was barring the way to the capture of Dresden.

When the battle started, Heinrici was able to call on fewer than 30 divisions to cope with Zhukov's and Koniev's army groups in the vicinity of Berlin. A separate offensive was launched in the north against von Manteuffel by Marshal Konstantin Rokossovsky's Second Belorussian Front. It was to be a very unequal contest.

Massive bombardment and blinding searchlights notwithstanding, the First Belorussian Front's surge westward out of the Küstrin bridgehead before dawn on 16 April soon slowed and halted. Stalin was furious; Zhukov, mortified. Heinrici, an expert in defensive tactics, had pulled

back his front-line troops on the eve of the attack, and the massive Soviet artillery effort had fallen on empty positions. The Ninth Army was dug in on the Seelow heights, blocking the main Küstrin-Berlin road, and was handing out terrible punishment to its attackers.

By sheer weight of numbers, Zhukov's forces carried the Seelow line on 17 April, but they were further slowed when they came up against more German defences, reinforced by General Karl Weidling's 56th Panzer Corps, Busse's last credible reserve. Stalin, fuming at the delay, ordered Koniev, whose offensive was making excellent progress, to turn northward with his tanks. Now major elements from two Russian army groups were pitted against the capital.

On 20 April, when von Manteuffel was assailed by Rokossovsky, Busse's Ninth

Army also started to disintegrate, and Zhukov, now only 35km/22mls from Berlin, began to shell the city with long-range artillery. Soon both the remnants of the Ninth Army and the battered metropolis were caught between the rapidly closing Russian pincers. Meanwhile, both Zhukov and Koniev had detailed spearhead forces to hurry on westward to the River Elbe, where first contact was made with the Americans at Torgau on 25 April.

Two days earlier Hitler had sent an impassioned plea to General Wenck to save Berlin. He implored him to disengage his Twelfth Army from its positions on the Elbe

The Soviet attack on Berlin, preceded by heavy air attacks, was launched from all sides on the morning of 26 April. Resistance by the Germans was ferocious, and they made skillful use of the ruined buildings and rubble to snipe at Russian sappers clearing paths for infantry and tanks. But overwhelming Soviet numerical superiority guaranteed the ultimate collapse of German resistance.

By the evening of 29 April, the garrison had been cut off and isolated in three areas and the great prize of the Reichstag building was within reach. Its capture was entrusted to Major-General Perevertkin's 79th Rifle Corps. The

attack was mounted in three stages: first, the Moltke Bridge was captured and held, then the Ministry of the Interior building (HQ of the Gestapo) was taken. Once these were secured, on the morning of 30 April, General Perevertkin decided to storm the Reichstag, but

attacks at 04.30 and 11.30 were repulsed by concentrated German small-arms fire. Then, at 18.00, a new assault was launched after a heavy artillery bombardment.

The Reichstag (2) was defended by SS and Volkssturm troops, augmented by a Naval School detachment and supported by artillery batteries sited in the Zoological Gardens.

The Germans had turned the Reichstag into a fortress. The lower storeys had been reinforced with steel rails and concrete, and windows and doors bricked up (3) except for loopholes. In front of the building, trenches and an anti-tank ditch (6) had been dug and flooded; streets leading to the Reichstag were barricaded and mined.

In the square, several 88-mm guns (4) had been ranged on the Moltke bridge to try to prevent the Russians bringing up reinforcements.

The dome (1), gutted and reduced to a steel framework, was enveloped in smoke and dust. Whole sections of the building had been wrecked by high-explosive shells.

The Russians suffered heavy losses breaking into the Reichstag. Desperate fighting took place for each room, the Germans using every weapon they could lay hands on—rifles, pistols, bazookas, grenades and machine-guns. Their weapons became so hot with ceaseless firing that they could not be touched. Fighting continued until the morning of 2 May, when the last of the Germans, those who were trapped in the basement, finally surrendered. Of the 5,000 defenders, around 2,500 were killed and the rest taken prisoner.

Through the rubble, on 30 April, Captain S.A. Neustroyev led his men to the Reichstag; one carried the Red Flag (5) and secured it to a column at the main entrance at 14.25. Later, some Russian soldiers broke out on to the roof and raised it there, to flutter triumphantly over the ruined city.

around Magdeburg and march to the relief of the city. It is forever to Wenck's credit not only that he attempted this manoeuvre but that he got so far. By 28 April, he had reached Potsdam, on the outskirts of the capital, where he finally encountered overwhelming Russian resistance. Wenck, however, managed to extricate his command and link up with what was left of the Ninth Army south of Berlin. This mauled and spent force then set off westward, hoping to capitulate to the Americans.

While Hitler raved about the treachery of his generals and his armies, Zhukov's and Koniev's troops closed in to mop up what Goebbels's Propaganda Ministry was describing as 'Fortress Berlin'. It was a myth. A large proportion of the 90,000-strong garrison, commanded in the opening stages of the battle by Major-General Hellmuth Reymann and latterly by General Weidling, consisted of poorly armed elderly men of the Volkssturm (Home Guard) and boys of the Hitler Youth. They occupied hastily prepared defences and used overturned tramcars filled with rocks as makeshift barricades.

And nearly two million Berliners, contriving still to go about their daily business in the beleaguered city, knew that talk of a fortress was nonsense. A current joke summed up their feelings: 'The Russians will take exactly two hours fifteen minutes to capture Berlin. Two hours laughing their heads off and fifteen minutes breaking down the barriers.'

As the Russians neared the city, many members of the Nazi hierarchy—including Goering and Himmler—left Berlin, but Hitler resolved to stay. For a while he had continued to operate as if the situation could be retrieved, issuing a stream of orders which bore no relation to reality. Then, as 15,000 Soviet guns rained shells on his helpless capital, he dropped all pretence of playing the warlord and announced his intention to take his life before the Russians arrived.

His Third Reich, which he had boasted would last a thousand years, was literally crumbling around him in its twelfth year. While Russian troops fought their way into the city, the Führer, in a final fit of venom, stripped Goering and Himmler of their offices—the former for trying to grab power prematurely, the latter for putting out peace feelers—and named Admiral Karl Dönitz as his successor. After dictating his will and political testament, Hitler and Eva Braun, his wife of one day, retired to their quarters in the afternoon of 30 April and committed suicide. Their bodies were burned in a

A defeated German soldier, all hope gone, sits amid the rubble surrounding the devastated Reichstag. He was one of only 2,500 German soldiers to survive the ferocious fighting. Remaining German troops elsewhere in the city surrendered on 2 May. Many later perished in captivity in Russian camps.

The headline in the *Daily Mail* on 2 May brought the news the free world had been waiting for: Hitler was dead and the war virtually over. But his successor, Admiral Dönitz, was resolved to continue the struggle. 'My first task', he said in his broadcast announcing Hitler's death, 'will be to save the German people from the advance of the Bolshevist enemy. For this aim only, the military struggle continues.'

The day after Hitler's death, Goebbels telegraphed Dönitz, the new Reichspresident. He did not specify the manner of Hitler's death, and Dönitz—who did not suspect suicide—broadcast to the Germans that Hitler had died leading his troops in battle. Even at this late hour, the Nazi leaders did not tell the truth, either to each other or to Germany.

The Commanders

Koniev

Heinrici

Busse

Wenck

Marshal of the Soviet Union **Ivan Koniev** (**1897–1973**) joined the Communist Party and then the Red Army in 1918. A tall, outspoken man, he had fought for the Tsar before joining the revolutionaries. His career followed much the same pattern as Zhukov's, but there was a distinction: Koniev joined the army with the powerful rank of commissar while Zhukov had always been a regular soldier.

Koniev, though considerate of his officers and men, was barbarous toward the Germans. During the Dnieper campaign, he called for the surrender of several German divisions which his men had surrounded. When this was not immediately forthcoming, he ordered his Cossacks, armed with sabres, to attack and cut down the Germans; even those hands raised in surrender were severed.

Colonel-General Gotthard Heinrici (**1886–1971**) took over command of Army Group Vistula from Himmler at precisely the moment when the Russians cut off the 20th Panzer Division, which had for months held open a corridor between the Russian bridgeheads either side of Küstrin on the west bank of the River Oder. The Soviets now had a large forward base for the assault on Berlin. Heinrici had conducted the retreat through the Carpathians to Silesia and was well versed in fighting against the Red Army. By the end of the war, he had become Germany's leading exponent of defensive warfare, a field in which most German commanders—trained for attack—were weak. He saved manpower by withdrawing his front line before the Soviet bombardment so that the shells fell on empty positions.

General Theodor Busse (**1897–**), commander of the German Ninth Army, a bespectacled man of 47, defended the eastern approaches to Berlin. A conventional commander, he never retreated until ordered to do so, thinking that independent action might be regarded as treasonable.

In the last days of the war, **General Walther Wenck** (**1900–82**) was appointed to command the Twelfth Army, then fighting on the River Elbe. Hitler had inflated hopes of this army's saving Berlin by an advance from the southwest. 'The army of General Wenck', Hitler repeatedly said in the Bunker, 'is moving up from the south. He must and will drive the Russians back long enough to save our people.' But Wenck's was a depleted army and he did not have the strength for such a feat, although he did try to reach Berlin.

The Russians paraded captured Germans through the streets of Moscow as a spectacle for civilians and for publicity films. They were then marched eastward to prisoner of war camps in the frozen wastes of Siberia. Few survived the abominable conditions—intense cold, inadequate diet and clothing, brutal treatment by Russian guards and outbreaks of typhus. Of the 91,000 Germans taken prisoner at Stalingrad, for example, only 5,000 survived to see Germany again.

shallow trench in the Chancellery garden. Later that night Zhukov's victorious soldiers raised the Red Banner above the Reichstag, the German parliament building. This, incidentally, was a bitter blow to Koniev. His troops had been denied the kudos of this symbolic act by Stalin, who had ordered the First Ukrainian Front to halt a short distance away from the Reichstag building.

Although there were still pockets of resistance amid the ruins, the Russians effectively controlled Berlin, a fact acknowledged by those remaining in the bunker, who now tried to negotiate terms. The Soviets refused to treat, demanding unconditional surrender, which General Weidling duly offered to General Vasili Chuikov of the Eighth Guards Army on 2 May. Within a few days, German forces everywhere had laid down their arms, hostilities ceasing officially at midnight on 8 May.

As the Soviets took over the capital, there followed an orgy of rape and looting which the victors sought to justify as revenge for atrocities committed by German forces in the USSR. It was an ugly conclusion to a short but bitterly fought campaign.

Nobody knows how many soldiers and civilians perished between 16 April and 2 May. Estimates put the German dead at more than 200,000, the Russian at 150,000, which reflects the ferocity with which the Ninth Army fought. Tens of thousands on both sides were wounded. The inner city was reduced to rubble and its surviving population cowed; but by the time the first American, British and French troops arrived in July to man the previously agreed zones of occupation, the Russian savagery had been checked.

Now Churchill's forecast of 'grave and formidable difficulties' was realized. The Russians, who felt that they had shouldered the biggest share of the war in Europe, made life awkward for their other partners in the Four-Power Control Council set up to administer post-war Berlin. The British, American and French contingents were marooned in a sea of Soviet domination, which, by common consent, now extended 160km/100mls west of the capital. Stalin did not disguise his distaste for the presence of the Western Allies deep in the heart of the Russian zone of occupation, which was later to grow into Communist East Germany. Relations became frigid, deteriorating into what became known as the Cold War, a conflict of ideologies which has been waged ever since between the Western nations and the Soviet Bloc.

General Jodl, watched by his compatriot Admiral von Friedeburg, signs the instrument of total unconditional surrender at Rheims, to take effect on all fronts at 24.00 on Tuesday 8 May. Alfred Jodl, the most intractable opponent of surrender, had played for time during the preliminary negotiations, hoping to win concessions from the Allies. Eisenhower, exasperated, then threatened to seal his lines on the Western Front, thereby preventing further Germans from escaping from the east. So Jodl had no option but to signal Dönitz, the new President, for permission to sign; this was promptly given.

In Berlin, in the early hours of 9 May, Field Marshal Zhukov, *centre*, signs the formal ratification treaty on behalf of the Supreme Command of the Red Army. Next to him sits Vyshinsky, Stalin's delegate. He is watched by several interpreters, the British Colonel Strong, *standing*, and Field Marshal Sokolovsky, *right*. Air Chief Marshal Sir Arthur Tedder signed the document on behalf of General Eisenhower, and Field Marshal Keitel on behalf of the German High Command.

Victory in Europe

Churchill and Harry Truman, the new US President, proclaimed 8 May, 'Victory in Europe Day', a public holiday. In London, people gathered in all the main squares and avenues in enormous numbers. From the balcony of the Home Office in Whitehall, Churchill addressed a huge crowd—'This is *your* victory'—while the Mall up to the gates of Buckingham Palace was crammed with civilians and servicemen on leave, singing and dancing and cheering the King and Queen when they appeared on the balcony. Church bells were rung through-

out the land and even in small villages there were celebrations to express relief and gratitude that the fighting in Europe was over. In New York, people poured in their thousands into central Manhattan, particularly Times Square, and celebrated until daybreak.

It was otherwise in Berlin. Food of any sort was scarce; many services, notably electricity, had ceased to exist and throughout the almost totally ruined city centre there was no water supply. For the women, however, there was something worse. The

Russian front-line troops who had captured the city were in the main disciplined, but the thousands following up at once indulged in unrestrained pillage and rape. Gangs of soldiers would assault a single woman; then, as often as not, shoot her. Age gave no security: children and the elderly suffered equally. Medical estimates suggest that as many as 100,000 German women were raped in Berlin. Soon, in fear and despair, women throughout the city were committing suicide; in a single district, 215 cases were recorded in three weeks.

Germany was divided into zones of Allied occupation and Berlin was jointly occupied and administered by a combined commission. It was isolated in the Soviet zone, but the Western Allies insisted on air corridors—a crucial factor in 1948 when the USSR sealed all roads from the west into the city.

An Allied publicity photograph of US occupation units entering Berlin. The city was divided into four zones of occupation—British, American, French and Russian. Spandau Prison, where senior Nazis were to be incarcerated, was, and still is, under the control of each of the Allied powers on a monthly rota basis.

Homeless civilians wandering in the ruins in front of Berlin's wrecked Anhalter Station. Most carry their remaining possessions and are muffled and wearing goggles for protection against the dust and smoke, generated by intense bombardment.

Revellers in Trafalgar Square, London, on VE night, waving flags and celebrating the end of the war in the European theatre.

Okinawa/*April-June 1945*

In the spring of 1945, the successful American island-hopping campaign against the Japanese in the Pacific entered its final phase with the invasion of Okinawa—the last stop before Japan itself.

Enemy resistance had been intensifying as the battle drew closer to home, so United States forces were expecting to meet fanatical opposition in their bid to capture this unprepossessing, but strategically invaluable, rocky outcrop, 97km/60mls long and 30km/18mls across at its widest part. This island—the largest of the Ryuku chain—lying just 563km/350mls south of the Japanese mainland, offered excellent harbour, airfield and troop-staging facilities. It was perfect as the main base from which to launch a major assault on Japan.

In order to secure it, the Americans thought that they would have to take on and defeat about 65,000 enemy troops, three times the number which had caused so much difficulty on Iwo Jima in February and early March. But their reconnaissance, conducted at long range by high-flying aircraft, had erred on the low side. Awaiting them on Okinawa was General Mitsuru Ushijima's Thirty-second Army, nearly 120,000 strong. In addition, the Japanese committed some 10,000 aircraft to the defence of the vital island and the navy, though short of fuel, sent a task force, including the *Yamato*, the largest battleship ever built.

For 'Operation Iceberg', as the attack on Okinawa had been codenamed, the United States had assembled a formidable array of combat-hardened units. The landing force, the biggest of the Pacific war, comprised Lieutenant-General Simon Buckner's Tenth Army—three Marine and four Army divisions totalling upward of 155,000 men. By the time the battle ended, however, more than 300,000 American soldiers were to be involved in the vicious fighting.

US naval operations were conducted by Admiral Raymond Spruance's Fifth Fleet, which had been subdivided into a number of task forces. The biggest was the main invasion fleet, commanded by Admiral Richmond Turner: TF51 comprised about 300 warships and more than 1,000 transports and landing craft. TF 58, four powerful, fast carrier groups led by Vice-Admiral Marc Mitscher, and TF 57, a Royal Navy carrier force under Vice-Admiral Sir Bernard Rawlings, were to screen Turner's fleet and operate offensively against the Japanese.

TF 52, commanded by Vice-Admiral William Blandy, was ordered to commence the preliminary bombardment of

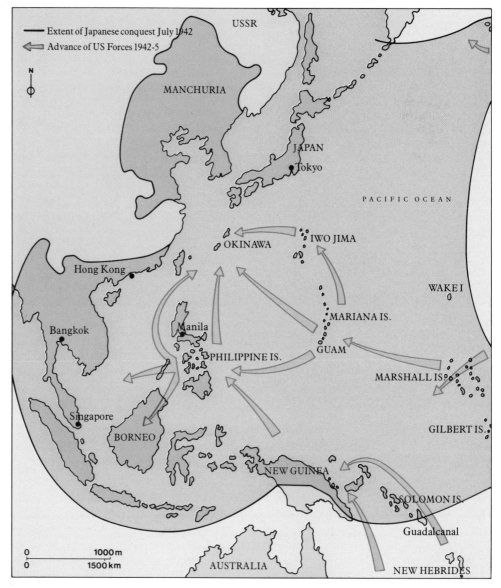

Map legend:
— Extent of Japanese conquest July 1942
← Advance of US Forces 1942-5

USSR · MANCHURIA · JAPAN · Tokyo · PACIFIC OCEAN · OKINAWA · IWO JIMA · Hong Kong · WAKE I · Bangkok · Manila · MARIANA IS. · PHILIPPINE IS. · GUAM · MARSHALL IS. · Singapore · BORNEO · GILBERT IS. · NEW GUINEA · SOLOMON IS. · Guadalcanal · AUSTRALIA · NEW HEBRIDES

0 — 1000m
0 — 1500km

By the end of 1942, Allied forces had stemmed the Japanese advance in the Pacific, and the long and costly process of 'island-hopping' began. The Japanese were pushed back, step by step, by taking one Pacific island at a time, then using it as a base from which to take the next. With air and naval superiority, the Allies were able to isolate Japanese island garrisons and eliminate them individually.

Guadalcanal fell in February 1943, and on 21 June US Marines opened the campaign for the islands of the central Solomons. Bougainville was the next target, then the Gilbert and Marshall Islands. The Marianas were taken in July 1944.

On 26 March 1945, the US 4th and 5th Marine Divisions, after the bloodiest fighting in their Corps' history, finally took Iwo Jima. The way was then open for the last action before the invasion of Japan, the occupation of the island of Okinawa.

Men of the 1st US Marine Division landed on Okinawa, *left*, on 3 April 1945.

The leading Marine has a Thompson sub-machinegun, the other a flame-thrower.

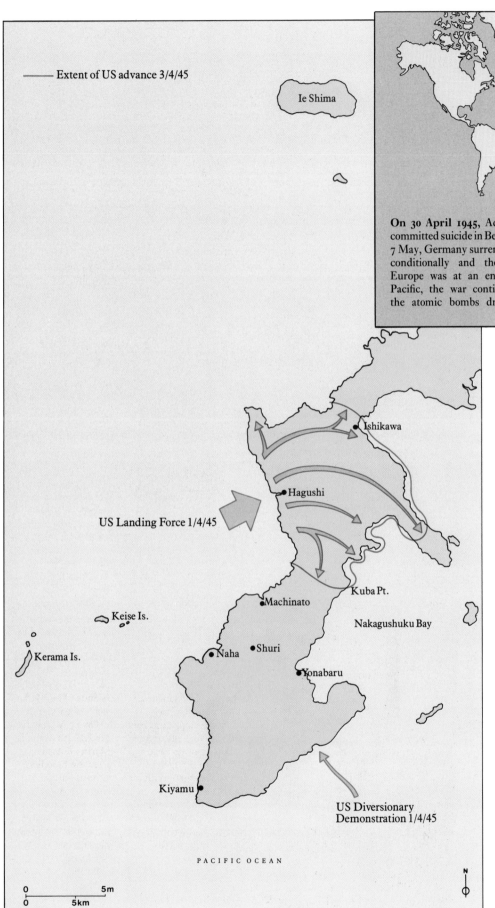

—— Extent of US advance 3/4/45

Ie Shima

Ishikawa

Hagushi

US Landing Force 1/4/45

Kuba Pt.

Machinato

Keise Is.

Nakagushuku Bay

Kerama Is.

Naha   Shuri

Yonabaru

Kiyamu

US Diversionary
Demonstration 1/4/45

PACIFIC OCEAN

0   5m
0   5km

N

N

OKINAWA

0   15m
0   20km

Admiral Nimitz as Commander-in-Chief Pacific Ocean Areas. His absolute priority was air superiority, which he insisted should be established before the Marine landings began.

Once this was achieved, the plan called for the 77th Division to capture the Kerama and Keise Islands to the West of Okinawa. This would give the Expeditionary Force a good, secure anchorage, a seaplane base and a point from which logistic support could be given to units of the fleet.

The campaign on Okinawa itself was to be divided into three phases. First, the southern part of the island was to be seized, then Ie Shima and northern Okinawa. This was due to be followed by the third and last phase—the capture and subsequent development of airfields and depots on other islands in the Nansei Shoto area.

After the landings, however, it was the northern sector that fell first.

The Allied plan for the conquest of the Ryukus, a chain of islands between Taiwan (Formosa) and Japan, was first to seize Okinawa so that airstrips could be built from which bombers could attack the Japanese mainland.

Once Okinawa had been strategically isolated by carrier- and land-based aircraft, naval gunfire and air strikes were to destroy Japanese defences and airstrips. The waters around the landing sites were then to be cleared of mines and any other defences to ensure the safe approach of the heavily laden transport ships.

Planning for 'Operation Iceberg' began in October 1944, the scheme being overseen by

Okinawa and to clear the extensive minefields laid in the approaches to the chosen landing beach at Hagushi on the west side of the island.

The invasion was set for 1 April, Easter Sunday, and from 18 March onward the Americans began a series of harassing attacks on the enemy. They struck hard at naval and air bases on the mainland; on the outer islands, Okinawa's defences were subjected to ever-increasing bombing and shelling, and the nearby Kerama Retto islands were overrun to provide a forward base for the main assault. The 77th US Infantry Division, which took the Keramas, also captured intact more than 200 Japanese suicide boats packed with explosive, thereby neutralizing a serious threat to the invasion fleet.

All this, however, was not achieved without Japanese resistance and retaliation. The carrier groups were the main targets for their air force, particularly the suicidal kamikaze pilots, who were first used extensively at the Battle of Leyte Gulf in October 1944, and four of the flat-tops were damaged in the prelude to the landings.

Shortly after 04.00 on 1 April, Marines and GIs crowded into landing craft to begin the four-and-a-half-hour run into Hagushi beach, which had just been made safe by the massive minesweeping operation by Blandy's TF 52. Going in under an umbrella of intense naval gunfire, the leading troops hit the beach at 08.30 and, to their astonishment, encountered no opposition. By the end of that first uneventful day, Buckner had 60,000 men ashore on a beachhead perimeter 13km/ 8mls wide and up to 4.8km/3mls deep. A feint made by a Marine division on the opposite side of the island also drew no fire. 'Where the hell are the Japs?' everyone wanted to know.

Over the next 48 hours, American patrols carefully probed farther inland, occupying the central zone of the island which included two airfields. Then Intelligence officers learned from the locals the answer to the question puzzling the US troops—Ushijima and the bulk of his army were waiting in strongly defended positions in the southern part of Okinawa.

Major-General John Hodge's 24th Corps swung toward the enemy and made contact with the Japanese forward positions on 3 April. For the next 80 days American soldiers were to see more than enough of Ushijima's command, which had sworn to sell itself dearly in a war of attrition it knew it could not win.

While the big confrontation was developing in the south, Buckner sent the 6th

Yamato l.o.a.: 263m/863ft; maximum speed: 27kn; armament: nine 18-in guns, twelve 6.1-in guns, twelve 5-in guns, four 13-mm guns and (finally) one hundred and forty-six 25-mm anti-aircraft guns; 6 aircraft.

Death of the *Yamato*

At 72,908 tons the battleship *Yamato* was the largest warship ever built. *Yamato* carried formidable armament, notably, by 1945, one hundred and forty-six machine-guns. On 6 April, the *Yamato*, the light cruiser *Yahagi* and eight destroyers were sent on what was, inevitably, a suicide mission to Okinawa; for although their tanks carried virtually all of the Japanese Navy's remaining supplies of oil, there was insufficient fuel for the ships to make the return voyage to Japan.

The flotilla was ordered to beach itself at Okinawa and then fight until eliminated. When halfway to their objective, however, they were sighted by US submarines and the next day they were attacked by carrier-based bombers.

The *Yamato* sustained seven bomb and 12 torpedo hits within two hours, finally blowing up and sinking. During the same period, the *Yahagi* and four of the destroyers were also sunk. This was the last Japanese naval action of the war.

The top-scoring naval ace of WWII was the US flier Donald McCampbell. Here he is seen in the cockpit, proudly displaying the 21 Japanese flags painted on the fuselage of his aircraft to denote his 'kills'. By the end of the war he had shot down 34 aircraft in all. McCampbell also held the record for shooting down the most aircraft in a single aerial engagement—nine.

Kamikaze—the last resort

Japanese kamikaze suicide squadrons, the brainchild of Vice-Admiral Takijiro Ohnishi, commander of the First Air Fleet, were first employed at the Battle of Leyte Gulf in October 1944. He believed that Japanese shortage of ships and aircraft, a result of the battles of attrition and a lack of pre-war planning for a prolonged war, could be offset by aircraft laden with explosives plunging on to American ships, especially carriers. The aircraft were piloted by fanatically patriotic young men who introduced a chilling and dangerous twist to the war to sea.

The tactical value of kamikaze, meaning the 'Divine Wind' and referring to a typhoon which fortuitously blew an invading fleet away from Japan's shores in the Middle Ages, was quickly established. By January 1945, several squadrons had been formed. Although American fighters and anti-aircraft fire usually proved effective against kamikaze attacks, some pilots inevitably got through and US losses in ships and men began to mount. British aircraft-carriers were better able to withstand these suicide attacks than their American equivalents because, in almost all instances, their decks were more heavily reinforced, so they were not crippled by a direct hit.

By the time of the Battle of Okinawa, however, it was becoming less easy for the Japanese to find men willing to sacrifice themselves, and there was a growing tendency for pilots to return to base and report that they had seen no enemy ships. To put a stop to this practice, kamikaze sorties were sometimes accompanied by a fighter escort to ensure that the pilots did their duty. In all, the kamikaze sank 30 US ships and damaged 368; they killed almost 5,000 soldiers and sailors.

0 ——— 5ft
0 ——— 1m

The carrier-borne Zero, *top*, so called because its makers designated it 'Type oo', was extremely manoeuvrable but flimsy by Western standards. Initially, these were the aircraft flown by kamikaze pilots. By April 1945, the Japanese had designed an aircraft especially for kamikaze use. The Oka, or Cherry Blossom, *above*, had three rocket engines and carried a pilot and some 2,041kg/4,500lb of high explosives. It was conveyed to its target slung underneath a bomber; when released, the pilot— who had no means of escape—dived at his target at a speed of nearly 966kmh/600mph.

**The *hachimaki*, or headband, *top*, worn by all kamikaze pilots was a samurai symbol of courage. The samurai were originally members of the warrior class which arose during the 12th century. They cultivated indifference to pain or death and complete loyalty to their overlords.

The USS Franklin, *above*, was set on fire in an attack by Japanese suicide bombers, causing more than 1,000 casualties. Though severely damaged and listing dangerously, she managed to reach port in the USA, where she was repaired.

A suicide pilot, *right*, adjusting a comrade's *hachimaki* before a kamikaze operation. Young men such as these were treated by the Japanese people as demi-gods.

Okinawa/3

Marine Division north to clear out enemy positions and the 77th Infantry Division to capture Ie Shima Island off the north-west coast; here there was an airfield which Buckner wanted to provide increased air cover over Okinawa.

It took the Marines 17 days to achieve their objective against extremely tough opposition. And on Ie Shima, which was defended by 2,000 Japanese, the GIs of the 77th fought possibly their fiercest action of the war, over a five-day period from 16–21 April, before they were able to claim the island.

Having recovered from the disrupting American strikes against their bases in March, Japanese air and naval forces began to take a direct hand in the fight for Okinawa on 6 April, when the first of a series of ten major bombing and kamikaze attacks was launched against the US fleet and the Hagushi beachhead. In addition, the strongest squadron the fuel-starved Imperial Japanese Navy could muster set sail for the island on what was expected to be a one-way mission.

Despite heavy losses, enemy aircraft managed to penetrate the American naval defences to sink six ships and damage 21 by crashing into them. But next day it was Japan's turn to lose half a dozen ships in what turned out to be the Imperial Navy's last action.

Shortly after midday on 7 April, the 64,000-ton giant battleship *Yamato*, the light cruiser *Yahagi* and eight destroyers were steaming toward Okinawa without air cover when they came under concerted attack from a huge force of dive- and torpedo bombers, flown off from carriers of TF 58. Vice-Admiral Seiichi Ito's squadron, which had been cold-bloodedly ordered to do as much damage as possible to the American fleet before succumbing, did not stand a chance. *Yamato*, *Yahagi* and four destroyers went to the bottom without ever sighting a US warship. The other four destroyers, two badly damaged, turned away and ran for home.

From 5 April, when the first heavy fighting against the Japanese in the southern part of the island began, until 12 April,

the American advance grew progressively slower in the face of their determined resistance. Then, Ushijima, who had suffered ten times the casualties of the 24th Corps in the week-long grinding battle, without giving up too much ground, suddenly went over to the offensive in a bid to catch his enemy off balance. For 48 hours banzai attacks buffeted the American positons, but in all instances they were repulsed, and the Thirty-second Army, further depleted, reverted to a grim defensive role.

For more than a month thereafter Buckner's efforts were concentrated on breaking into the main Japanese lines, a cunningly prepared island-wide defensive zone centred on the old city of Shuri. In this heavily fortified region, the enemy had gone to great lengths to provide their strongpoints with interlocking fields of fire, making them extremely difficult and costly to overrun. These ridges and hills, identified by the Americans by unwarlike names such as Sugar Loaf and Chocolate Drop, became killing grounds.

The southern tip of Okinawa, looking southwest

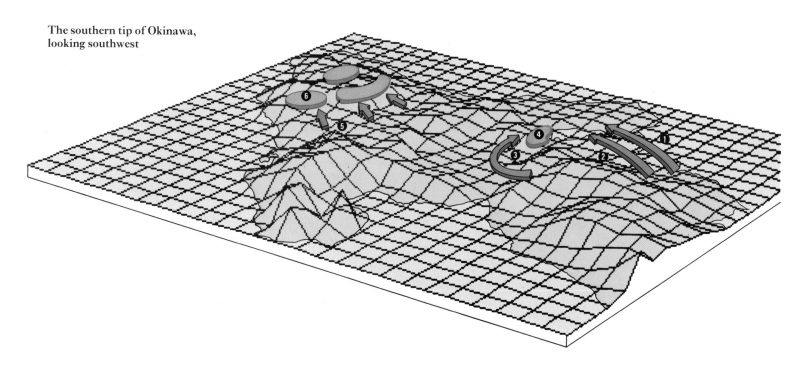

On 4 June 1945, two US Marine Corps divisions—the 4th (1) and the 29th (2)—made an amphibious landing on the Oroku Peninsula in the southwest of the island of Okinawa to link up with the 22nd Marine Division (3), which was advancing overland from the opposite direction. Their objective was to overcome the strongly armoured and well-provisioned remnants of the Japanese Naval Base Force (4) which had taken up defensive postions in a large complex of tunnels and undergound rooms, where they had vowed to fight to the death. The battle lasted for 10 days.

Meanwhile, in the hilly country farther south, the main body of the US Tenth Army (5) was hammering at the three heavily fortified areas (6), Yaeju-Dake, Yuza-Dake and Kunishi Ridge, chosen by General Ushijima for his last stand. The fighting continued there until 22 June.

The Commanders

Turner

Buckner

Ushijima

Vice-Admiral Richmond K. Turner (1885–1961), commander of the Amphibious Force, had been ordered to the Pacific early in 1942 and saw service at Guadalcanal, Iwo Jima and other landings. An opinionated man of caustic tongue and intemperate language, he often aroused antagonism among his army colleagues by instructing them in their duties.

Lieutenant-General Simon Bolivar Buckner (1886–1945)—son of the celebrated Confederate general of that name—commander of the Tenth Army, the US landing force on Okinawa, had previously been responsible for organizing American defences in Alaska. Buckner inaugurated a campaign of psychological warfare in the island by dropping some 8,000,000 leaflets on it, designed to win the confidence of civilians and spread despair among Japanese soldiers. When his invitation to the Japanese commander to surrender was spurned, Buckner tried to make capital out of the general's decision to commit his entire force to certain death. Buckner was killed when a Japanese shell exploded directly above an observation post he was visiting and a splinter of flying coral penetrated his chest.

The commander **Lieutenant-General Mitsuru Ushijima** (1887–1945) was a calm and capable officer, who was held in extremely high regard by his troops. He had commanded an infantry group in the early stages of the Burma campaign and later served as commandant of the Japanese Military Academy in Zama.

Even when the Thirty-second Army defending Okinawa was disintegrating, Ushijima was contemptuously amused by calls for his surrender, which would have been inconsistent with his honour as a samurai. When defeat became inevitable, he took the traditional course and, having bowed in reverence toward the eastern sky, knelt on a quilt covered with a white cloth and committed suicide with a sword in the honoured Japanese rites of *hara-kiri*.

Men of the 1st Marine Division, *below*, pouring fire into Japanese defence positions on Okinawa. The Marine in the foreground is armed with a carbine; to his left, a comrade fires an MI Garand semi-automatic rifle. Beyond and behind them, other men operate a Bazooka rocket-launcher.

A frightened Okinawan peasant, *above*, leaves his hiding place to surrender to US Marines who are clearing out enemy positions. The Marines are alert and ready to shoot, for almost all cornered Japanese troops were prepared to fight to the death. Of the enemy's original strength on Okinawa of 120,000, all but 10,000 perished. Decades after the war ended, many lone soldiers were found throughout the Pacific islands, still with their weapons.

On 4 May, Ushijima once again tried to seize the initiative by counter-attacking. Despite a few successes, his dwindling forces were unable to sustain the initial momentum of their offensive and within three days were back on the defensive.

For the next two weeks American pressure was applied on the flanks of the Japanese lines, slowly bending them inward, until they threatened to encircle Shuri. By 21 May, Ushijima had decided to withdraw to the southern tip of Okinawa to make a final stand. Heavy rain turned the front into a mud-bath, and while the Japanese rearguard continued to battle it out with the Americans, the Thirty-second Army made an orderly retreat to its new line, unimpeded by US aircraft, grounded by the bad weather.

Shuri eventually fell on 31 May, and the US Tenth Army prepared for the last push. Marines made an amphibious attack on the Oroku Peninsula on the southwest coast to take out a major airfield and a strong pocket of resistance, while Buckner's main body moved on Ushijima's positions on the Yaeju-Dake ridge, using flame-throwers and high explosives to force their way in.

During a week of heavy fighting, the Japanese line began to crumble; then on 18 June the Americans, on the brink of victory, lost their commanding general. Simon Buckner died from a wound sustained on a visit to one of his forward positions. Within three days Ushijima was dead, too, but by his own hand. He had scorned an American offer to surrender and spare the lives of his remaining forces, and on 21 June he and his Chief of Staff had knelt outside the Japanese headquarters and then committed ceremonial hara-kiri. The 82-day-long battle for the stronghold of Okinawa was over, except for mopping-up operations.

Out of an army of nearly 120,000 men, the Japanese lost a staggering 110,000 killed. The US Tenth Army had 7,203 dead and just over 31,000 wounded, while naval losses amounted to almost 5,000 dead and about the same number injured.

With Okinawa at last secure, American eyes turned towards the Japanese mainland and plans were laid for an enormous invasion, with a proposed launch date of 1 November. However, this conventional means of fighting the enemy to the finish—inevitably costly in terms of loss of men—was soon rendered unnecessary with the dawn of the nuclear age in August 1945. Japan surrendered after two atomic bombs had annihilated the cities of Hiroshima and Nagasaki.

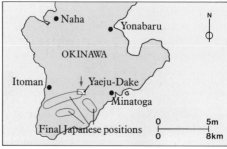

American forces finally penetrated to the southern tip of Okinawa more than two months after landing on the island. Here, the remaining troops of General Ushijima's command were preparing to fight the final battle in a series of bitter and bloody conflicts.

Troops from the US 96th Infantry Division are seen on 12 June, advancing on strong Japanese positions on Yaeju-Dake ridge. This area was overrun two days later, but it was another 10 days before the Americans could declare Okinawa secure.

Yaeju-Dake (1), known to the Americans as 'Big Apple', formed the eastern flank of the main Japanese defence line occupying a ridge some 64km/40mls long.

The survivors of the Japanese 24th Division (2) directed heavy fire on the advancing Americans from strongpoints on top of the ridge, as well as from fortified caves in the slope of the hill.

The US infantry marked their forward positions with large yellow cloths (5) to let their air support know exactly where enemy territory began. The Japanese were often attacked by Corsair fighters and Avenger bombers.

The infantry were assisted in clearing out enemy postions by Sherman tanks fitted with flame-throwers (3). There were only two ways to neutralize firing points: to throw charges of high explosive into them or to use flame-throwers.

Infantrymen from the 96th Division (4) edge toward Japanese positions on the lower slopes of Big Apple. American forces did not capture the strongly held ridge until 14 June. Casualties were high, because of the enemy's intention of killing as many US troops as possible before dying themselves.

A new era: the atom bomb

The Allies had been forewarned on their island-hopping campaign of the ferocious, fanatical reception they were likely to receive if they invaded mainland Japan. But the Americans now had at their disposal a new and terrible weapon: the atomic bomb. On 6 August 1945, one was exploded over Hiroshima; three days later, on 9 August, another was exploded over Nagasaki. Both cities were destroyed, and their inhabitants either killed or horribly mutilated.

On 9 August, too, Russia declared war on Japan. For almost a month the Japanese continued to resist American and Soviet attacks on shipping, airfields and some island bases. Finally, however, they became convinced of the uselessness of continued resistance, so sparing the lives of countless Allied—and Japanese—combatants. On 3 September, the Japanese formally surrendered on board the US battleship *Missouri*, which was anchored in Tokyo Bay.

Bibliography

This list includes a selection of those books consulted by the Publishers in the preparation of *Great Battles of World War II* and also some suggestions for further reading. Many of these books are available in a paperback edition also.

The Western Theatre

Ambrose, Stephen E. *Pegasus Bridge* Allen & Unwin, London, 1984

Barker, A.J. *Dunkirk, The Great Escape* J.M. Dent & Sons, London, 1977

Belchem, David *Victory in Normandy* Chatto & Windus, London, 1981

Blaxland, William G. *Destination Dunkirk* William Kimber, London, 1973

Broome, Jack *Convey is to Scatter* William Kimber, London, 1972

Calder, Angus *The People's War* Jonathan Cape, London, 1969

Collier, Richard *Eagle Day: Battle of Britain* Hodder & Stoughton, London, 1966

Costello, John and Hughes, Terry *The Battle of the Atlantic* William Collins, London, 1977

Deighton, Len *Fighter*, 1978; *Blitzkrieg*, 1979, *Battle of Britain*, 1980; Jonathan Cape, London

Divine, David *The Nine Days of Dunkirk* Faber & Faber, London, 1959

Eisenhower, Dwight D. *Crusade in Europe* Heinemann, London, 1948

Eisenhower, John S.D. *The Bitter Woods* Robert Hale, London, 1969

Elstob, Peter *Hitler's Last Offensive* Secker & Warburg, London, 1971

Grenfell, Russell *The Bismarck Episode* Faber & Faber, London, 1948

Harman, Nicholas *Dunkirk, the Necessary Myth* Hodder & Stoughton, London, 1980

Harris, John *Dunkirk* David & Charles, Newton Abbot, 1980

Hastings, Max *Overlord* Simon & Schuster, New York, 1984

Haswell, Jock *The Intelligence and Deception of the D-Day Landings* Batsford, London, 1979

Held, Werner *Fighter!* Arms & Armour Press, London, 1979

Horne, A.A. *To Lose a Battle: France 1940* Macmillan, London, 1969

Howarth, David A. *Dawn of D-Day* Collins, London, 1959

Kennedy, Ludovic *Pursuit: The Chase and Sinking of the Bismarck* William Collins, London, 1974

Lord, Walter *The Miracle of Dunkirk* Allen Lane, London, 1983

Macdonald, Charles B. *The Battle of the Bulge* Weidenfeld & Nicholson, London, 1984

Marwick, Arthur *The Home Front* Thames & Hudson, London, 1976

Mason, Francis K *Battle over Britain* McWhirter Twins, London, 1969

Montgomery, Bernard Law *Norman-* *dy to the Baltic* Barrie and Jenkins/The Arcadia Press, London, 1947

Müllenheim-Rechberg, Baron Burhard von *Battleship Bismarck* The Bodley Head, London, 1981

Perrett, Bryan *Lighting War* Panther, London, 1985

Piekalkiewicz, Janusz *Arnhem: 1944* Ian Allen, London, 1977

Price, Alfred *The Battle of Britain: The Hardest Day* Macdonald & Jane's, London 1979

Rutherford, Ward *Blitzkrieg 1940* Bison Books, London, 1979

Ryan, Cornelius *The Longest Day* Victor Gollancz, London, 1960

Ryan, Cornelius *A Bridge Too Far* Hamish Hamilton, London, 1974

Strawson, John *The Battle for the Ardennes* Batsford, London, 1972

Toland, John *Battle: The Story of the Bulge* Frederick Muller, London, 1960

Townsend, Peter *Duel of Eagles* Weidenfeld & Nicolson, London, 1970

Tute, Warren, Costello, John and Hughes, Terry *D-Day* Sidgwick & Jackson, London, 1974

Turnbull, Patrick *Dunkirk: Anatomy of a Disaster* Batsford, London, 1978

Whiting, Charles *Ardennes: The Secret War* Century Publishing, London, 1984

The Mediterranean Theatre

Attard, Joseph *The Battle of Malta* William Kimber, London, 1980

Blumenson, Martin *Anzio, The Gamble That Failed* Weidenfeld & Nicolson, London, 1963

Bradford, Ernle *Siege: Malta 1940–43* Hamish Hamilton, London, 1985

Ellis, John *Cassino: The Hollow Victory* Andre Deutsch, London, 1984

Forty, George *Desert Rats at War* Ian Allen, London, 1980

Graham, Dominick *Cassino* Ballantine, New York, 1971

Hay, Ian *The Unconquered Isle* Hodder & Stoughton, London, 1943

Hibbert, Christopher *Anzio: the Bid for Rome* Ballantine, New York, 1977

Hogan, George *Malta, The Triumphant Years* Robert Hale, London, 1978

Jackson, W.G.F. *The Battle for Italy* Batsford, London, 1967

Lewin, Ronald *The Life and Death of the Africa Korps* Batsford, London, 1977

Lloyd, Hugh *Briefed to Attack* Hodder & Stoughton, London, 1949

Lucas, James *The War in the Desert* Arms & Armour Press, London, 1982

Majdalany, Fred *Cassino: Portrait of a Battle* Longmans, Green & Co., London, 1957

Micallef, Joseph *When Malta Stood Alone* Interprint, Malta, 1981

Montgomery, Bernard Law *El Alamein to the River Sangro* Barrie and Jenkins/The Arcadia Press, London, 1948

Moorehead, Alan *The Desert War* Hamish Hamilton, London, 1965

Piekalkiewicz, Janusz *Cassino* Orbis, London, 1980

Pitt, Barrie *The Crucible of War: The Western Desert 1941* Jonathan Cape, London, 1980

Schmidt, Heinz *With Rommel in the Desert* Harrap, London, 1957

The Air Battle of Malta HMSO, London, 1944

Smith, E.D. *The Battles for Cassino* Ian Allan, London, 1975

Strawson, John *El Alamein* Dent, London, 1981

Verney, Peter *Anzio 1944: An Unexpected Fury* Batsford, London, 1978

The Eastern Theatre

Chuikov, Vasili I *The Beginning of the Road* Panther Books, London, 1963

Clark, Alan *Barbarossa: The Russian-German Conflict 1941–1945* Hutchinson, London, 1965

Erickson, John *The Road to Stalingrad* Weidenfeld & Nicholson, London, 1975

Jukes, Geoffrey *Kursk: The Clash of Armour* Ballantine, New York, 1969

Parotkin, Major-General (Ed.-in-Chief) *The Battle of Kursk* Progress Publishers, Moscow, 1974

Piekalkiewicz, Janusz *Moscow: 1941* Arms & Armour Press, London, 1985

Ryan, Cornelius *The Last Battle* Collins, London, 1966

Thach, Joseph Edward *The Battle of Kursk, July 1943: Decisive Turning Point on the Eastern Front* Ann Arbor, Michigan University Microfilms, 1971.

200 Days of Fire Accounts by participants of the Battle of Stalingrad. Progress Publishers, Moscow, 1970

Carell, Paul *Hitler's War on Russia*, 1964; *Scorched Earth*, 1970; George G. Harrap, London

The Pacific Theatre

Allen, Louis *Burma: The Longest War 1941–45* Dent, London, 1984

Bateson, Charles *The War with Japan* Barrie & Rockliff, London, 1968

Costello, John *The Pacific War* Collins, London, 1981

Esposito, Vincent J. (Chief Editor) *The West Point Atlas of American Wars 1900–1953* vol. II Frederick A. Praeger, New York

Evans, Geoffrey and Brett-James, Anthony *Imphal: A Flower on Lofty Heights* Macmillan, London, 1962

Fuchida, Mitsuo and Okumunya, Masatake *Midway: The Battle that doomed Japan* US Naval Institute Annapolis, Md, 1955

Kilduff, Peter *U.S. Carriers at War* Ian Allan, London, 1981

Leckie, Robert *Challenge for the Pacific* Hodder & Stoughton, London, 1966

Lucas Phillips, C.E. *Springboard to Victory* Heinemann, London, 1966

Macfetridge, Charles H.T. *Tales of the* *Mountain Gunners* William Blackwood, Edinburgh, 1973

Manchester, William *Goodbye, Darkness* Michael Joseph, London, 1981

Morison, Samuel Eliot *The Two-Ocean War* Atlantic, Little, Brown, Boston, Ma, 1963

Prange, Gordon W. *Miracle at Midway* McGraw-Hill, New York 1982

Preston, Anthony (Ed.) *Decisive Battles of the Pacific War*, Hamlyn, London, 1979

Slim, William *Defeat into Victory* Cassell, London, 1956

Spurr, Russell *A Glorious Way to Die* Sidgwick & Jackson, London, 1982

Swinson, Arthur *Kohima: The Turning Point* Cassell, London, 1966

General

Airborne Operations Salamander, London, 1978

Arnold-Foster, Mark *The World at War* Collins, London, 1973

Bullock, Alan *Hitler: A Study in Tyranny* Odhams, London, 1952

Butler, James M. (Ed.) *History of the Second World War*, United Kingdom Military Series (26 vols) HMSO, London, 1952–1976

Churchill, Winston S. *The Second World War* Vols. I–VI Cassell, London, 1948–1954

Dear, Ian *Marines at War* Ian Allan, London, 1982

Dollinger, Hans *The Decline and Fall of Nazi Germany and Imperial Japan* Odhams Books, London, 1965

Frankland, Noble and Dowling, Christopher (Eds) *Decisive Battles of the Twentieth Century* Sidgewick & Jackson, London, 1976

Goodenough, S. *War Maps* Macdonald, London, 1982

Hogg, Ian V. *The Guns: 1939/45* Macdonald, London, 1970

Humble, Richard *Hitler's Generals* Arthur Barker, London, 1973

Jane, F.T. *Jane's Fighting Ships* Samson Law, Marston, London, 1945

Morison, Samuel Eliot *History of United States Naval Operations in World War II* (vols I–XV) Oxford University Press, London, 1948–1962

Pearcy, Arthur *Dakota at War* Ian Allan, London, 1982

Pitt, Barrie (Ed) *History of the Second World War* Purnell, London, 1972 *et seq*

Ramsey, Winston (Ed) *After the Battle* Battle of Britain Prints, London, 1973 *et seq*

Shirer, William L. *The Rise and Fall of the Third Reich* Secker & Warburg, London, 1973

U.S. Army in World War II, (23 vols) Chief of Military History, Department of the Army, Washington DC, 1948–7

Wingate, John (Gen Ed) *Warships in Profile* Profile Publications, Windsor, 1973

Index

Page numbers in **bold** print indicate major references to the Battles; captions to illustrations, diagrams, and supplementary text are shown in *italic*. Lower case Roman numerals in italic refer to the gatefold between pages 136 and 137.

Index

Index

Acknowledgements

The publishers are particularly indebted to Mr James Lucas, Mr Paul Kemp, Mr Alan Williams, Mr M.J. Willis and Mr Peter Chamberlain for their specialist advice. They are also grateful to the staff of the Imperial War Museum, London; the RAF Museum, Hendon; the London Library; the School of Oriental and African Studies, London; and the Public Record Office, Kew. Mr F. Tomkins of the Burma Star Association; Mr J. Lyndhurst of the Warnham War Museum and Mr John Stanford kindly provided us with additional research material and objects for photography. Invaluable assistance was given by Mr Thomas G. DeClaire, Geography and Map Division, Library of Congress, Washington, DC; Mr Haberlein, the Naval Historical Center, Washington, DC; The German Historical Institute, London; The Goethe Institute, London; the Militärgeschichtliches Forschungsamt, Freibourg, and Dr Ian Gow, Japanese Business Policy Unit, Warwick University. Maps were provided by Edward Stanford Ltd; the Instituto Geografico Militare, Florence, and the Royal Geographical Society, London. Thanks are also due to Pat Hunter and Vivienne Quay for their most useful editorial assistance.

Additional artwork by Roy Huxley, Andrew Stanford, Mark Franklin, Hayward and Martin
Maps by Creative Data Ltd
Index by Valerie Lewis Chandler

Picture Credits

l = left; *r* = right; *t* = top; *c* = centre; *b* = bottom

1–8 Warnham War Museum; 9*t* Robert Hunt Library; 9*c* Imperial War Museum; 9*cr* Bundesarchiv/MARS; 13*tl* Robert Hunt Library; 13*tc* The Photo Source; 13*tr* The Photo Source; 13*b* Imperial War Museum; 16*t* Imperial War Museum; 16*c* Imperial War Museum; 13*b* South Eastern Newspapers/MARS; 17*t* Imperial War Museum; 17*c* Imperial War Museum; 17*b* Imperial War Museum; 18*t* MARS; 18*c* Imperial War Museum; 18*b* MARS; 19*t* (map) Imperial War Museum; 19*t* Bundesarchiv/Robert Hunt Library; 19*c* John Frost Newspaper Collection; 19*b* Imperial War Museum; 21*l* Imperial War Museum; 21*tr* Imperial War Museum; 21*br* Imperial War Museum; 25*bl* The Photo Source; 25*br* Bundesarchiv/MARS; 26*t* MARS; 26*b* Illustrated London News; 27*l* Imperial War Museum; 27*t* Imperial War Museum; 27*b* (cigarette cards) Paul Wilkinson; 28*tr* Illustrated London News; 28*b* Illustrated London News; 29*tl* Imperial War Museum; 29*tc* Imperial War Museum; 29*tr* Imperial War Museum; 29*bl* Kent Messenger Group; 31 (badges) Paul Wilkinson, Jeff Burke; 32 Blohm & Voss; 35*r* MARS; 35*l* MARS; 35*r* MARS; 37 Imperial War Museum; 41*l* Bundesarchiv; 41*c* Bundesarchiv/Robert Hunt Library; 43 The Photo Source; 44 The Photo Source; 48*t* Novosti; 48*c* MARS; 49*l* Bundesarchiv; 49*c* Bundesarchiv; 49*r* Novosti; 50*t* MARS; 50*c* MARS; 50*b* MARS; 51*t* Bridgeman Art Library; 51*br* Auckland Collection; 51*bl* MARS; 52*t* Bundesarchiv; 52*b* Novosti; 53 Novosti; 56 Imperial War Museum; 60*t* Imperial War Museum; 60*b* Imperial War Museum; 61 Imperial War Museum; 63 Imperial War Museum; 64 USN/MARS; 68 USN/MARS; 69*l* USN; 69*c* Robert Hunt Library; 69*r* USN/PPL; 70*t* MARS; 70*b* MARS; 71*t* MARS; 71*br* MARS; 71*bl* MARS; 72*t* US Army/MARS; 72*b* USNA/MARS; 73 USNA; 78 MARS; 78 (badges) Warnham War Museum; 79 MARS; 81 Imperial War Museum; 82*t* MARS; 82*b* MARS; 83*l* Bundesarchiv; 83*r* Imperial War Museum; 83 (badges) Paul Wilkinson, Jeff Burke; 84*t* Imperial War Museum; 84*b* Imperial War Museum; 89 (both) Imperial War Museum; 92*t* The Photo Source; 92*c* Novosti; 92*b* Novosti; 96*t* Novosti; 96*c* Bundesarchiv; 96*b* Novosti; 97*tl* Novosti; 97*tc* Robert Hunt Library; 97*tr* Novosti; 97*b* Bundesarchiv; 100*t* Bundesarchiv; 100*b* Novosti; 105*tl* Bundesarchiv; 105*tc* Bundesarchiv; 105*tr* Novosti; 105*b* Novosti; 108–109 USNA; 109 Imperial War Museum; 112*t* Bundesarchiv/Robert Hunt Library; 112*c* Robert Hunt Library; 112*b* Imperial War Museum; 113*tl* Bundesarchiv; 113*tc* Imperial War Museum; 113*tr* Imperial War Museum; 113*b* Imperial War Museum; 114*t* Auckland Collection; 114*c* Auckland Collection; 114*b* Imperial War Museum; 115*t* Bundesarchiv; 115*c* Imperial War Museum; 115*b* Bundesarchiv; 116*t* Imperial War Museum; 116*c* Imperial War Museum; 116*b* Imperial War Museum; 121 Imperial War Museum; 122 Imperial War Museum; 128 Imperial War Museum; 129 Imperial War Museum; 130*t* Imperial War Museum; 130*c* Imperial War Museum; 130*b* Imperial War Museum; 130 (medal) Burma Star Association; 131*tl* Imperial War Museum; 131*tc* Imperial War Museum; 131*tr* Robert Hunt Library; 131*b* Imperial War Museum; 132*tl* COI; 132*b* Imperial War Museum; 136 Imperial War Museum/MARS; 137 Imperial War Museum/MARS; 140 Robert Hunt Library; 141*l*-to-*r* Imperial War Museum; Imperial War Museum; Bundesarchiv; US Army/MARS; Imperial War Museum; Imperial War Museum; 141*b* USAF; 144*t* Imperial War Museum; 144*b* Imperial War Museum; 148*t* Imperial War Museum; 148*c* Imperial War Museum; 148*b* Imperial War Museum; 149*l* Imperial War Museum; 149*r* Imperial War Museum/MARS; 152*t* Imperial War Museum; 152*c* Imperial War Museum; 152*b* Imperial War Museum; 153*tl*-to-*r* The Photo Source; Imperial War Museum; Imperial War Museum; Bundesarchiv; 153*bl* Bundesarchiv; 153*b* Bundesarchiv; 155 Imperial War Museum; 155*tr* (all portraits) Imperial War Museum; 155*b* Bundesarchiv; 155*br* Paul Wilkinson; 156*t* Imperial War Museum; 156*b* Imperial War Museum; 160*t* Imperial War Museum; 160*c* Imperial War Museum; 160*b* Imperial War Museum; 161 Imperial War Museum; 164 Imperial War Museum; 165*r* Imperial War Museum; 165*l* US Army; 166 Imperial War Museum; 167*tl* Robert Hunt Library; 167*c* Bundesarchiv; 167*r* The Photo Source; 167*b* US Army/MARS; 168*t* USArmy/MARS; 168*b* Novosti; 173 Robert Hunt Library; 176*t* Novosti; 176 USNA; 177*t* Imperial War Museum; 177*b* Novosti; 178*t* Novosti; 178*b* The Photo Source; 179*t* Associated Press; 179*bl* Robert Hunt Library; 179*br* BBC Hulton; 180 USMC/MARS; 182 USNA; 183*l* USN/MARS; 183*r* USN/MARS; 185*tl* The Photo Source; 185*tc* The Photo Source; 185*tr* USN; 185*bl* USN; 185*br* USMC. GATEFOLD: i*l* USN/MARS; i*c* USMC/The Photo Source; ii*l* Imperial War Museum; ii*r* Bundesarchiv; vii USN; viii*c* US Coast Guard; viii*bl* Imperial War Museum; viii*br* Imperial War Museum.